Stan Ovshinsky and the Hydrogen Economy: Creating a Better World

George S. Howard, Ph.D.
University of Notre Dame

Also by George S. Howard, Ph.D.

Stan Ovshinsky and the Hydrogen Economy: Creating a Better World

George S. Howard, Ph.D.
University of Notre Dame

Academic Publications
Box 187
Notre Dame, IN 46556

Published by Academic Publications,
Box 187, Notre Dame, IN 46556

Library of Congress Cataloging In Publication Data
    Howard, George S.
Stan Ovshinsky and the Hydrogen Economy: Creating a Better World

ISBN 0-937647-05-5

    1. Biography—Stanford R. Ovshinsky. 2. Hydrogen Economy
    3. Science—Amorphous and Disordered Materials 4. Energy
    Conversion Devices

Printed in the United States of America

Cover photo by Steven Dibner
Book design by Peggy Swanson

This biography is not a recommendation to buy any particular stock or group of stocks. Investing in securities involves risk and anyone wishing to make such investments should consult with an advisor or do his or her own due diligence to assess the risks involved and whether a particular investment meets the needs, goals and risk tolerances of the investor.

Information contained in this biography is taken from sources assumed to be reliable; however the author can not guarantee its accuracy.

Thanks is extended to Elsevier Science B.V. for permission to reprint S.R. Ovshinsky (1994) "The material basis of efficiency and stability in amorphous photovoltaics." *Solar Energy Materials and Solar Cells* (93) 128-134. Thanks is given to the American Association for the Advancement of Science for permission to reprint S.R. Ovshinsky, M.A. Fetcenko and J. Ross (1993) "A nickel metal hydride battery for electric vehicles." *Science* (260) 176-181. Finally, the author is greatful to the Society of Glass Technology for permission to reprint H. Fritzsche (2006) "Why chalcogenides are ideal materials for Ovshinsky's Ovonic threshold and memory devices." *Physics and Chemistry of Glasses* (in press).

Dedicated to

Stan's love, Iris   and   My love, Nancy

Table of Contents

Foreword

Are all life stories created equal? Probably not. Some lives intrigue us because the tales deal with the outcomes of epic struggles. That's why readers never seem to tire of biographies of leaders like Roosevelt, Hitler, Stalin and Churchill. The world came very close to succumbing to the powers of totalitarianism—the stakes were enormous, the outcome uncertain. Reading about the leaders of the warring countries can give us a front row seat for what was arguably the most important struggle of our time.

Other life stories intrigue us because these people made marvelous scientific breakthroughs. Think of Einstein, Newton, Darwin and Steven Hawking. Would you like to examine the inner workings of the minds of extraordinary scientists like this group? These stories can be both edifying and humbling. We come to see them as humans like us, but humans who made intellectual leaps that, even after hundreds of years, can still leave us breathless.

Another interesting type of story involves individuals who profoundly altered the world we live in. Here I think of Edison, Ford, the Wright brothers, and Louis Pasteur. It is hard to imagine a world without electricity, automobiles, airplanes and, most importantly, milk in the refrigerator.

Some books tell of good men and women who dedicate their lives to a set of admirable guiding principles, such as Mahatma Gandhi, Mother Teresa, and Eleanor Roosevelt. Reading stories about their lives and work serves to remind us of how good, how truly noble, humans might become.

A few stories tell us about remarkable relationships. I recently read *Franklin and Winston* which demonstrated how two driven, quirky heads of state slowly built a relationship that literally saved our world for democracy. Scientific versions of this type of biographical sketch might be Watson's *The Double Helix* or Pierre and Marie Currie's biography entitled *Currie*.

So where does *Stan Ovshinsky and the Hydrogen Economy* fit in this taxonomy of life stories? Remarkably, Professor Howard claims that Stanford Ovshinsky fits all of the categories I've delineated above. I leave it to each reader to determine whether or not this implausible claim is adequately substantiated in this book. However, a few obvious and remarkable observations about Ovshinsky's life and work can be offered.

First, Ovshinsky is wrestling with what might well be society's most important issue in the twenty-first century. There is no doubt in my mind that we must move from the age of burning hydrocarbons to the hydrogen/electrical energy systems of the future. This conclusion is true both for reasons of supply (e.g., Peak oil) and waste by-products (e.g., global warming). Ovshinsky's story offers readers a ringside seat to the Herculean struggle between forces tied to our hydrocarbon-dominated past and the prospects of a clean and renewable energy future. For what it's worth, there is no doubt in my mind that on this issue, Stan fights on the side of the angels.

Please allow me a brief digression, as I note a passing similarity between Stan and myself. Many years ago, as we faced our first energy crisis, I had an idea for three very large, gossamer-like, thin film photovoltaic collectors that would float geosyncronously with three great world deserts at an altitude several hundred miles above the earth. The sun would always shine on one or two of these solar energy-collecting space stations. Thus, we would have around-the-clock access to solar power. It gratifies me to know that Energy Conversion Devices (ECD) has developed the ultra-lightweight photovoltaic cells that now might allow my fuzzy dream to become a reality. Of course, Stan's terrestrial solution to obtaining photovoltaic energy rendered my space energy collectors idea unnecessary.

We have the testimony of a bevy of notable physicists (some Nobel Laureates) that Stan's work with disordered materials is seminal. He clearly is a scientific genius. *Stan Ovshinsky and the Hydrogen Economy* also made me think of Gandhi. The Mahatma was actually very similar to our scientist, Stan Ovshinsky. The title of Gandhi's autobiography simply states his method, *The Story of My Experiments with Truth*. Gandhi was a scientist just like Stan. However, the Mahatma's content area was the spiritual domain of humans, whereas Stan roams the fields of disordered and amorphous materials.

I wager that Gandhi would have loved Stan's aphorism "In God we trust—everyone else must show data." Gandhi knew he wasn't God. Thus, he needed some justification (or warrant, as the philosophers say) for his spiritual principles. Gandhi's warrant lay in the results of his experiments with life (practicing nonviolence in his life, celibacy in marriage, observing dietary restrictions). Gandhi came to know the nature of his truth—and also the nature of sin.

After reading *Stan Ovshinsky and the Hydrogen Economy*, you will know the nature of sin as understood by Stan Ovshinsky. Sin resides in the ways of the world that Stan avoided, including elitism, sexism, racism, and the like. For Gandhi, sin occurred when one failed to balance two related "goods." For example, Wealth without Work; Pleasure without Conscience; Knowledge without Character; and Religion without Sacrifice are four of Gandhi's seven sins. But his remaining three sins sound positively "Ovshinskyian" to me: Politics without Principle; Commerce without Morality; and Science without Humanity.

Perhaps you are leery that I mentioned someone you've heard little about—Stanford Ovshinsky—with the Thomas Edisons and Henry Fords of the world. Recall that thirty years ago, if I'd said Einstein, Newton, Darwin and Steven Hawking, all would have exclaimed, "Steven who?" This is precisely Professor Howard's wager. He believes that three decades from now we will better recognize Ovshinsky's place among the Edisons and Fords of the world, and wants to tell the story of Stan's contributions to science, to industry, and to our planet. This book seeks to elaborate that bold but plausible claim.

While this book is about Stan Ovshinsky, there is another presence who at every turn lurks between the pages—Iris Ovshinsky. Stan and Iris are a wonderful team. This book is as much a tribute to Iris as it is to Stan. Father Ned Joyce was my colleague and friend for over 50 years—about as long as Stan and Iris have been partners. But the parallels go deeper still. Father Ned was every bit as responsible for what Notre Dame has become as am I. However, it was Father Ned's choice to labor a bit more in the shadows. Iris Ovshinsky also is more comfortable just outside the spotlight's glare. But anyone who knows ECD knows that it is as much Iris' creation as it is Stan's. One of the great blessings of my life was to have found a "great soul" like Father Ned to share the work of our common vision for building Notre Dame. For, as we all know, a shared burden is a lightened burden. Stan was similarly blessed in having his soulmate, Iris.

In a very real sense, *Stan Ovshinsky and the Hydrogen Economy* is a love story—love for science, love for coworkers, love for all of humanity, and Stan's love for Iris. And so with apologies to Mr.

Shakespeare, I'll simply close with a gloss on the ending of his greatest love story,[1]

    For rare is a story, more important to man
    Than this of sweet Iris, and her loving Stan.

Theodore M. Hesburgh, C.S.C.
Notre Dame, IN

Preface

To See Further

In a letter (Feb. 5, 1676) to Robert Hooke, Sir Isaac Newton, the father of celestial mechanics and the creator of the calculus, wrote, "If I have *seen further* than others, it is by standing on the shoulders of giants." A scientific genius humbly bestowing credit on his intellectual forebears—the stuff of which scientific legends are constructed.

But wait. The reality of Newton's remark is not nearly as simple and heroic as it appears. The letter in question did not deal with celestial mechanics or the calculus, rather its topic was Newton's work on optical theories. So Newton would not be thinking of genuine "giants" like Copernicus or Galileo, who inspired his work on celestial mechanics. Instead, Newton's intellectual debt in the optics would be to men like Rene Descartes and Robert Hooke. While Sir Isaac genuinely appreciated the contributions of some of his intellectual forebears, he was already embroiled in a bitter, long-running feud with Hooke. Newton earlier had wiped Hooke's name from the Royal Society records and also destroyed Hooke's portrait. So it would be very strange indeed for Newton to deliver anything but scorn for Hooke. "Standing on the shoulders of giants," is such a wonderfully generous image—until one realizes that Hooke has been described as one whose, "crooked posture and short stature made him anything but a giant, especially in the eyes of the extremely vindictive Newton."[1]

Successful scientists are often canonized for their intellectual contributions. For example, Alexander Pope wrote of Newton, "Nature and Nature's laws lay hid in night: God said: 'Let Newton be!' And all was light." However, closer scrutiny of the lives of scientific giants often reveals quite ordinary human frailties.[2,3]

This book considers another great scientist—Stanford Ovshinsky. Like Newton, he is not a demigod. However, I view his life and work with an appreciative eye. Ovshinsky is a fascinating man who has made truly extraordinary contributions to science and to the world. In fact, I believe him to be the world's most important contributor to the fight against looming environmental problems. Yet, speaking of standing on the shoulders of giants, it is interesting that both Hellmut Fritzsche, Ovshinsky's closest collaborator and past head of the Department of Physics of the University of Chicago, and Sir Nevill Mott, Nobel Laureate, characterized Stan as coming from nowhere, his work not anticipated by anyone. Ovshinsky's work is so original that there are no scientific forebears to thank.

I chose him for this book because I am eager for the world to know the nature of his contributions. Part I of *Stan Ovshinsky and the Hydrogen Economy* deals with the life and loves of this remarkable man, and the company, Energy Conversion Devices (ECD), that he and Iris created to usher humanity into the hydrogen economy of the twenty-first century. In Part II we relive his truly extraordinary scientific odyssey. Finally, Part III looks at the larger picture of Stan's place in the scientific and business world, and presents some thoughts on the future. Comments and stories by Stan and a number of his colleagues, collaborators, and employees are included, which serve to provide a richer account of the breadth and depth of Stan's mind, heart, and soul. I'd like to note that each included comment is representative of many more like it.

Who should write a biography? Most biographies are written by historians. Their goals are usually to shed light on some historical period and to give readers a deeper glimpse into the life of an interesting historical figure. The historical period of interest for *Stan Ovshinsky and the Hydrogen Economy* is the late twentieth century and early twenty-first century—the time that marked the end of the era of burning hydrocarbons and the birth of the hydrogen economy. Readers who desire further historical analysis of that epochal shift might read Jeremy Rifkin's *The Hydrogen Economy* (1999, New York: Penguin), or Peter Hoffmann's *Tomorrow's Energy* (2001, New York: MIT Press).

Why would a psychologist write a biography? Psychologists tend to probe a person's motives, experiences, and belief systems, rather than the characteristics of an historical period, in elucidating why a person acted as he or she did. The hope is that in knowing the Ovshinskys—their beliefs, values, hopes and visions—one can see more clearly: how the science of disordered and amorphous materials developed; how ECD developed into a most extraordinary company; and how our world transitioned from the age of hydrocarbons to the age of hydrogen. Perhaps a psychologist can show how an important vision (i.e., the complete hydrogen loop) combined with a half-century of exciting scientific work and struggle can serve to create an entirely new and better world, one powered by hydrogen.

The contributions of others to this book have been invaluable. Two people stood head and shoulders above all others—Iris Ovshinsky and Nancy Gulanick. I am thankful for countless interviews with Stan Ovshinsky, Bob Stempel, Hellmut Fritzsche, Morrel Cohen, Tyler Lowrey, Herb Ovshinsky, Rosa Young, Nancy Bacon, David Strand, Subhendu Guha, Alastair Livesey, Dennis Corrigan, Kevin Fok, Srini Venkatesan and many others of Stan's and Iris' colleagues who make up ECD. Stan and Iris have requested to include their acknowledgements, which can be found in Appendix 11 on page 283. The quality of this book has also profited from the fine contributions of Judy Stewart, Kate Halischak, Peggy Swanson, Jay Van Dyke, Tom Kanzcuzewski, Ed Smith, Nathan Vogel, John Cernak, Bob Rupholdt, Ray Bowman and Freya Saito to whom I am extremely grateful. With helpers such as these, work is a true joy.

Part I

The Man

Plugging into the sun

Chapter 1

Success!

Someday, Stanford and Iris Ovshinsky are likely to be remembered by history in much the same vein as Thomas Edison and Nicolas Tesla. Their discoveries of amorphous materials have helped pave the way to a more energy efficient society.

EV World, February 23, 2005

It happened in 2005 during the month of August. A very important corner was turned for Energy Conversion Devices (ECD)—the company Stan and Iris Ovshinsky founded in 1960 to facilitate our transition to the hydrogen economy. Like many inflection points in life, I only recognized the change in direction in retrospect.

For more than ten years I studied this small, alternative energy and information[1] company located in suburban Detroit that develops photovoltaics, batteries, solid hydrogen storage, and fuel cells—products useful for the hydrogen economy. Throughout that decade I spoke about the possibility of a hydrogen economy in the following manner, "*If* we change from a hydrocarbon economy to a hydrogen economy…" But on the final day of August, 2005, I caught myself saying, "*As* we change to the hydrogen economy…" That change of one word represents a huge conceptual shift. Some event must have occurred, or some blazing cognitive shift have taken place, to prod me to go from seeing the hydrogen economy as *a possibility* to knowing it had *already begun*. However, upon reflection, there was no startling event nor blinding cognitive revision. Like so many other profound attitudinal shifts, the corner was turned so slowly and smoothly that I never sensed I was changing my mind.

August, 2005

ECD's stock price began August, 2005, at approximately $25.70 per share, and closed out the month eight dollars higher. A 31% price increase in one month certainly suggests that I was not the only person to sense the change in the company's prospects. Still, numerical increases do not furnish answers as to why the change came about. Perhaps reviewing ECD's official announcements for August might put some meat on the bare bones of this inflection point.

ECD owns a solidly profitable photovoltaic business (United Solar Ovonic) that has six months of back-orders for product, and in mid-July broke ground for its second 25/30 MW Ovonic solar production plant. The Secretary of Energy of the United States, Samuel Bodman, spoke at this event, stating:

> *...I came to know of the famous Ovshinsky pair many years ago when I was a young teacher of engineering at MIT. I started reading about things going on in Michigan. It was striking because I always thought of Michigan, in those days, as the center of manufacturing technology and greatness in manufacturing. The idea that we were having greatness in the physical sciences caught my attention. So I was particularly pleased to get a chance to meet with the inventor of all this.*
>
> *Today's groundbreaking underscores the successful collaboration of Government and Industry to promote the manufacturing and growing market penetration of photovoltaics... The technology embedded in the product is one of the most advanced and promising technologies developed today...companies like Uni-Solar [United Solar Ovonic] are showing how we can harness science and technology in innovative ways to become global leaders in new and growing industrial opportunities...*

It is now clear that in about a year United Solar Ovonic will become much more profitable. Further, on August 15, the Air Force announced additional funding for space applications of Ovonic solar cells. By the end of August, the future for ECD's photovoltaic activities looked dazzlingly bright.

COBASYS (ChevronTexaco Ovonic Battery Systems—ECD's 50-50 joint venture with Chevron for Ovonic nickel-metal hydride batteries) prepared for August by expanding its licensing terms and extending the duration of its agreement with the Panasonic/Toyota battery joint venture. August then witnessed a blitz of startling announcements regarding these batteries:

- August 4. COBASYS and Motorola announce hybrid electric vehicle component agreement.

- August 11. COBASYS achieves ISO/TS 16949 global automotive supplier certification.

- August 17. Ovonics battery subsidiary grants patent to Intellect Battery Co. of China.

- August 29. COBASYS confirms contracts for hybrid electric vehicle programs.

This represents a stunning array of announcements in a single month. Clearly Ovonic nickel-metal hydride (NiMH) batteries had also turned a corner.

ECD's solid hydrogen storage division, Ovonic Hydrogen Systems, was likewise active in August. On August 15, ECD announced that it planned to open a solid hydrogen test facility in Akron, Ohio. At the announcement ceremony, ECD exhibited a hybrid electric automobile, a Toyota Prius (which already has Ovonic nickel-metal hydride batteries) whose internal combustion engine was powered by *hydrogen*—not gasoline. A large banner stated simply: *Anything That Burns Can Be Replaced With Hydrogen*. ECD also displayed its mobile Ovonic hydrogen service station, the first solid hydride service station in the world. To say the two vehicles were a big hit with the Akronites is to lie by understatement. It looks like the solid hydrogen storage division is turning its own corner.

ECD's Fuel Cell Division also had some good news to report in August. They were awarded a $400,000 grant by the Michigan Public Service Commission to support a program to prepare ECD's fuel cell for commercial uninterruptible power and emergency power applications. This grant represents a large step forward.

Finally, in terms of the information side of the business, Ovonyx (ECD's joint venture with Tyler Lowrey and Intel) announced an agreement on Ovonic Universal Memory (OUM) with Elpida, an important Japanese semiconducting company.

Taken together, the developments in August clearly suggest that a new day has dawned for ECD. But the changes in ECD represent only about half of the reason to believe that we are now part of a whole new energy world—one that acknowledges the birth of the hydrogen economy.

As you know, the first prediction of the theory of global warming is that we will see more (and more devastating) weather events, such as hurricanes. The residents of Florida, Louisiana, and other Gulf Coast states have strong opinions about recent changes in hurricane activity. As you also know, the chief cause of global warming is the CO_2 released wherever one burns hydrocarbons. The recent run of devastating hurricanes suggests that we might be victims of our own hydrocarbon-dominated energy system. However, global warming is not the only problem raised by the United States' addiction to foreign oil.

Our economy is now dependent upon imported oil. Many have asserted that the United States' most recent wars have taken place in the Middle East because it controls the bulk of our planet's remaining oil reserves. Sadly, hurricanes and oil touch one another in a second way. On August 29, 2005, Hurricane Katrina stormed ashore in Louisiana—the entry point for approximately 30% of the oil and natural gas in this country. The devastation included: pipelines damaged, oil rigs in the Gulf of Mexico sunk or damaged, oil refineries shut down, oil unloading terminals damaged, and so forth. The petroleum market's reaction was almost instantaneous—in two days, the price of unleaded gasoline in my town went from $2.50/gallon to an unprecedented $3.40/gallon—a price almost unimaginable a short month earlier.

In retrospect, I now understand why August, 2005, was a tipping point for America's energy future, and an important step on the road to the hydrogen economy. Yet, while you and I might be newcomers to alternative energy, Stan Ovshinsky's road to the hydrogen economy was already more than 45 years in the making.

Bob Stempel (ECD's Chairman and CEO) appeared on the *Bloomberg Business Report* on the last day of August, 2005. He made a subtle, yet telling, comment that suggests his wisdom. He noted that while gas prices were quite high, ECD was built to be profitable with gas prices far lower than they are currently. Because of Bob, Stan, and Iris, ECD is not simply today's fad. It is, in all likelihood, the company that will lead the world into tomorrow's hydrogen economy.

Figure 1-1 traces in broad brushstrokes Stan's and Iris' vision for a totally clean and renewable hydrogen economy. Simply stated, the sun is the sole energy source for this system. Ovonic thin film photovoltaic cells convert the sun's rays into electricity. The electricity

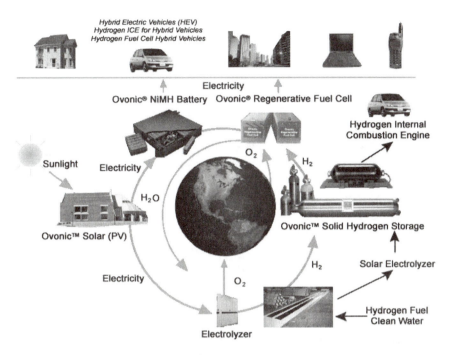

Figure 1-1

can either be used immediately, used to generate hydrogen from the electrolysis of water (which is then stored in Ovonic solid hydrogen powders), or stored in Ovonic nickel-metal hydride batteries.

Virtually any work can be accomplished with one or more of the above carriers of energy. Take, for example, the propulsion of an automobile. General Motors' EV-1 was a plug-in electric automobile. Electricity was delivered to its Ovonic nickel-metal hydride battery which ran the electric motors used to propel the car. Or, for example, ECD has utilized its hydrides to store hydrogen in a solid, replacing the gas tank of a hybrid automobile and having the internal combustion engine run on hydrogen rather than gasoline. Together with its standard Ovonic nickel-metal hydride batteries, it becomes an all-hydrogen car. Of crucial importance is the fact that the burning of hydrogen propels an auto without producing the unwanted by-products of gasoline powered autos (e.g., CO_2, SO_2, NO_x). Finally, hydrogen can be delivered to an Ovonic Regenerative Fuel Cell, which chemically converts the hydrogen gas back into electricity in a car. This electricity can then be used to run electric motors which propel the automobile.

A moment's reflection reveals that anything that burns—wood, coal or gasoline— can be replaced by hydrogen. One can appreciate then that many other tasks (heating or cooling our homes, running appliances, lighting, etc.) can also be accomplished with hydrogen. The entire system depicted in Figure 1-1 runs completely pollution-free, and is totally renewable because the sun generously bestows its bounty upon us daily. Of course, there are other renewable means of producing hydrogen such as via wind, tides, hydroelectric, geothermal and so forth. In addition, reforming hydrocarbon-based fuels (e.g., natural gas, oil, kerosene) can also produce hydrogen. However, these energy sources usually produce some pollution and are, of course, non-renewable.

So there you have it—Stan's and Iris' plan for a hydrogen economy, in a nutshell. Appendix 1, entitled "The Hydrogen Loop—The Means for Making the Hydrogen Economy Realistic," further discusses the technologies and products that flow from this hydrogen loop. Even if you do not choose to read it now, you might want to peruse its pictures and graphs in order to see the technologies and products which will be described later in this book.

Science Done the Old-Fashioned Way

Silly me. When I arrived at ECD that first time years ago, I thought Stan was giving up his whole day just to provide me with a tour of the ECD businesses. In a way he was, but in a more important way Stan was checking in with his numerous collaborators on a wide range of scientific/industrial "experiments." Those scare quotes are necessary because Stan's research typically doesn't follow the procedures for conducting experiments that scientists are taught during their graduate school years.

Stan's research style seems more akin to the natural philosophers who lived and worked prior to the twentieth century. These were men and women who conducted research out of pure curiosity. Science wasn't their profession; but it certainly was their passion. Some were lucky enough to be independently wealthy; others had benefactors who supported their work; and for others it was what they did after a hard day's work as a merchant or shoe maker. These natural philosophers sometimes gathered in societies of like-minded individuals, such as the Royal Society of London. In the twentieth century, the more typical career path was graduate school training to become a scientist and then employment in business, academia, or government.

Stan has a high school and trade school education, but no college or graduate experience or degrees. Yet, ECD was founded to develop advanced science and technology to build new industries. And in fact, so important are his scientific contributions that he's been awarded several honorary degrees and numerous awards.

…we walk up to a machine. It's a pretty big machine, and I have no idea what it does. Stan smiles as he approaches the man hunched over the open face of the machine.

"Hi, Stan."

"How's it going?"

"Not so good. See, I'm trying to get this to work like this but when I grind it down…"

Stan scrambles to get a better look at the machine's settings. He makes a quick adjustment and says, "Try that."

The worker nods, and we're off to the next machine.

"What's he doing?"

"We're building equipment to make nickel-metal hydride batteries. That one's going to Inner Mongolia."

"Where?"

Stan smiles and says, "The Chinese are some of our best customers. They wish to build their country on science and technology. And we believe that by recognizing the potential of China and working with them, we are opening up possibilities for China to become even more modernized so that they can take their place in the world community."

…and we move on to see another huge machine that makes the powders for solid hydrogen storage.

My tour does not include "the suits," since Stan has (correctly) pegged me as a science-guy. As one who can't stand getting dressed up, I comment on the "flannel and jeans" uniform of ECD workers.

"In addition to doing science, we're also building industries. That's often dirty work. Suits have no place here in our factories."

"But Stan, you're wearing a suit."

"I might be the only president of a company who is a member of a union. I'll show you a plaque in my office that was given to me by my union.[2] At ECD, we not only make the research breakthroughs, we also build the machines that will turn the breakthroughs into products. Then we make the earth-saving products themselves. You know: batteries, photovoltaic shingles, solid hydrogen storage products …"

I was quiet as Stan went on. But then Stan began an unrelated thought.

"George, at ECD we really believe in equality. If a worker can do the job, and he's handicapped, who cares? But that also extends to race, gender, nationality, sexual orientation, you name it. We must have well over thirty-five different nationalities represented on ECD's work force. Everything we do here is designed to change the world for the better. We hire and retain workers who are smart, talented, hard-working, loyal and considerate of others ..."

"Considerate? That's a job requirement?"

"Yes! We really want ECD to be the kind of community where everyone feels they are a part of the ECD family . . ."

"And how successful are you in creating that sort of community?"

"You'll be the judge of that. Talk to anyone here that you want to. That's just the scientific method: In God we trust, everyone else must show data."

All I could do in reply was to smile and wonder—which is, I believe, most people's first reaction to Stan Ovshinsky.

Consider this description of the first meeting of a University of Chicago physicist with Stan in the early 1960s, which was included in the book compiled for Stan entitled *Reminiscences & Appreciations.*[3]

...Max Powell picked me up and I looked in vain for a big sign saying Energy Conversion Devices, Inc. on the big buildings we passed on the way from the airport. Max said, "They haven't put up a big sign yet." Soon I was sitting across from Stan at his storefront office at 14121 W. McNichols Rd. Without much talk we went to his lab and Stan crossed two wires coated with some material, which created a completely symmetric current-voltage characteristic of switching and, after adjusting the variac, of some memory action into insulating and conducting states on the screen of his oscilloscope. I was flabbergasted, puzzled, astonished and very curious about the thin coating of the wires. Stan told me the approximate composition. "The percentages don't have to be exact and there are many compositions," he said. Stan watched me carefully but, "that is absolutely new" was all I could say...

Hellmut Fritzsche, *R&A*

Drawing the Hydrogen Loop, 1960

Stan with hydrogen tank, 1960

Iris as a little girl

Stan on pony with sister

Stan as a little boy

Iris and Stan on their porch in Detroit, 1960

Stan's high school graduation

Iris with her mother

Stan's "Alma Mater"

Steven, Ben, Sylvie, Robin, Iris, Stan, Dale,
and Harvey recently in California

Brother Herb, Father Ben, Sister Mashie,
Mother Bertha, and Stan(age 12)

Chapter 2

Stan and Iris

Scientific American Frontiers: Working as a team is not usually the easiest. How do you make it work?
Stan: By being in love I think.
Iris: We're very, very lucky because many people over the years have sort of said to us, "Oh my God, I couldn't work with my wife, et cetera. How do you do it?" And we just like to be together.

One of my trips to ECD took place the day after Stan had given an address to the Roundtable in Akron, Ohio. Akron was Stan's hometown, and his hosts had taken him to see his old home, park, school, and library. When I met Stan and Iris for lunch that day, they were in the mood to reminisce about their childhoods.

"...My (Stan's) father was a member of the Bund, the Jewish workers party born in the 19th century, in Eastern Europe before the Second World War. Stalin killed their leaders. They were also devastated by Hitler and the Germans. So they got it from both sides. In elections in Poland, the Bund's candidates received the most votes of any party that represented Jews. But they were pretty much all wiped out during the Second World War...

"My family lived on top of a hill in Akron, then the rubber capital of the world. I remember bicycling up and down that hill in all kinds of weather—rain, snow, whatever. I was the delivery boy for all of the pies and other food that my mother cooked for some of our relatives who needed it. And we always had relatives living with us because of the Depression. Mom was a 'red cross' for the neighborhood, but especially for the family. Family always came first for us, whether it was cousins across town or immigrants who were trying to make a start in Akron. It was a close group, a mutual aid sort of thing of immigrants helping each other."

"Did your father stay with relatives when he came to America?" I asked.

Stan smiled and said, "When he arrived in Chicago, he stayed with his sister and her husband. He was just a teen with no money and had to work right away. He became a teamster, which in those days meant driving wagons with horses. Then he went out to the Northwest (the Dakotas, Montana, Wyoming). I understand that at times his brother-in-law and older nephew traveled with him. His brother-in-law worked in the Mesabi Range mines and sailed the Great Lakes working on the ore boats. His nephews became plumbers, and fought very successfully in the Golden Gloves tournaments. They were a really tough bunch...

"My father loved Duluth, Minnesota, and went up through the Northwest laying railroad track and telephone poles. While he was out West, he broke wild horses. He loved horses all his life, and decided to break them more gently than everybody else. He felt others were too cruel as they broke horses. My father was known to 'talk' to horses and had a special way with them. As I was growing up in Akron, he was sought out by people to give advice about sick horses, what horse to buy, whatever... A cousin from New York taught my father how to drive a truck in the early 1930s, and when he had to stop, the first thing he'd do was say 'whoa'...

"So, anyway, my father moved across the West, working with horses, and returned to Chicago where he did various other kinds of jobs. Then he went on to Akron, Ohio, to take a job in a rubber factory at the beginning of World War I. He was a laborer, a very intelligent man, very socially conscious, and a leader for those who needed help.

"...In Akron, my father met my mother through her brother, a butcher, who was a friend of his. She was a very sociable and good-looking person, and very proper. She worked at many jobs, beginning with a metal stamping factory in her very early teens, a rubber factory (where I later worked), and a fruit market. She liked every place she worked. And at every place she worked, they liked her. My mother and father were both active in The Workmen's Circle, an organization promoting Yiddish language, culture and education, friendship, mutual aid and the pursuit of social and economic justice. My father was a founding member of the Akron branch... Although he had no formal education, my father was interested in culture, in Yiddish theatre—he performed with Paul Muni—and had fond memories of people he worked with in the theatre. On Saturday, he used to come home from work and listen to the opera."

"Stan, when did your father come to America?"

"After the 1905 revolution. For a better life. I remember the story of how he got the dent in his head."

"Dent in his head?"

"Yes, the Cossacks were running protesters down, and one of their horses stepped on his head and left this big dent like a hoof print at the top of his forehead. In Akron, when I was a child, my father used to wear his hair pulled forward to cover the dent. And because I was a child, I liked to push his hair back to see the horse's hoof print. I was told that my dad's friends spirited him out of the country and sent him to America...but my dad sure loved horses. I know this is true because several people in Akron told this story to me. In the winter, when the hills were really icy, my father would unhitch the horse from the wagon and he would pull the wagon up the hill himself. Imagine that..."

"Didn't your father get his love of horses from his father?" Iris asked.

"Yes. My grandfather served in the cavalry for 30 years. He was impressed... nobody wanted to be in the Russian army. They would ride into town, and the adults knew they were after 'recruits,' so they would run away. But sometimes the children weren't quick enough to run, so I guess they got him..."

"Kidnapped?" I asked in disbelief.

"Yes, as a young boy. And after 30 years in the Russian army, he came back and they let him have the rights to operate a local stage coach line."

I wanted Iris to reminisce also, so I asked, "Iris, what are some of your fondest memories of the years with Stan?"

"Oh, there are lots of them. One of the happiest is Stan's being in the dictionary! 'Ovonics,' the new field of physics he founded, is named after Stan. I'm especially proud of that because of my love of language. I also think back to our earliest years and the fun we had in the storefront (ECD's first office), just the two of us. We set up a wet lab and did some neurophysiology experiments with various elements that could change phase. Stan made some of his first switches and we wrote proposals to the government for funds.

"Sometimes we were successful, and that was gratifying. Other times it was very disturbing. For example, we once wrote a grant for government support. A while later, someone from the Westinghouse Corporation called to say that the government was funding Westinghouse to study our idea. Can you imagine that? This person wanted us to help him to study our ideas. Of course, that didn't happen just to us—in general the government liked to work with larger companies back then.

"I didn't work all day. I'd go home early to be with the kids when they came home from school. And we actually got the kids pretty involved. We had this Robin-device which she pressed. And Steven would practice the violin in the lab. We did it because the lab was close to our home... And we did things together, with the five kids. Stan's kids would come over and we'd do things as a group."

"Were Stan's three children older than your two?" I asked.

"Yes. Ben was born in 1946, Harvey in 1948, and Dale in 1949. Robin was born in 1952 and Steven in 1954. And they are all so different and so wonderful. They are all very close—we're one family. We're going to California next week, and we'll get to see two of them.

"Ben, the oldest, and his wife Eileen, a fantastic cook and gardener, live in Berkeley, California where he is ECD's West Coast representative and also teaches total quality management and does some consulting. Harvey and his wife Cathie live in Ann Arbor, just an hour away. Harvey is an award winning TV and film documentary writer, director and producer. Cathie is Associate Professor of Hospice Education at Madonna University in Livonia. Their daughter, Natasha, is Director of Physical Education at Grosse Pointe Academy, and their son Noah, who graduated in political science from Kalamazoo College, is a freelance radio and television producer. Our next son, Dale, lives in Miami, Florida and has worked for many years at a Publix grocery store. Our daughter, Robin Dibner, is a physician—she is Associate Program Director of the Department of Medicine at Lenox Hill Hospital. She lives in New York with her 17 year old daughter, Sylvie Polsky, who is a student at Brearley. Steven Dibner, our youngest son, now 51, has been for many years the associate principal bassoonist of the San Francisco Symphony and teaches both at Aspen and Marlboro.

"I am an only child. Stan had an older sister, Mashie, who died recently, and of course, you know his younger brother Herb."

"Iris," I said, "didn't you grow up in New York?"

"Forty miles north of New York, right near Peekskill in Mohegan Colony, which was formed by socialists, anarchists, and, feminists...

Later communists became part of the scene, and this caused a great deal of trouble between them and the others."

"I didn't know there was a radical strand in your family too," I offered.

"Oh yes," she replied. "They wanted us kids to have a progressive education, and the community was built around the Mohegan Modern School, modeled after the Ferrer School in New York. When I left the school in the sixth grade, they wanted me to go into sophomore year of high school. I resisted because I thought it wouldn't be good to jump so many years."

"I'd say you made the right choice," I said. Iris graduated from Swathmore College with a BA in zoology, received an MS in biology from the University of Michigan, and a Ph.D. in biochemistry from Boston University, which recently named her one of its distinguished alumni.

"My father—I don't know if there was such a thing as a conscientious objector at that time—but my father did not want to fight in the First World War. He left France for the United States in order to not go to war. He became a translator. You could give him a page in English and he'd read it to you in French, Spanish, Italian, any Romance language, with no hesitation." Iris was clearly proud of him.

I inquired about Iris' mother.

Iris began to laugh, "He met her through the Ferrer School..."

"In France?" I guessed.

"No, in New York. Francisco Ferrer was a Spaniard who fought for progressive education. He was actually garroted—do you know what garroting is?"

I nodded affirmatively. But then I made the mistake of stretching for a joke, "Was he for progressive education before or after he was garroted?" And Stan and Iris were kind enough to chuckle at my feeble attempt.

"...So in the early 1920s, my mother and father met at the Ferrer School in New York, which sponsored discussions and dances and such. My mother became a teacher—actually she left college when she met my father. When I was little, she went back to college, and finished her degree as a French teacher. There were few jobs because of the Depression, and by the time she got to the top of the list of prospective teachers, she had turned forty, and that was too old for new teachers at the time, so she worked as a secretary working with French and English. I remember that she worked for the French government in exile for a while."

Just then the waitress arrived carrying a tray of deserts. And even though I shouldn't have done so, the "To Die For Chocolate Cake" looked so good…

Returning our discussion to Stan, Iris mentioned that in the early 1980s, Stan received an honorary Doctorate of Engineering from Bowling Green State University. "In his short acceptance speech I remember him saying, 'I've worked on Ohio's farms, I've worked in Ohio's factories, I got my education in Ohio's public—and he paused—*libraries*.'"

Stan joined in excitedly, "I was very much interested in every-thing—science, technology, history, art and literature, politics, poetry and girls. I was not interested in school but was very excited by learn-ing and found that I could do it much better on my own… I spent so much time at the tiny public library on Wooster Avenue that they waived the 2 books limit for me so I could take out as many books on any subject that I wanted. It was my second home as a child. One day, when I was about eight, I carried out a stack of books so high that the librarian said, 'Stanford, what will be left to read when you grow up?'" [A picture of Stan's "Alma Mater" can be found on page 12.]

Herb Ovshinsky's memories of his older brother Stan include the young scientist scooping water from mud puddles so that he could look for one-celled animals under the microscope of the trea-sured chemistry set, as well as the socially conscious activist willing to stand up to bullies of all ages. One time he even broke a buggy whip that a teacher had used against a student. There were hours reading H. G. Wells' *Outline of History* and the *Henry Ford Trade School Machinist Training Manual*, as well as incredible discussions on life, politics, science—the revolutionary automatic high speed lathe, the revolutionary vision of the brain as a physiological device, and later the revolutionary vision of synapse-like devices (chemical, then electronic). In describing his brother, Herb says, "That's just Stan. That's who he's always been. Now I know how unusual he is. But back then, since he was my only brother, I thought all brothers were like him."

However, Stan and Iris are far from ordinary. They have traveled together throughout the world to introduce Stan's Ovonic technol-ogy. And it doesn't take long, when you're with Stan and Iris, to see the strong, deep, and tender connection between them. It's easy to understand that what attracted them to each other in the 1950s is still very present today. For Stan, his love of Iris has been his sustenance and inspiration, and he flatly declares that he'd be nothing without her. Iris recalls Stan's being so handsome and brilliant, and her desire and resolve to be able to work with him. After having been apart geographically, the excitement they felt when Iris finally arrived in Michigan for Stan's birthday in November, 1959—where they've been together ever since—is still clearly present in this couple who have loved together and worked together for more than 45 years.

On December 6, 2004, in New York City, The Workmen's Circle honored Iris and Stanford Ovshinsky as renowned scientists and socially responsible entrepreneurs who have "lived their entire lives devoted to the principles of The Workmen's Circle/Arbeter Ring—creating *a shenere un a besere velt* (a more beautiful and better world)."

As Laura Ashley's article for the program summarizes,[1]

...Armed with their Workmen's Circle values, they set upon a goal—to create a new science and technology that solves society's problems rather than causes them. Starting with inventive genius, Stan and Iris were able to realize this vision with their own personal qualities of fearless creativity, dogged tenacity, and vision...

In 1960, Stan and Iris together founded Energy Conversion Devices (ECD) to commercialize Stan's ground breaking (sic) scientific inventions in energy and information. They initiated and pioneered the field of amorphous and disordered materials, building new industries, creating jobs and catalyzing new areas of education. Since the problems were global, they operated internationally and their products have become the enabling technology in photovoltaics (solar cells) and their Ovonic nickel-metal hydride batteries are used in consumer products and enable all hybrid vehicles. This is not a long way from their roots as they have done all these things to make for **a shenere un a besere velt** *by working to reduce pollution, climate change and wars over oil...*

In Akron, Stan was elected chairman of the Jewish Young Adult Council, representing all of the young people of the Jewish community. A confirmed Yiddishist and an opponent of all totalitarian movements; he is the living legacy of The Workmen's Circle ideals. As a tool-maker he was a member of the International Association of Machinists, of which he is now an honorary member...

Stan's and Iris' interest in global affairs and helping third world countries improve their living conditions has been a driving force in their work. The small, thin film, light-weight photovoltaic cells that Stan invented were used on the Mir Space Station operation to generate electricity from sunlight. But they are also used to bring electric power to the most remote areas on the earth, allowing the poor and isolated to learn to read and write, store food and drugs through refrigeration, build new industries, and build better lives.

In 1988 the PBS science program, **Nova,** *aired a documentary on Stan entitled "Japan's American Genius." The small, powerful, nickel-metal hydride batteries that Stan created at first did not impress American manufacturers, but Japanese electronics giants embraced the technology. Last year, 1 billion, 250 million NiMH batteries were utilized in computers, cell phones, and other gadgets including those hand-held calculators that we rely on everyday. Most of these were developed through licenses on the more than 300 patents that Stan holds. In the 1980s the Japanese licensed his patents to produce rewritable CDs and digital video discs, revolutionizing the information age. Today Stan and Iris and ECD, working with American carmakers, are in the forefront of the battle to apply the nickel-metal hydride batteries as the energy source for electric and hybrid cars. This will revolutionize our use of fossil fuels and help defeat the threat of pollution.*

In 1999 **Time** *magazine named Stan a "Hero for the Planet" for his work in "healing the earth," he was awarded The Karl Boer Solar Energy Medal of Merit jointly by the University of Delaware and the International Solar Energy Society and he was given the Sir William Grove Award by the International Association of Hydrogen Energy. He and Iris were named "Heroes of Chemistry" in 2000 by the American Chemical Society, for having "made significant and lasting contributions to global human welfare." A street in Springboro, Ohio was named Ovonic Way by the Governor of Ohio.*

"Healers of the earth"—this is a good way to describe Stan and Iris. They have shown us, through their life work, how science and technology, marshaled by visionaries, can build **a shenere un a besere velt.**

A more beautiful and better world, indeed.

Stan's and Iris' reply was a simple,

*Two billion people in the world are without electricity. [Alluding to the photo found below.] A barefooted young woman carries our Ovonic photovoltaics up a steep mountain bringing electricity to her village. She has the future on her back and the future in front of her. Let us all join her in the struggle to make **a shenere un a besere velt.***

We are honored to be honored by the Arbeter Ring which has always been with the oppressed against the oppressors.

Stan and Iris

Stan building his Benjamin automatic center drive machine (Toledo, circa 1947)

Chapter 3

An Industrialist at Heart

In 1907, Carl Sandburg represented the Wisconsin Social Democratic Party, whose platform "found a design" for the kind of society he envisioned: reformed government; the elimination of corrupted power; the prohibition of child labor; protection of rights of women in the labor force; the right of literate women to vote; tax reform, including a graduated income and property tax; urban renewal; free medical care and school textbooks; public works projects to improve the environment and provide work for the unemployed; state farm insurance; pensions; workmen's compensation; municipal ownership of utilities; higher wages and shorter hours for working people; better living and working conditions for everyone. With the Wisconsin socialists, Sandburg had found a new forum from which to "agitate and educate".

Penelope Niven (1991)
Carl Sandburg, A Biography

Stan Ovshinsky has always loved machines—building them, running them, fixing them. He remembers that, as a boy, he was always working with his father cleaning up at the various machine shops and foundries in Akron, Ohio. His first job was as a machinist, and he was not only excited by it, but actually saw art forms and sculpture in what other people might have thought of as merely castings or machines. To Stan, however, a machine was beautiful.

Stan started out as a worker, and he has never lost his solidarity with the common worker. The Social Democracy of Eugene Victor Debs, Carl Sandburg, and Norman Thomas is one of the intellectual roots from which he's grown. Although what's important to Stan is not the politics, but the values that drove such a movement that it became a massed voice for people all over the world—values of true social responsibility and equity, where human beings are treated with dignity, and where they can grow to their potential.

What Stan believes in doesn't represent any political party or movement affiliation. He can't be pinned down by a label. In fact, Stan is against ideology of any sort because of the rigidity of thought and action that it imposes. He feels that change is inevitable for progress, and uses the example that one would not practice medicine now as one did in 1910. Stan is quick to say, "I only belong to my conscience. What I stand for is not a party, but an ideal." For Stan, no single party—Left, Right, or Center—really understands the problems of the world's energy systems or the alternative energy systems, the problems of our global economy, the problems having to do with endemic joblessness. And no one political party understands what we must do to reindustrialize America in the 21st century—that we innovate and create new industries or we perish.

As a problem solver who believes that America needs to be a manufacturing dynamo, Stan is an industrialist at heart. Particularly concerned about erosion of the industrial base of the United States, he believes that we will always have joblessness and poverty and social problems if we do not build new industries that are what the 21st century and beyond require, based on the most advanced science and new technology—based on *innovation*. Stan has said that energy and information are the two areas that are fundamental to our society and to our global economy. That's why he picked those two areas for making revolutionary changes.

Stan wants to build huge new industries, not by doing the same thing over and over, which he sees as contrary to progress, but by continually advancing new ideas that build industries that are responsive to the needs of the global population—that are "green," like photovoltaics, like the hydrogen economy. His aim is to solve problems of pollution, climate change and wars over oil while providing high quality manufacturing jobs, like those at ECD, and offering new ideas for curricula to the education system. He sees the value of jobs that bring out the potential of human beings and uses the human reservoir of talent—not just a small segment, but the larger community—to solve the problems we all face.

Stan has always been a big believer in education. For example, as a young worker, he pushed to educate workers about the coming changes of automation, so that rather than being frightened of change, they might be better prepared to change with the times. He also organized book review sessions as part of the factory routine. This was done to promote the welfare of workers as an integral part of the work place.

A recent example of the way ECD encourages employees to continue to learn would be Kevin Fok, who works at the Fuel Cell Division. He was an engineer at the Battery Division who decided to get an MBA. ECD paid for the degree, gave him time off to take the classes, and encouraged him to rethink his job at ECD. Now he's the business manager at Fuel Cell. Kevin has many good things to say about the way ECD encourages employees to improve themselves.

Being influenced by Social Democracy suggests that one would feel a degree of empathy with the common working-stiff that has almost vanished from our contemporary worldview. Consider the structure of American businesses today. With rare exception, businesses are constructed to be of benefit primarily to the owners and/or the management. Today we tend to think of ourselves as members of some "management team," and our goal in life is to help our corporation (or university, in my case) become successful. From this contemporary management perch, labor looks like just one more "cost" incurred in our business' struggle to become profitable (along with the costs of materials, capital, etc.). Not so for Stan.

The welfare of labor (or *all* of the people who make up a corporation) has to have equity with all other values. When speaking with the employees of ECD, one quickly realizes the degree of commitment employees feel toward the company's goals. Stan believes that bringing out the creative potential of his colleagues makes for the unusual culture of achievement that has raised ECD above the very large companies where labor is a disposable commodity. What is not recognized is that this culture creates great value and, in the end, greater profitability and return to the stockholder.

I'd like to highlight several themes that recur often with Stan Ovshinsky: his ability to imagine possible science and technology inventions long before they become technically feasible, his mission to make ECD a colleague-oriented business that provides solutions to society's most pressing needs, his solidarity with all workers, and his commitment to defending the human rights of all people. The comments of a few of the people associated with ECD help to illustrate these themes.

*Stan treats his employees like an extended part of his family. He's never used titles and everyone is addressed by their first name, including himself. He would never judge a person by their degree, race, or anything else, but by their talent. Stan gives everyone the opportunity and time to develop their individual potential. In addition, he uses the concept of the Round Table, in that everyone is equal, and carries that belief into the ECD main conference room where you will actually find a large, **round** table. He always tells us "you are working with me, not for me"…*

Ben Chao, *R&A*

This is not about Stan's acknowledged genius, commanding presence and creative leadership. Nor is it about his strength and grace under fire. These are a given. Rather this is about the Stan whose insight and compassion have led him to recognize talent and potential in people where others less gifted have failed. What follows is but one of the many Stan stories that for me illustrate the qualities I mentioned.

One day, an applicant for a technical position is introduced to Stan for an interview. It is painfully apparent the gentleman is seriously physically challenged and has, as well, a pronounced speech impediment. Stan reviews his resume/c.v. noting that the man's Ph.D. was awarded before the onset of this tragic affliction. He further learns of the dogged determination of the fellow in his pursuit to find a position prior to applying at ECD, i.e., countless interviews followed by the agony of countless rejections. Stan's sensitivity and perspicacity plumb below the reaches of the obvious stumbling blocks to employment. Rather, based on his assessment, he sees a person of intelligence and promise whose grit and dignity merit consideration and an opportunity to prove himself.

The applicant was hired, he proved to be diligent and productive and was enveloped with warmth and an appreciation for his skills by Stan and Iris and the welcoming family of ECD friends…

Pat Dahlin, *R&A*

Stan has a unique ability to bring out the best in people… The ECD culture, in my view, is the opportunity for people with diverse backgrounds to work together in an environment where we work for a common good—society, our shareholders, each other…I have observed Stan motivate extraordinary effort not by cracking the whip but by inspiring people. This culture allows anyone and everyone to achieve great things, and to take pride in what we accomplish. It is the ECD culture from Stan that allowed me to rise through the ranks from vacuum technician to jr. engineer, engineer, sr. engineer, manager of technology, director of technology, vice-president of technology to Sr. Vice-President of the battery company. I recall the progression not to bring credit to myself but to illustrate the unique environment Stan and Iris have created where such a progression is possible...

Mike Fetcenko, *R&A*

This next quote speaks of the unusual melding of novel scientific concepts with a truly unique research/development and production-oriented company. As Stan says, "We invent the materials, we invent the products, and we invent the production technology."

When I first joined ECD, my work centered on amorphous silicon and photovoltaics. I remember testing thousands of small devices, the size of a pinhead, and was astonished when Stan held a company meeting and declared that ECD was going to make amorphous silicon photovoltaics by the mile. And I wasn't the only one as I looked around the room. Today, in Auburn Hills, there stands an ECD amorphous silicon deposition machine that does just that! Unbelievable, but true.

The next program I worked on was thin film microelectronics. Again Stan had a vision of incorporating amorphous silicon into large areas and this time it was displays. Stan believed that amorphous silicon could be used to make displays for TVs and computers and he was right again. Today, almost all portable displays for PDAs and laptop computers use amorphous silicon active matrix technology.

The last and current program is my favorite. This program calls for the development of memory devices based on phase change in chalcogenide materials. Stan started this work back in the '60s, when computer memories were unheard of. As a matter of fact, neither were computers. But Stan had a vision and he was right again. Today, almost everyone has a computer, and no computer has enough memory. They all want more.

The program started after I had written several SBIR (Small Business Initiative Research) proposals that were rejected by the government as too good to be true. But I had only written what Stan believed in and he had convinced me that it was attainable. Just after the program started, I specifically remember going to

Stan one day with negative results. I had to tell him that the memory devices that we had made would not switch. When I told him that, he wasn't discouraged. He asked me what pulse widths I had used and sent me back to the lab to try narrower pulses. Again, Stan was right, but I was getting used to it by then. With narrow pulses, almost six orders in magnitude, we got switching and launched the new phase change memory era at ECD. Today, this technology is pursued by Ovonyx with companies like Intel, STMicroelectronics and BAE as licensees...

Wally Czubatyj, *R&A*

The reader will likely note the incredible lengths of time that workers stay at ECD. They might have the lowest turnover rate in the country.

Our family is one of the many families that has been inspired and elevated through our association with Stan and ECD. When we were a very poor family living in Waterloo and our father was a teaching assistant at the University of Waterloo, he visited ECD on the urging of Dr. Eisenberg, who was a consultant to ECD at the time. When he met Stan, he was so impressed and so excited. Wanting to negotiate for a better life for his family, our father made what he thought was an impressive request for a high salary. Stan, with characteristic generosity, told our father he would pay him twice as much, and our father joined immediately. This was 32 years ago. My father still works at ECD.

Our mother [Momoko Ito], who was a housewife at the time, asked whether she could get a clerical position at ECD. She began working in the personnel department, but also started helping Stan on negotiations with the Japanese. ECD was rapidly increasing activity with Japan at the time, and she was quickly promoted to VP of International and board member. Stan was able to see the hidden potential in a housewife with no experience in business, and coached and supported her in becoming a rare instance of a Japanese woman executive and one of the chief negotiators for deals for ECD. This could only have happened with Stan at ECD. We watched our mother expand her repertoire from a great mom to a successful and confident businesswoman. She eventually moved on to establish and run Japan ECD for almost a decade. Stan's uniquely unprejudiced view of a young Japanese woman transformed the company, her life and ours...

Joichi Ito and Mizuko Ito, *R&A*

...Our relationship goes back more than forty years. Over that time, much of the world has finally come to appreciate all those things we already knew existed.

Recognition. Some individuals strive for recognition. The unimportant will settle for fleeting notoriety or their "fifteen minutes of fame." Others want more. A select few hope to make an indelible mark in history, a mark that will be recognized by not only their peers, but by the world at large. Such is the case with Stan Ovshinsky. But recognition for this man is not about ego or self-indulgence. Rather, it is the progressive realization of ideas.

Perseverance. Few men have experienced the true nature of perseverance. For the better part of five decades, Stan Ovshinsky forged ahead with a clear eye on the future. Disregarding the slings and arrows of detractors, Stan plowed ahead, running the gauntlet and, more importantly, emerging victorious. And now, celebrating his eightieth year, his eyes are still clear and still fixed on tomorrow.

Vision. A rare quality, possessed by few, envied by all. What gave Stan the unique powers of a visionary? If we could answer that question, we would all be standing in line waiting our turn to receive that power. But one thing is certain. Stan Ovshinsky is unique. He combined an innate genius for science with the perceptiveness of a gambler. He merged his quest for knowledge with a natural intuitiveness that would make a fortune-teller green with envy. His vision allowed him to see a future that the rest of us had trouble comprehending. For Stan Ovshinsky, looking ahead twenty, thirty, forty years into the future was like writing next week's schedule...

Daniel Davidow & Elihu Nemiroff, *R&A*

Stan created a truly unique culture and organization at ECD which minimized bureaucracy and optimized creative opportunities to bring out the potential of people in the organization. Stan feels that the entire company, built both on his contributions and on his business strategy, requires the talent, creativity and contributions of his colleagues and collaborators. He is very proud of the culture and the family feeling that is the heart and soul of ECD's success. He points out that teams of dedicated, committed and talented people in the various parts of ECD interact and exist harmoniously, knowing that their efforts and contributions are appreciated. He gives them the opportunity to represent the company globally, and they make the company internationally respected.

Stan is the first to say that ECD is not just his and Iris' company; rather that ECD truly represents his talented colleagues and collaborators. Since its beginning, ECD has had many outstanding Directors on its Board.[1] Particular acknowledgement goes to Bob Stempel's important contributions and company leadership. Former CEO of General Motors, Bob had risen from being an engineer on the drawing board to become internationally recognized for his contributions to the automotive industry and business community. His contributions to the environment were early shown by his problem solving talent of initiating catalysts that significantly cut down on automotive pollution. He was and is a pioneer and leading figure in making possible electric and hybrid vehicles, and continues to be the spearhead of building the new automotive industry.

Initially serving as a senior business and technical advisor to Stan, Bob joined ECD in 1993. He works so well in tandem with Stan that several years back, Stan felt that Bob should be properly recognized as chairman and CEO of the company. Stan and Iris consider him to be an outstanding leader, engineer, partner, and person, and express deep respect, admiration, and affection for him. Stan and Iris continue the work that they are doing, Stan now being president, chief scientist and technologist, and the basic inventor of the materials, products and technology for every division of ECD.

I see the roots of Stan's philosophy in his parents' qualities—integrity, compassion, and hard work—and in the social democratic values Stan internalized as a youth in the Akron Workmen's Circle. He is against totalitarianism of any sort, Communist or Fascist. He refers to his philosophy as Social Responsibility (instead of Social Democracy) in order to be better understood, and gives the following quote by Damon Darlin in *The New York Times* (December 4, 2005) as an example of what he means:

But, as they [the founders of Hewlett-Packard] fiddled with the oscillators in that garage, the men were hammering out new ideas about how companies should be run, including an egalitarian emphasis on employees' happiness as a means toward generating innovation. That worked not only for their company, but also as a model for Intel, Sun Microsystems and other successful giants of Silicon Valley.

It is clear that Stan combines a love of building new industries based on invention, science and technology with the human and social values espoused by the nineteenth century Social Democratic movement, wedded to the influence of two thoroughly decent Russian immigrant parents in Akron, Ohio near the dawn of the twentieth century.

Always An Idealist

Harley Shaiken, now a professor and authority on global labor and economic issues, knew Stan and Iris from those early days when he was a young apprentice who ran ECD's small machine shop in a garage at one end of ECD's old back building. As he recalls:

> *I first met Stan and Iris in the late spring of 1960. We were in the basement of a bank at the corner of 7 Mile Road and James Couzens in Detroit attending a founding meeting of the Congress of Racial Equality (CORE) in Detroit. The sixties were unfolding and the civil rights movement that would transform the decade was beginning to stir. Stan gave an impassioned, inspiring talk on the value of rights and the importance of supporting those who were taking up this cause.*
>
> *To know Stan and Iris, then as well as now, is to engage ideas, to embrace human values, to challenge cant and hidebound orthodoxy. It is to be inspired in fundamental ways. I still remember the excitement of reading for the first time writers as different as Thoreau and Orwell; John Reed and Bertold Brecht; Shakespeare and Kropotkin. I was introduced to them all through Stan and Iris. In a world of increased academic specialization which funnels into narrowness, Stan embodies the breadth of the Renaissance.*
>
> *Stan was very impressed with the Reverend Martin Luther King so we would talk about the roots of his non-violence, hence Henry David Thoreau; Stan introduced me to Orwell as embracing freedom amidst a darkening totalitarianism; and throughout there was a sense of discovery and excitement. Stan embraced many ideas but a constant thread ran through them all; people fulfilling their promise and having a greater say in their future.*
>
> *All this would have been heady enough, if Stan had been a philosopher, a writer, a poet, a politically committed person—all of which he is—but he is also a scientist. I soon found out that the values that motivated his humanistic view of the world also propelled his scientific quest. Soon after I met Stan, I worked briefly*

at ECD when it was a storefront on Six Mile Road in Detroit and had just hired its first full time employee. Those were the days in which science could take place during the day, young people from CORE might meet in the evening, and more science could take place in the early hours of the morning.

Stan spoke about the role solar energy might play in addressing the problems of the most impoverished and marginalized. He spoke of a vision of development and hope and the science that could fuel the transformation. The vision was extraordinary then, and far more vital now.

Stan's remarkable genius as a scientist and his defining achievements in science embody his passion to change the world. At times, making the world a better place requires the courage to sit down at a lunch counter when that simple act might put your life at risk; at times it means bringing solar energy to a remote village in Chiapas or clean energy to Los Angeles or all the remarkable things ECD has produced under Stan's guidance.

Harley Shaiken, *R&A*

Stan is an idealist through-and-through. Yet, while he has no hesitancy in proclaiming his core values, he is a tough realist. I suspect that Stan's coming up with a fundamentally new area of science while not having a conventional academic background was threatening to some people in science and in business. Institutions have built-in inertia and do not change suddenly. Although Stan is always quick to say that the support he received from numerous giants of science and business more than made up for whatever lack of institutional support he experienced.

As best I can tell, Stan is the "real deal"—a committed idealist with a clean soul. Unusual and amazing, indeed. Of course, Stan's commitment to his scientific and business values would serve as a rebuke to any scientist or businessperson who was less scrupulous in his or her observation of those values. This rebuke would be present, whether or not Stan intended to deliver it.

"In God We Trust

. . . everybody else must furnish data." You've already heard that Stan-ism. If I've heard it once, I've heard it a thousand times. And, indeed, he's correct. If you believe something to be true, then that belief must be ready to withstand the scrutiny of a fair, empirical test. That statement represents every true scientist's commitment to empiricism. And if Stan is anything, he is a scientist. So is there a fair, empirical way we can test Stan's basic commitment to the principles of equity and fairness?

In a sense, the explicit testimony of his lifelong colleagues represents such a test. And there, he seems to pass with flying colors. However, a recent article in *The New York Times* stimulated an idea for an even tougher test of Stan's level of commitment to these principles. The article was written by Gretchen Morgenson (January 25, 2004, Section 3: Money and Business) entitled, "Explaining (or not) Why the Boss Is Paid So Much: Looking at Chief Executive Pay Expressed as a Multiple of the Employee Average Pay at that Company for 2003."[2]

That figure (CEO pay/average employee pay) for all companies headquartered in Japan, for example, was 10. Thus, if the employee average for a company in Japan was $25,000, then the chief executive would make (on average) $250,000. Values for the other highest ranking countries of the world are: Germany (11), France (16), Canada (21), Britain (25), Mexico (45), and Brazil (57). The burning questions, then, are: "What is the comparable figure for companies in the USA?" and "What is the ratio for Stan Ovshinsky relative to the salary of the average employee at ECD?"

A moment's thought suggests that someone influenced by the principles of Social Democracy would have a smaller ratio than average for his or her country, believing that all workers should share fairly in the success of their company. In fact, as *The New York Times* article describes,

> *Daniel J. Steininger, Chairman of the Catholic fund, submitted a proposal to limit the chief's pay to a figure that is 100 times that of the average worker. Steininger's rationale for the salary cap is, "We're trying to get at the notion of economic injustice in what the C.E.O. is making compared to the average worker." It's bad for the long-term performance of a company because it breaches the trust between top management and the people who work for them.*

The ratio for the average American business in 2003 was an obscene 531! The ratio for Stan and the average ECD salary in 2004 was 5! I trust those data would make even a Eugene Victor Debs or a Carl Sandburg smile in solidarity.

I'll close with a colleague's explicit comparison of Stan's management style with a manager from the Canon Corporation.

In 1990, ECD and Canon formed a joint venture company called United Solar Systems to further amorphous silicon photovoltaic technology and expand its manufacturing capacity. Like many others, I became part of United Solar. The first president, Mr. K., was from Canon, a well-known Japanese company with a traditional hierarchy. One day, Mr. K. and I had a one-on-one discussion. We had different opinions on many issues. He was frustrated that I didn't share his views. "Tell me, what is the difference between my management style and Mr. Ovshinsky's." I looked into his eyes and said slowly but firmly, "We call you Mr. K., and you consider us your subordinates. We call Mr. Ovshinsky STAN, and he considers us his colleagues and collaborators." There was silence for a long time.

Jeffrey Yang, *R&A*

Stan was named a "Hero for the Planet" by *Time* magazine, 1999

Stan in his lab

Chapter 4

The Vision of a Genius

"Hellmut," I implored, "you've worked with Stan for forty-five years. How can a self-educated man pioneer an entirely new field of science?" After thinking for a few moments, Professor Fritzsche replied, "Perhaps one key to Stan's genius or success is the fact that academic training did not confine him to only one specialty field such as physics, chemistry or engineering. Perhaps a self-taught person is better able to think outside the box."

Did you wonder why I spoke of Isaac Newton in the Preface of this book? It was because I believe that Sir Isaac Newton and Stanford Ovshinsky have a lot in common. Most scientific men and women of genius simply take the tools at their disposal and employ them to make some conceptual breakthrough. That is often enough to gain for themselves their share of immortality.

Still others, like Michaelangelo and Leonardo Da Vinci, practice their brands of genius over such a wide array of fields (painting, sculpture, science, anatomy, etc.) that it strains our imaginations to appreciate how they might achieve these feats. I am told by many that Stan is conversant with a similar wide range of disciplines. Alas, I am ill-equipped to measure his skill in fields such as art, literature, poetry, and the like. However, I have allowed myself to be convinced by others of his expertise in these diverse fields.

I believe that Newton and Ovshinsky share a common ground that even most other people of genius do not. When Newton created his vision of a mechanical universe, the movement of whose celestial bodies was governed by his "inverse-square" law, he also realized that no mathematics then available could handle the necessary calculations. So Newton created the calculus, which made the calculation problems of his mechanical universe tractable. This second level of genius is very rare indeed in the history of science.

Stanford Ovshinsky reminds me of Newton because he not only envisioned the hydrogen economy described in Chapter 1, but he also created the science of disordered and amorphous materials to furnish his unique technological solutions to our environmental challenges. While there are, for example, non-amorphous batteries and photovoltaic cells, Stan's batteries, photovoltaic cells, computer memory, fuel cells, and so forth are quite different because they are based upon his science of disordered and amorphous materials. As Newton offered both the Newtonian worldview and the calculus to express the vision mathematically, Ovshinsky offered his vision of the hydrogen economy and the science of disordered and amorphous materials to produce the technological achievements necessary to bring his vision to fruition. Prior to Ovshinsky, solid state physicists, inorganic chemists, and materials science engineers studied atomically ordered materials—as if they were the most important of all substances. After Ovshinsky introduced the utilization of disorder as a means of providing new degrees of freedom to synthesize new materials and develop new chemical, physical and electronic mechanisms, materials scientists were able to follow his lead. For example, even in the 1950s, he was using thin films in the angstrom range. What is now called nanotechnology was something that he was already working in. He called it atomic engineering and was particularly interested in the properties of materials as they reached the quantum limits.

A "liberation-constraint" dichotomy goes far beyond the choice of subject matter by scientists. "Liberation" and "constraint" are often two sides of the same coin. For example, automobiles liberated many millions of us to travel the country freely. However, we are now constrained by some unintended negative consequences of autos—traffic congestion, haze, acid rain, global warming, wars for dwindling supplies of oil, and the like.

Or, think instead of grid-produced electricity. It is now 3 AM, as I write this chapter. Doing so would be almost impossible without power supplied to me by the Indiana & Michigan Power company. I look at other aids to living that now surround me and bestow a degree of freedom—refrigerator, microwave, television, computer. And while I am loathe to forfeit these conveniences, they do tie me to the vicissitudes of I & M Power, the Anaconda coal company, the Encana (natural gas) corporation, as well as other parts of the North

American Power grid which might precipitate a massive blackout that affects me. After the automobile, the electric utility system is North America's largest polluter.

Stan's creations weigh in on the side of liberation. Photovoltaic cells on the roof free us from the perils and pollution of the electric grid. Similarly, fuel cells and hydrogen free us from most of the limitations of the internal combustion engine (although traffic congestion will still remain). Stan's creations typically offer maximum freedom with a minimum of attendant constraints.

Change Doesn't Come Easily

Foresight (or the power to imagine possible futures) is both a creative and a practical human skill. Part of Stan's genius was to foresee the emerging hydrogen economy almost a half-century before it began to develop. Unfortunately, during those five decades, the United States lived under a different vision—the dream of energy produced through the burning of cheap hydrocarbons.

Oil companies, natural gas companies, coal companies, and electric companies make enormous profits from people's various needs. These business giants have a vested interest in keeping people un-liberated in the energy domain. Such collusion to impede radical change is not new to our country. For example, the monied interests behind the making of horse-drawn carriages, buggy whip manufacturers, and the like, opposed the mass production of automobiles almost a century ago. Even if the hydrogen economy is a better idea for the world of the twenty-first century, our hydrocarbon-based corporations do not simply step aside and fade into history. After all, they are fighting for their business-lives.

An example of this can be seen in why the hydrogen economy did not take off after the initial Arab oil embargo of the 1970s. An issue this complex defies a simple answer. However, a few contributing factors can be mentioned. First, the oil companies were extremely powerful and they realized that expensive oil—while it would hurt consumers—would actually enhance their profits. [This is the era which created the phrase "obscene profits," a term that oil company executives joke about to this day.] Thus, the 1980 presidential election proved to be a pivotal event. Ronald Reagan's campaign, supported by the enormous wealth and power of the energy and automobile corporations, worked to portray Jimmy Carter as weak and ineffective, shivering in the White House as he called for conservation.

Our country rejected the path toward the hydrogen economy—and also rejected freedom from cheap, Middle East oil. Our choice hurled the world toward increased air pollution, global warming, a hastened Peak oil crisis, Gulf wars, and a perilous energy future. How different a world it would be had we greeted the creation of OPEC with a sustained effort to bring about the hydrogen economy. Instead, for twenty-five more years, we fiddled while oil burned.

A Dark Vision of the Future

The oil companies themselves have been aware of the ultimate need for a transition away from burning hydrocarbons.[1] Back in the 1960s, M. King Hubbert was a petroleum geologist for the Shell Corporation. He was asked to model the productive life of a typical oil *well.* His findings suggested that the graph of production was roughly a bell-shaped curve that peaked (the year of highest production) when approximately one-half of the well's reserves had been produced. These were interesting results, but nothing shocking. Next, Shell asked Hubbert to model the productive life of an oil *field.* For example, Spindletop was a "whale" (a gigantic field) in east Texas that had thousands of wells producing during the first half of the twentieth century; Ladyfern was a large oil field in Western Alberta in the 1990s. Hubbert's model revealed that an oil field's productive life looked eerily like the curve for a single well.

While Shell didn't ask Hubbert to continue this line of research, he naturally wondered about a *country's* productive oil life. In modeling oil production in the United States, Hubbert predicted the peak production of oil would arrive sometime in the 1970s. Since oil peaks can only be known retrospectively, Hubbert's results became known in the 1980s. Oil production peaked in the United States in 1970—the point at which half of our reserves had been harvested—and production has steadily declined since then. While this finding was troubling for oil geologists, as long as other parts of the world were increasing their oil production, there was no crisis.

In the late 1990s, Colin Campbell tried to ascertain the Hubbert Peak for *global* oil production.[2] Startlingly, the oil peak was predicted to be sometime early in the 21st century. There are many consequences to an oil peak. The two most troubling are that global oil consumption *must* begin to decline and that the price of crude *must* increase dramatically for both geological (it is always much more expensive to produce the second half of an oil field than to produce the first half) and economic (supply-demand imbalances always produce higher prices) reasons.

In his book, *The Hydrogen Economy* (2002),[3] Jeremy Rifkin describes some secondary consequences of world peak production of oil:

> *...the world's leading geologists...warn there really is an oil crisis looming on the horizon, and when it hits it will be permanent. So where are we headed in the next few years?*
>
> *If global oil production were to peak some time in the next decade or so, followed shortly thereafter by a global peak in natural-gas production, it could set off a cascade of events that could unravel much of our industrial way of life. Two developments, in particular, are likely to figure prominently in the coming oil equation.*
>
> *First, while the experts disagree about when global oil production is likely to peak, they agree that when it does, virtually all of the remaining untapped reserves will be left in the Muslim countries of the Middle East, potentially changing the current power balance in the world. The juxtaposition of dwindling oil reserves and growing militancy among many of the world's younger Muslim population could threaten the economic and political stability of every nation on Earth. Political leaders and policy analysts are particularly worried about the escalating conflict between the Israelis and the Palestinians and the possibility that, in the future, Islamic fundamentalists might pressure their governments to use oil as a weapon against the United States and other Western nations for supporting the Israelis.*
>
> *Second, if global oil and natural-gas production peak, catching the world unprepared, countries and energy companies are likely to look to the dirtier fossil fuels—coal, heavy oil, and tar sand—as substitutes. With Earth's temperature already projected to rise by 2.52^0 to $10.44^0 F$ between now and the 22nd century, the switch to dirtier fuels would mean an increase in CO_2 emissions, a greater temperature rise than is now being forecast, and even more devastating effects on the Earth's biosphere than have already been envisioned.*

Donella Meadows and her colleagues, in their book *Beyond the Limits* (1992),[4] worked with the (reasonable) assumption, "What if the future is a continuation of past trends?" Using the actual data for most of the twentieth century to mathematically model global trends, she had the program make predictions for each of the years of the twenty-first century.

So what happens to our world according to those predictions? Catastrophe strikes. The population rises in mid-century to about 9 billion souls. Then in a few decades it declines to about 4 billion. One hundred million people were killed in World War II which was the worst catastrophe in human history as defined by loss of lives. One shudders to imagine how the population might be reduced by 5 billion people. In so far as math models can depict how this kind of loss of life might occur, it appears that pollution levels become so severe that per-acre grain production falls rapidly, which causes rapid loss of food production. Of course, math models cannot tell us whether the enormous loss of life is due to starvation, savage wars over dwindling food supplies, or the like. However, a world in the process of losing 5 billion people can only be depicted as nightmarish.

While other parts of the world have moved aggressively toward conservation, the United States has been singularly unresponsive until recently. Our country has generally shown an antipathy toward conservation. The economist Hal Varian (who serves as the Dean of the School of Information Management and Systems at the University of California at Berkeley) discusses how countries can easily facilitate conservation by considering the question, "What will happen if we tax gasoline like Europeans do?"[5]

> *First, it is a good idea to tax the consumption of goods that impose costs on other people. One person's consumption of gasoline increases emissions of carbon dioxide and other pollutants, and this imposes environmental costs on everyone. And even those who do not care much about the environment have to acknowledge that driving contributes to traffic congestion. Increased taxes on gasoline would reduce consumption, cutting both pollution and congestion.*
>
> *But, you might argue, we already have taxes on gasoline: federal, state and local taxes average about 41 cents a gallon, or 28 percent of the price of gasoline. Isn't this enough? The problem is that the tax is used mostly to pay for road construction and maintenance. True, the gasoline tax decreases the use of gasoline, but the road subsidy increases its use.*
>
> *If we subtract the subsidy from the tax, we end up with a net tax rate on gasoline in the United States of about 2 percent, which is much, much lower than net gasoline taxes in the rest of the world.*

Paying at the Gas Pump

The price of premium unleaded gasoline may vary around the world, but it is taxes that take the biggest bite in Europe. Average prices shown are for the week ended Oct. 16, 2000.

Cost for a gallon of gas		Percentage to taxes	Amount (per gallon) to taxes
Britain	$4.35	**76.3%**	$3.32
France	3.50	**68.3**	2.39
Germany	3.37	**67.5**	2.27
The Netherlands	3.82	**65.1**	2.49
Belgium	3.43	**65.0**	2.23
Italy	3.58	**63.4**	2.27
United States	1.71	**22.4**	.38

Source: Energy Information Administration

There is another, quite different reason to tax oil products.

Economists like to tax things that are in fixed supply because the same amount is available whether or not the tax is imposed. World oil supplies wax and wane in the short run depending on how effectively OPEC is enforcing production quotas. But in the long run, there is only so much oil. Taxing petroleum products will not reduce the total amount of oil in the ground, it will just slow the rate at which it is discovered and extracted.

Taxes on gasoline reduce the demand for oil, thereby reducing the price received by the suppliers of oil. And most of those suppliers are foreign: the United States now imports 56 percent of its oil, and OPEC countries control about three-fourths of the world's proven reserves. Taxing foreigners is popular both economically and politically—they do not vote. Of course, domestic oil producers not only vote, they contribute to campaigns, and a tax on gasoline would be unpopular with them. But deals can be made—taxes can be traded for depletion allowances and other accounting goodies to make such a plan politically viable.

A gasoline tax in a small country falls mostly on the residents of that country. The world price of oil is essentially independent of the taxing policies of most countries, since most countries consume only a small fraction of the amount of oil sold. But the United States consumes a lot of oil—almost a quarter of the world's production. That means it has considerable market power: its tax policies have a major impact on the world price of oil, and economic analysis suggests that in the long run, a significant part of a gasoline tax increase would end up being paid by the producers of oil, not the consumers.

Nearly 20 years ago, Theodore Bergstrom, an economist who is now at the University of California at Santa Barbara, compared the actual petroleum tax policies of various countries with policies those countries would adopt if they wanted to transfer more OPEC profits to themselves. He found that if each major oil-consuming country pursued an independent tax policy, the tax rates in European countries should be somewhat lower than they are now, while the tax rate in the United States should be much higher. If the United States, Europe and Japan all coordinated their oil-tax policies, they would collectively want to impose net tax rates of roughly 100 to 200 percent. This is not as scary as it sounds since such a coordinated tax increase would mostly affect oil producers; the price at the pump would increase much less.

Mr. Bergstrom's analysis was focused entirely on transferring profits from oil-producing to oil-consuming nations. If we factor in the pollution and congestion effects mentioned earlier, the optimal petroleum taxes would be even higher. In the past, Al Gore has advocated increasing gasoline taxes for environmental reasons, though he has been pretty quiet about this proposal lately. George W. Bush does not think much of oil taxes, but he likes the idea of a tax cut.

Let me propose a bipartisan plan: raise the tax on gasoline, but give the revenue back to taxpayers in the form of an income tax credit. Average consumers would be about as well off as they are now, but the higher price of gasoline would tend to discourage consumption—giving us environmental, congestion, and tax-the-foreigner benefits. It would make sense to phase the tax in over several years, so that the next time drivers trade in their sport utility vehicles, they would have an incentive to buy those fuel-efficient cars that Detroit has promised to produce.

Increasing the net tax on gasoline by, say, 2 percent a year for the next 10 years would be pretty painless for most people. Oil prices would almost certainly drop back down in the next few years, tending to reduce the price of gasoline back toward historical levels. A higher gasoline tax would just mean prices would not drop quite as far as they would otherwise.

If something must be taxed, it makes a lot of sense to tax something that is costly to the environment, costly to the users and mostly controlled by foreigners. The United States is passing up a big opportunity by not taxing gasoline at a higher rate.

Of course, Professor Varian is correct. We ought to be paying almost twice what we now pay for a gallon of gasoline. Doing so would instantly make hybrid electric, electric, and fuel cell autos a smart business decision. We could easily reverse the regressive nature of a gas tax (i.e., imposes a disproportionately worse effect on the poor than on the rich) through a tax rebate or a generous grant to poorer people who purchase fuel-efficient autos.

Our imports of foreign oil would drop precipitously. The Peak oil phenomenon would be pushed into the future by a considerable amount. The price of a barrel of oil would drop. The United States' balance of payments with foreign countries would improve substantially. Our domestic auto producers would achieve the same competitive position as countries like Japan and Germany in the race to produce the clean and efficient autos of the future. Atmospheric pollutants would be reduced. Fewer greenhouse gases would be produced by automobiles. There would be less reason to engage in military actions in the Persian Gulf region. The percentage of our taxes devoted to the military could be reduced. Our government would be flooded with new tax dollars that could be used to lower tax rates, pay down our national debt, rescue a wounded Social Security system, fund projects to enhance the nation's educational competitiveness, etc., etc.

A Future Full of Light

Stan's hydrogen economy (depicted in Figure 1-1) converts free (from the sun) energy into the satisfaction of human needs in a completely non-polluting manner. Thus, the severe pollution levels that trigger the catastrophe in Donella Meadows' mathematical model of our future might never occur. Our society transitions nicely from burning ever scarcer hydrocarbons to the pollution-free harvesting of hydrogen. Remember, anything that burns can be replaced by hydrogen *now*. Middle East oil-related entanglements do not occur. Americans prosper by producing the infrastructure and products required for the hydrogen economy. Detroit could produce hybrid hydrogen autos, not only waiting for the fuel cell to become accepted, but also utilizing the basis of the present automobile industry, the internal combustion engine; Dayton might focus upon manufacturing nickel-metal hydride batteries; Akron could develop solid hydrogen storage industries; and so forth. This is clearly a half-full glass, when contrasted with the dark vision where we remain addicted for too long to a rapidly declining, polluting hydrocarbon economy.

Stan saw these problems emerging forty-five years ago. One can only begin to appreciate the mountain of frustration endured by someone who has fought against the forces that have resisted the hydrogen economy for half a century. He, Iris, Bob Stempel, and ECD took on the long, onerous task of developing the products and systems required to bring about the hydrogen economy. Stan Ovshinsky deserves enormous credit for making ECD an international company and shepherding it through the dangerous shoals where so many businesses have foundered.

Stan and Iris honored as "Heroes of Chemistry" in 2000

The ECD Team

Chapter 5

An Extraordinary Company

I am prouder of the organization and working climate
that we have built than of any of my inventions.

Stan Ovshinsky
1998

A Hot Summer's Day

It was very hot as Max Powell drove down McNichols Street in
Detroit one summer day. A lot was happening. Civil rights and school
integration were burning issues. But Max mostly thought about getting a few more jobs so that his fledgling office cleaning business
might survive.

Max drove his old truck past a man in a white shirt and tie who
was mowing the small strip of grass in front of his store. Within
two blocks, Max had decided to make a U-turn and try to speak to
this amateur lawn-care specialist. If he mowed his own lawn, Max
reasoned, he might not have hired someone to clean his office, either.
When he turned his truck around, Max actually made a U-turn in his
life.

The man was Herb Ovshinsky, and mowing grass in the summer
sun made the idea of hiring a handyman quite appealing to Herb. So
Max was engaged to clean the ECD offices about twice each week.
Max dealt with Herb primarily, but he saw both Stan and Iris from
time to time as they went about their different activities.

One day Herb asked Max to stop by Stan's office to discuss a
full time job with ECD. Over forty years later, a ninety-five year
old Max Powell, who has served as Vice-President of African Affairs
since 1995, chuckles as he thinks back to that summer day and that
U-turn in his life. A timeline depicting significant events in ECD's
history can be found on the company's website *www.ovonic.com*.

Harvey Leff connects Stan's Akron years with ECD's early years.

...I was born and grew up on Moon St. in Akron, Ohio, where all of the residents were immigrants, many of whom had a horse in the garage (barn). At first nobody had a car or truck. Benjamin & Teibel, Stan's parents, also lived there in the early '30s. His father started peddling scrap with a horse and wagon and was probably the first one on the street to buy a truck. In fact, he had a reputation from the old country as a horse specialist extraordinaire. He was considered very bright as he spoke at least five languages. It was common knowledge that most machine shops in Akron exclusively did business with Ben because of his reputation as a man of integrity and reliability. Teibel, Stan's mother, had a reputation as a very kind and hospitable person who often invited neighbors and friends to stop by for conversation and food.

Stan inherited all these traits "in spades." He was considered a genius by all his friends and neighbors. He was friendly to everyone and always hard working. He read profusely and was so involved in expanding his knowledge base that he went to trade school while attending high school. He had a passion for machinery...

At the age of 21, Stan already showed his creativity and entrepreneurship. One of his early ventures was a shop he opened to rebuild and overhaul carburetors, generators and brakes. All of his good friends were offered jobs if they needed work. Shortly after that he invented the "Benjamin Center Drive Lathe," named in memory of his father, which created lots of interest and was then licensed to a national company. This lathe was considered a major advancement at that time...

As one of his first investors in 1960, I am constantly amazed as to Stan and ECD's accomplishments. Of course, I remain a major stockholder today as I am convinced that all his dreams of ECD changing the world will definitely happen.

I can still remember my first visit to Sohio in the early '80s where I tried to arrange for their technical staff to meet with Stan. They had absolutely no interest but agreed to a preliminary meeting. After that visit, Sohio, now BP, had a love affair with Stan and ECD. After investing nearly 80 million dollars they decided to go it alone where they are still today. But recently I was told that Stan is still revered by BP, and if it were not for him they would probably not be in the solar energy business today...

Harvey Leff, *R&A*

Takeo Ohta traces the period from the late 1960s to the 1990s.

It was 1968 when I first heard about Stan Ovshinsky through the media. The newspapers reported that he had discovered the Ovonic switching phenomena in amorphous thin films. It was quite a different process from anything in crystalline silicon semi-conductors, and I started to study amorphous thin films.

Then, in 1971, he announced his phase-change optical memory. At the time, I was developing laser modulation devices of Kerr and Pockel's effect investigating ferroelectric materials. I proposed, then, a new project in the Central Research Laboratory of Matsushita for developing high-density thin film optical memory devices. I attended the Japanese Applied Physics spring conference in Chiba, Japan, where I heard the lecture of "Physics of Amorphous Semiconductors" from Prof. H. Fritzsche of the University of Chicago. It was an exciting lecture about new phenomena in amorphous disordered materials; that summer in 1971, I discovered optical memory phenomena in sub-oxide films.

The program of our Central Research Laboratory at that time was to promote new research and development products of post-color TV. Many engineers were developing videotape recorders in the Central Research Laboratory at the time and the Laboratory promoted big, industrial products such as VHS in the late 1970s. In the 1980s, we were challenged to promote post-VHS product developments using amorphous optical memory films. The first product was sub-oxide write-once optical disk of Matsushita/Panasonic-IBM3363 in 1985 and the next was the phase-change rewritable optical disk of Matsushita/Panasonic LF71100 in 1990. Our high-density recording phase-change optical disk by thin substrate (0.6 mm) technology was introduced to the DVD technology in 1995. And, now, the phase-change optical disk comes to be the mainstream optical memory in the world as CD-RW and rewritable DVD.

Stanford R. Ovshinsky is the Great Father of Phase-Change memory.

Takeo Ohta, *R&A*

Japan has been a very important part of the history of ECD. ECD had been working successfully in Japan since the 1960s, for example with Fuji Film. Activity in Japan took off in the 1970s, when Momoko Ito joined the company. [See page 28.] Stan describes her as incredibly talented and a very important contibutor to ECD who was its ambassador not only to Japan but to the world. She was the President of Japan-ECD, and also served on the Board of Directors. ECD has worked with Asahi Chemical, Nippon Steel, Sharp, Canon, Matsushita, etc., some of the largest and best companies in Japan.

Internationally, the United Kingdom and Europe have been important to ECD from the beginning. Italy and Germany continue to be sources of growth. Furthermore, Japan, Korea, Taiwan, China and Russia have played and continue to play important roles in ECD's international activities.

Stan insisted that basic science must coexist with saleable products at ECD. Marc Kastner, head of the Physics Department of MIT, marvels at how theoretical physicists and others reveled in the ECD intellectual hot house.

*A condition of my job offer from MIT in 1973 was that I **not** work on amorphous semiconductors. The "experts" at Bell Labs had advised MIT that the field had no future. So I began research on other topics. Nonetheless, despite his shortage of funds at the time, Stan Ovshinsky asked me to consult at ECD, and I made several trips to Michigan with Dave Adler. Earlier, while I was a graduate student in Hellmut Fritzsche's group at the University of Chicago, I had suggested some ideas from chemistry that I thought could be useful in understanding chalcogenide glasses. Stan was the first to embrace these ideas, and his outspoken support did much for my self-respect. The discussions with Dave and Stan at ECD in the early '70s kept me aware of the scientific issues, even though I was not directly involved in the research.*

Then, in 1976, Stan brought Neville Mott to ECD for a visit. In honor of the occasion, Stan organized a workshop, which was attended by the leaders of the field. These were my heroes: Stan himself, Neville Mott, Hellmut Fritzsche, Morrel Cohen, Artie Bienenstock, Dave Adler and others who made seminal contributions to our understanding of disordered materials. I was in awe of these physicists, and was honored that Stan would include me, far less distinguished than the others and no longer active in the field. The most important question discussed at the workshop was related to a model Mott and Street had recently proposed to explain the absence of spins in chalcogenide glasses. They proposed a very high density of unsatisfied chemical bonds in the material, and that at these dangling bonds, electrons attracted, instead of repelled, each other. At one point Hellmut Fritzsche pointed out a flaw in the Mott-Street model, and Mott was trying to find a way around it, when I thought of a new way to explain what was going on.

*I did not put forth my idea at that moment, but on the airplane going home to Boston, Dave Adler and I wrote a first draft of a paper and, working with Hellmut, we completed the manuscript a few weeks later. That **Physical Review Letters** paper on the valence alternation model of defects in glasses is still my most cited paper. The response the work received from the community made it possible for me to work again on amorphous semiconductors, and the Kastner-Adler-Fritzsche model was the achievement that earned me tenure at MIT...*

Marc Kastner, *R&A*

Problems of size, funding, and the struggle for survival over the years are highlighted by Bob Johnson.

Stan and his work on amorphous devices first came to my attention as Vice President of Engineering at Burroughs with his fast switch. Fast switches are the backbone of computers, and Stan had a clever, new, and different idea. I never did figure out how to use his switch as a basic computer element, and when he told me he could make a thin film transistor, I asked him "What good is that?" It was slow and hard to connect for example. Main frame computer guys, and engineering VP's, were and are, hard to communicate with.

One of my favorite early recollections of Stan and Iris was when they appeared out of the cold on my doorstep at home one New Year's Day. Stan said he needed (as I remember it now) $100,000 by January 3. Could Burroughs and I help? We did, and I think that not only saved Stan's neck but got us at Burroughs seriously interested in the clever and useful things that Stan was inventing.

When leadership matters at Burroughs deteriorated, I took early retirement and joined Stan at ECD intending to make a thin film, foot square, NGEN, the next generation computer, on his production line for photovoltaic cells. That never made it, but the thing Stan had also started then, flat panel liquid crystal displays driven by his amorphous switches, did make it. ECD invented that device. With their essentially free capital in those days, the Japanese built the $200 million facilities necessary to produce FPLD's, and took the market away from us, the USA, and Europe. After 20 years, Asia still owns the FPLD market...

The problems of image, small company size, new and unproven (in production) technologies, are typical of the problems Stan has had with every one of his inventions…

Bob Johnson, *R&A*

The struggle for recognition has been a 45 year battle for Stan and ECD.

Over the years, I discovered that Stan left a very strong impression on people—strongly positive or negative—never neutral. This was particularly so in the scientific community where people either admired him for his bold imagination or would run him down. It is only since the mid eighties that even the doubting Thomases were willing to concede that they could have been wrong. As an outsider, people talked about their resentment quite openly in my presence when I happened to attend a couple of conferences in the early eighties. I was very puzzled, as I knew they were wrong and I could not understand the reasons for their resentment. I think that I finally understood the resentment they initially had towards Stan and hence ECD and will try to explain it briefly as I understand it.

America is a land of ideas—ideas are welcome irrespective of nationality, social status, and upbringing. The heroes that come to mind quite readily are yesterday's heroes—Edison, Ford, Bell. It is not an accident that they also happen to be Stan's heroes. But even in America, it is difficult for a Ph.D. from Harvard or Stanford, or wherever, to accept that somebody without that formal training could discover something of great importance that he could not. I believe this was the reason many people in the scientific community had difficulty accepting his claims. It is another matter altogether that there were many other members of the same community who did not have that difficulty. It was also maybe a product of the times. The seventies and eighties saw the NIH (Not Invented Here And Hence Presumably Unimportant) attitude in big corporations. It was only towards the end of the eighties that corporations (after being humbled by smaller competitors both from within and without the United States) redesigned their philosophy—NIH was no longer a bad word in a company. It is interesting, if not purely coincidental, that it was about the same time that many scientists—grudgingly at first, and later quite unequivocally—endorsed and accepted the progress and claims from ECD. I think that Stan was a victim of the times. His is also a story of perseverance through such difficulties. This really is a story of human beings and their weaknesses—a story constant through the ages—the more things change, the more they are the same. As a further aside, I find it very interesting that the latest product (I am familiar with) from ECD—the Nickel Hydride Battery—developed in the nineties faced no opposition or difficulties. Amorphous Silicon Solar cells did not enjoy as easy an acceptance and it took the community about ten years to accept ECD's supremacy—the chalcogenide switch faced the most difficulty—it is interesting for me to read that Motorola has tied up with ECD in 2002—37 years after the first discovery at ECD—to convert it into products. This, I guess, must be very satisfying for Stan.

K.L. Narasimhan, *R&A*

Finally, Stan Stynes, a former director of ECD, summarizes the scope and travails of Stan and ECD's 45-year adventure.

In a time when the image of corporate leadership is tarnished everywhere by the greedy unprincipled actions of a few, Stan has been a role model for the kind of creative leadership that finds ethical, moral action totally compatible [indeed essential] with good business practice. It has been my pleasure to be a part of ECD for over 25 years and never once have I seen Stan succumb to pettiness or vengeful action, although he has been sorely challenged by outsiders [even some insiders on rare occasions] hoping to usurp the creative accomplishments of the company. Individuals and major global giants have attempted to steal the ideas and literally the ownership of the company—while we have defended ourselves vigorously in the courts, Stan has always been willing to meet his adversaries more than halfway; frequently settling cases with agreements that benefited all involved, rather than pursuing a we-win, you-lose policy. His integrity and creativity are models for any executive's business style, indeed for anyone who aspires to lead others...

Stan Stynes, *R&A*

Business and the Environment

Does it take a most-unusual man, like Stan Ovshinsky, to create a most-unusual business? In the book *Collapse* (2005),[1] Jared Diamond describes the relationship between environmentalists and businesses in the following manner,

Issues of human environmental impacts today tend to be controversial, and opinions about them tend to fall on a spectrum between two opposite camps. One camp, usually referred to as "environmentalist" or "pro-environment," holds that our current environmental problems are serious and in urgent need of addressing, and that current rates of economic and population growth cannot be sustained. The other camp holds that environmentalists' concerns are exaggerated and unwarranted, and that continued economic and population growth is both possible and desirable. The latter camp isn't associated with an accepted short label, and so I shall refer to it simply as "non-environmentalist." Its adherents come especially from the world of big business and economics, but the equation "non-environmentalist" = "pro-business" is imperfect; many businesspeople consider themselves environmentalists, and many people skeptical of environmentalists' claims are not in the world of big business.

Because we live in an environmentally conscious age, the classic who-cares-about-the-environment business attitudes and practices of an earlier age have been suppressed. Because it's the law, every business is aware of environmental constraints—even if they are only viewed as impediments to be avoided or subverted. Most businesses now fall into a category whereby business is conducted in an environmentally proper manner—so long as it does not seriously impair profitability. An even better business approach consists of companies whose primary business is environmentally neutral, but who have developed strengths in environmental areas. For example, Sharp (electronics) and British Petroleum (oil and natural gas) are currently the two largest producers of photovoltaic cells. It is difficult to know whether their motivation to expand into pro-environmental domains was motivated by environmental values, the perceived profitability of the new domain, or both. Regardless of their motivations, such companies are to be credited for furthering the cause of environmental sustainability.

ECD is the prototype of a new category of company—businesses whose *raison-d-être* is to produce sustainable, environmental products. While some of ECD's businesses are not environmentally focused (computer chips, DVDs, etc.) its primary businesses are designed to foster the clean and renewable hydrogen economy (photovoltaics, batteries, hydrogen storage, fuel cells). Such companies' primary motivation is to design and manufacture products that are good for our world. Their primary ambition is to create a better world.

What Makes a Business Environmentally Problematic or Helpful?

There are many ways to tell scientific tales of the future. Perhaps the least controversial approach is simply to state current scientific theories and to plot the present trends of the variables implicated as important by those theories. Paul Ehrlich and Ann Ehrlich noted that the stress placed upon any ecosystem by humans can be determined by consulting the following formula, $I = P \times A \times T$ or PAT.[2] In this formulation, the impact (I) of any group is the product of the size of its population (P), its per-capita level of affluence (A) as measured by consumption of goods and services, and a measure of the damage done by the technologies (T) employed in supplying each unit of that consumption. An ecosystem's carrying capacity is defined as the population size that an ecosystem can sustain indefinitely. When the human population's total impact (I) exceeds the ecosystem's sustainable carrying capacity, the ecosystem begins to deteriorate. Unless human impact is reduced, an ecosystem pushed beyond its carrying capacity will deteriorate until it eventually crashes.

Counting the number of humans in a population is a reasonably straightforward task, and so, determining the value of P is relatively easy. Figure 5-1[3], on the following page, shows the course of P over the past thousand years. Any person who examines this graph will realize that our species is now experiencing out-of-control growth. The results of this growth might be catastrophic for the health of our planet's ecosystems.

Measuring the population's affluence level (A) is much more difficult because combining entities such as land, water, air, energy, and so forth into one overall measure is problematic. GDP (Gross Domestic Product) has traditionally been used to measure a population's level of affluence (A). The technology (T) term is often mistakenly thought to signify an anti-technology bias in the $I = PAT$ equation. However, T simply reflects the environmental *destructiveness* of the techniques used to produce the goods and services consumed. In fact, sophisticated technologies can obtain either high or low values assigned for T. For example, complex technologies, such as nuclear powered electric plants, can have high values for T because society cannot safely deal with radioactive waste for the thousands of years that it requires attention. Similarly, chlorofluorocarbons (CFCs) used as aerosol propellants, as cleaning detergents for microprocessors, and for heat transfer in cooling units once were considered to be commodities with a low assigned value of T. But CFCs' value for T first increased when they were found to be greenhouse gases, and then increased again when they were implicated in the destruction of the earth's ozone layer, which protects us from the sun's ultraviolet rays. Thus, the value assigned for T is always a function of science's state of knowledge of the entities and techniques in question. In Chapter 7 we consider a very complex technology—photovoltaic cells within roof shingles—that produces electricity and has a value for T of about 0.

Unfortunately, there is currently no accepted procedure for obtaining worldwide values for T. Values can be estimated only on a technology-by-technology basis. However, several scientists have suggested that a measure of a population's energy consumption serves as the best available index of the combination of affluence and technology (A x T). This is because several disparate entities (e.g., forests lost, oil burned) can be converted into energy unit equivalents with little distortion. Also, the amount of waste produced by human activities is now closely related to the amount of carbon-based energy consumed. What energy consumption (as a measure of A x T) hides is the fact that not all sources of energy stress ecosystems equally. For example, obtaining electricity from solar power stresses the earth far, far less than obtaining electricity by burning coal. What are the current paths of P, A, and energy consumption (A x T) in the above I = PAT formula?

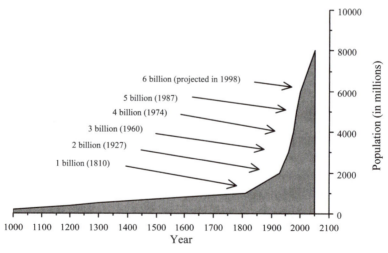

Figure 5-1. Global population growth.

I know of no worldwide figures of the growth in energy consumption and GDP. However, the growth in energy consumption, GDP, and population in developing countries over a 30-year period are shown in Figure 5-2.[4] Although a 30-year time span might be large for psychological studies, it represents a deceptively short span for the physical and biological trends that now threaten the planet. As with all restriction of range problems, one tends to underestimate the magnitude and importance of relations when they are assessed during a narrow window of time. Thus, population, GDP, and energy use *appear* to grow in a linear fashion as shown in Figure 5-2. Similarly, the standardization procedure performed on the dependent measures (using 1960 as the base year) in Figure 5-2 also tends to make the trends appear less dramatic than if the raw data had been presented. However, the trajectory of growth in the global human population can be interpreted as a *geometric* (or exponential) trend when considered over a much longer period of time—such as the second millennia of our common experience (See Figure 5-1). In reality, the increases in GDP and energy consumption in Figure 5-2 are even steeper than the growth in population depicted in Figure 5-1.

Since the Industrial Revolution, the planet's human population (P) and the amount of energy consumed by humans (A x T) have increased geometrically. This represents an inherently unstable situation that must be corrected. Kenneth Boulding, former president of the American Economic Association, stated the problem succinctly, "Only madmen and economists believe in *perpetual* exponential growth."

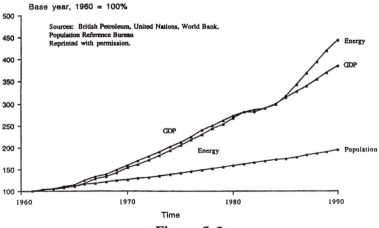

Figure 5-2

All of this is to reinforce the fact that growth in P and A has been staggering over the last 1000 years. Our ecosystems are condemned to succumb to the stress (I) we place on them unless we dramatically lower the T-term in the I=PAT formula. We've finally reached the crux of why ECD represents a new (and very unusual) type of business. From its start back in 1960, ECD has self-consciously worked to develop technologies that have infinitesimal T-values. We can have billions of people living relatively affluent lifestyles if and only if those levels of affluence are produced via technologies with extremely small T-values. Revisit ECD's overall plan for the emerging hydrogen economy presented in Figure 1-1. Every new technology in their clean and renewable cycle (e.g., fuel cells) replaces another frequently used technology (e.g., internal combustion engines) that possesses a dramatically higher T-value than ECD's alternative. ECD is an extraordinary company because it is dedicated to driving down the T-value of the technologies that provide our affluent lives.

ECD's Complete Hydrogen Economy Solution

Figure 5-3[5] presents the current organizational structure of ECD.

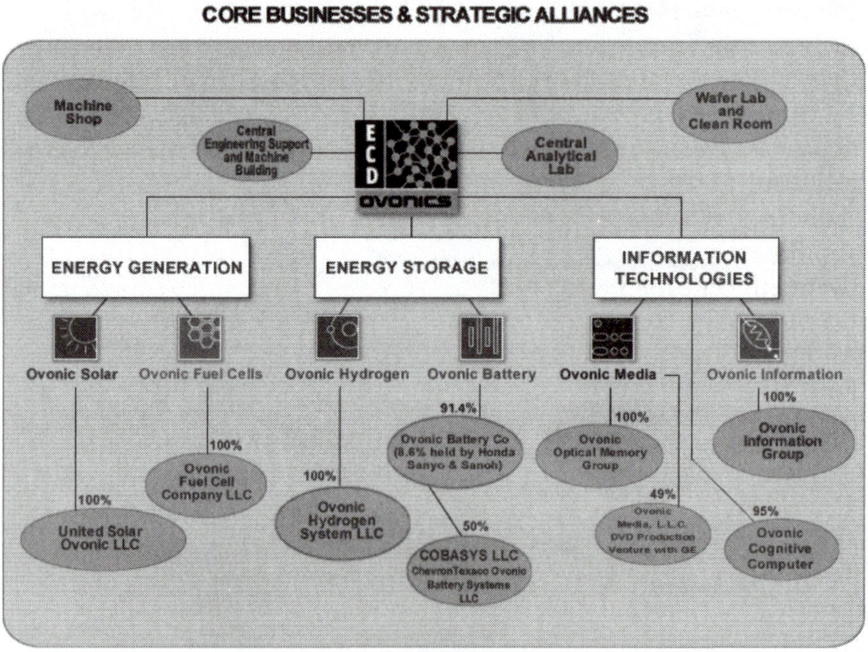

CORE BUSINESSES & STRATEGIC ALLIANCES

Figure 5-3

Ballard is to fuel cells as ECD is to the *complete* hydrogen economy. Sharp is to photovoltaic cells as ECD is to the *complete* hydrogen economy. Matsushita is to batteries as ECD is to the *complete* hydrogen economy. Finally, Quantum is to hydrogen storage as ECD is to the *complete* hydrogen economy. The four companies compared with ECD above are all "unusual" because they also strive to create and market low T-value products.

Where ECD is doubly-unusual is that it offers a total solution to our hydrocarbon-dependent society. It is the only company with the complete hydrogen loop. Ballard develops a fuel cell in the hope that some other companies will solve the hydrogen production problem, and the hydrogen transportation and storage problems. Even if Ballard succeeds, other difficulties might remain. Thus, the development of the hydrogen economy rests on a series of solutions to different problems being attacked by different companies. ECD engages in the exploration of all of these problems simultaneously in the hope of offering a complete solution to our waiting world. Comments by Stan's colleagues in several chapters of this book often mentioned the fantastic and brilliant scope of his vision. I think this is what they alluded to: Who dares to take on all of the problems of the hydrogen economy? Stanford Ovshinsky, that's who. And with each passing year of the twenty-first century, it looks ever more clear that ECD does have the complete hydrogen economy solution.

ECD might be to the twenty-first century what GE was to the twentieth. And because it offers competitive solutions to each of the problems of the hydrogen economy, ECD might be to the hydrogen economy what the combination of IBM, Intel, Microsoft, Cisco, and others were to the computer revolution in the second half of the twentieth century. Pretty heady stuff, indeed. Richard Tedlow's book *Giants of Enterprise* (2001),[6] chronicles the lives of seven pioneers: Andrew Carnegie (U.S. Steel), George Eastman (Kodak), Henry Ford (Ford Motors), Thomas J. Watson Sr. (IBM), Charles Revson (Revlon), Sam Walton (Wal-Mart), and Robert Noyce (Intel). Might Stanford Ovshinsky's name be added to this list? Small wonder that *Time* magazine recognized Stan as a "Hero for the Planet" in 1999.

Part II

The Science

The New York Times

NOVEMBER 11, 1968

Glassy Electronic Device May Surpass Transistor

Stanford R. Ovshinsky, scientist-inventor, whose work with amorphous materials is said to promise practical benefits beyond what the current transistor technology can offer.

By WILLIAM K. STEVENS

A Detroit inventor-scientist, in a long-awaited paper that is being published today, describes the production of electronic devices made from simple, inexpensive glassy materials that are said to promise practical benefits beyond what transistor technology can offer.

Stanford R. Ovshinsky, a 45-year-old, bushy-haired pipe smoker with the enthusiasm of a schoolboy, described the devices at a news conference in his office in Troy, Mich., last Friday, three days before the publication of his paper in Physical Review Letters, official journal of the American Physical Society.

Among the fruits of the versatile electronic components, Mr. Ovshinsky said, are expected to be small, general-purpose desktop computers for use in homes, schools and offices; a flat, tubeless television set that can be hung on the wall like a picture,

Continued on Page 42, Column 4

Chapter 6

A New Science

On November, 11, 1968 a front page story in *The New York Times* entitled, "Glassy Electronic Device May Surpass Transistor"[1] attracted a great deal of attention:

A Detroit inventor-scientist, in a long-awaited paper that is being published today, describes the production of electronic devices made from simple, inexpensive glassy materials that are said to promise practical benefits beyond what transistor technology can offer.

Stanford R. Ovshinsky, a 45-year-old, bushy-haired pipe smoker with the enthusiasm of a schoolboy, described the devices at a news conference in his office in Troy, Mich., last Friday, three days before the publication of his paper in **Physical Review Letters***, official journal of the American Physical Society.*

Among the fruits of the versatile electronic components, Mr. Ovshinsky said, are expected to be small, general-purpose desktop computers for use in homes, schools and offices; a flat, tubeless television set that can be hung on the wall like a picture, and missile guidance systems impervious to destruction by natural or man-made radiation.

He added that the devices were expected to cut the cost and size of electronic systems generally.

He said that his devices were made of amorphous materials—those with a disordered, irregular atomic structure—whose electrical properties were different from the atomically symmetrical, crystalline materials that transistors are made of.

Ordinarily, the amorphous glasses block the flow of electricity. But the balance of energy forces inside them is such that when a voltage of just the right minimum, or threshold, strength is applied it makes the material suddenly switch from an insulator to a conductor.

This property has been called the "Ovshinsky effect." The effect puts amorphous glasses in the class of semiconductors, which have been the foundation of the post-World War II electronics revolution.

Some of the world's leading solid-state physicists, interviewed last week, credited the discovery to Mr. Ovshinsky, viewed it as one of the most exciting developments in their field in some years and said it represented a departure in electronic technology.

"It is the newest, the biggest, the most exciting discovery in solid-state physics at the moment," said Sir Nevill Mott, director of the Cavendish Laboratory at Cambridge University in England, who was interviewed by telephone.

The discovery of the Ovshinsky effect was "quite unexpected," said Professor Mott, whose current interest is in the field of amorphous materials. He is an unpaid consultant to Energy Conversion Devices Inc., the company in Troy, Mich., that Mr. Ovshinsky founded to develop glass semiconductors.

Professor Mott said that the principle of the transistor, discovered in 1947, could originally have been figured out on the basis of old knowledge, but that the Ovshinsky effect represented totally new knowledge.

The reaction within the electronics industry to the possible applications of the devices has generally been one of caution. Although experts in some major industrial laboratories said last week that they believed the potential uses of the glass devices were exciting, they were reserving judgment until more was known and demonstrated.

Energy Conversion Devices, however, says that it has contracts or joint agreements with several major electronics companies who prefer not to be named for competitive reasons.

Mr. Ovshinsky said that electronic components smaller than one five-thousandth of an inch across, or one-third the size of the smallest transistors, could be made from the amorphous materials.

Such devices can be packed densely enough to produce a typewriter-size general-purpose computer for home use at relatively low cost, he said.

The paper in **Physical Review Letters**, titled "Reversible Electrical Switching Phenomena in Disordered Structures,"[2] describes devices that change from an insulating to a conducting state in 150 trillionths of a second when a threshold voltage is applied.

The action is something like the firing of a nerve cell. The threshold voltage for a device depends on its thickness and on which kind of glass is used.

Mr. Ovshinsky said that some of the materials returned to their nonconducting state immediately after firing, which meant that they had performed like an electronic switch.

Other kinds of amorphous materials stay in the conducting state indefinitely, without further need for electrical energy from outside, in which case they act like a computer memory storage mechanism by "freezing" in a given state.

This device can be restored to its previous insulating state at any time by feeding it a pulse of current.

This memory device is expected to be useful in computers. Mr. Ovshinsky said that it could be "read" without wiping out the information it carried; that no current was necessary to maintain the memory state, and that access could be gained to any given memory element instantly.

He said that no existing computer memory had all these capabilities, although some had one or two.

The technological importance of the discovery, Mr. Ovshinsky said, lies partly in the fact that the glass switches and memory elements are far simpler, cheaper, easier to make and smaller than conventional semiconductor components.

Semiconductors pass only a small electric current, compared with a metal. On the scale of conductivity, they lie between conductors and insulators.

Crystalline semiconductors, which have largely replaced vacuum tubes as basic electronic devices, are made to conduct electricity by adding small bits of impurities to the material.

This upsets the crystalline atomic structure slightly, in such a way that when an electric force is applied, a few electrons move from atom to atom through the material. This is conduction.

It is time-consuming and costly to grow semiconductor crystals and "inject" them with impurities. Often, too, many rejects result.

Since the conduction properties of amorphous materials are intrinsic, the need to grow a crystal or to "dope" one could be obviated.

Mr. Ovshinsky says this results in a higher yield of good devices and leads to lower costs.

The amorphous switching device described in today's **Physical Review Letters** *is made of 48 per cent tellurium, 30 per cent arsenic, 12 per cent silicon and 10 per cent germanium.*

Unlike crystalline semiconductors, the glass devices pass current in two directions. In handling alternating current, the kind that comes into most homes, it is not necessary therefore to fabricate complex and expensive devices, as is the case with crystalline semiconductors.

Unlike conventional semiconductors again, Mr. Ovshinsky said, the glass materials are unaffected by radiation. Energy Conversion Devices, in one of four military contracts it holds, is developing radiation-proof computer circuits for use in the guidance systems of Air Force missiles.

Another promising application, the inventor believes, will be in flat-screen television sets to be hung on the wall like pictures.

Operating on household current, the "ovonic" devices—the name chosen by Mr. Ovshinsky—can withstand the high voltages that must be borne by the switching elements that would activate light cells on the electroluminescent screen.

In the company's modest, one-story plant on the northern outskirts of Detroit, a pilot production line has been set up on which workers each day turn out 150,000 ovonic devices in the form of glass film 1-20th the thickness of a human hair.

Thin film technology has been around for some years but has never achieved its potential largely because crystalline semiconductor devices have not been successfully produced in that form. Entire circuits and entire computers can now be made of the film, Mr. Ovshinsky said.

Mr. Ovshinsky has talked generally of his findings before— some would say he has evangelized about them—and others have made glass semiconductors experimentally since the discovery of the Ovshinsky effect in the early 1960s.

But until today's publication in **Physical Review Letters***, none of the scientific data had been disclosed. Mr. Ovshinsky said that publication had been delayed until patents had been obtained.*

The company's 10 scientific consultants, some paid and some not, include Dr. Mott; Dr. Hellmut Fritzsche, professor of physics at the University of Chicago's James Franck Laboratory and a vice president of the company; Dr. Isidor I. Rabi of Columbia University, 1944 Nobel prizewinner in physics; Dr. Morrel H.

Cohen, director of the James Franck Institute, and Dr. David Turnbull, Gordon McKay Professor of Applied Physics at Harvard University.

William K. Stevens (1968)

The atomic structure of a crystalline material repeats itself many times over. Thus, if you have a piece of pure silicon and wish to study its atomic structure, it would not matter where in the material you looked first. The answer (the basic atomic configuration observed) would be the same from any part of the material. A characterization of any part of the material reveals all one needs to know about the structure of the entire material.

Scientists love simple rules that can explain a broad array of phenomena. For example, $E=mc^2$. What could be a simpler characterization of the relationship between energy and mass? Einstein was especially attracted to such simple scientific laws. For a while, philosophers of science suggested that "simplicity" was one of the basic characteristics (along with predictive accuracy, internal consistency, external coherence, etc.) of good scientific theories. However, science in the last half of the twentieth century demonstrated that many areas of nature cannot be reduced to a few basic laws. Thus, simplicity is no longer considered a necessary requirement for good scientific explanations.

It was scientists' affection for simple explanations that drew them to the study of crystalline materials. That is, the regular periodic repetition of the basic structural elements made a theoretical and mathematical treatment of a substance possible. The repetition of a basic atomic structure throughout a material composed of trillions of atoms held the promise of some simple scientific explanations for each substance.

While the existence of disordered materials (and of glasses) was known for thousands of years, their disordered atomic structures discouraged further scientific scrutiny. It seemed unlikely that such materials would easily yield simple scientific explanations. However, in 1955, Stan and Iris turned their attention to the study of disordered and amorphous solids. They felt the most exciting physics lay in exploring this vast, unexplored ocean, using the periodic table as their nautical chart and their physical intuition as their compass. The remainder of this chapter will present an overview of the world of amorphous materials. While some parts may be challenging for readers with little science background, a precise understanding of the science is not necessary to appreciate the applications discussed in later chapters. For individuals who would like a more scientifically detailed explanation, Appendix 2, entitled "Amorphous and Disordered Materials—The Basis of New Industries," discusses the role of disorder.

What are the basic differences between crystalline and amorphous solids? Figure 6-1[3] gives pictures of amorphous and crystalline materials, showing differences between the two. In crystals, atoms are arranged in a regular, orderly fashion. This allows for the growing of, for example, silicon crystals that can then be sliced into (in the hundreds of microns range) wafers such that the marvels of modern electronic circuits can be etched and diffused into them. Such wafers are used for making solar energy collection cells as well as for making semiconductor chips.

 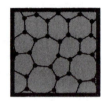

Figure 6-1

In contrast, the positioning of atoms in amorphous materials is completely disordered except for the nearest neighbors. And, very importantly, materials can be made much smaller than 100 angstroms, depending upon one's purpose. Furthermore, because they are noncrystalline, these materials, can be made over a very large area. For example, the Ovonic photovoltaic solar cells are manufactured by the mile as multi-layered thin films in a continuous process.

Back in the 1960s, scientists had no idea of how to characterize the properties of amorphous semiconductors. Whatever had been learned about solids was theoretically based on the crystalline, orderly arrangement of atoms. Disordered materials was not simply a new area, it required the development of a whole new science. Stan and his collaborators had to develop new concepts, design new experiments, and so forth, to understand the electronic processes in amorphous, disordered materials.

Ovshinsky staked out an entirely new, unexplored territory of materials science. Academics at the finest universities on several continents (e.g., Stanford, Chicago, Yale, Brown, Penn State, Harvard and MIT in the United States) dropped what they were doing to study Stan's new, amorphous materials. These came to be known as Ovonic materials. According to Webster's dictionary, the etymology of "Ovonic" derives from OVshinsky + electrONIC = OVONIC.

Sir Nevill Mott, then the head of the Cavendish Laboratory at Cambridge University, met Stan in 1967. He was immediately challenged by Ovshinsky's discoveries and switched his research program to Ovonic materials. Ten years later, when Sir Nevill received the Nobel Prize for his work on amorphous materials, he thanked Stan in his acceptance speech, "for saving me from the stagnation of theoretical solid state physics at the time."

Two University of Chicago physicists, Hellmut Fritzsche (an outstanding experimental physicist) and Morrel Cohen (a brilliant theoretical physicist) have also been longtime collaborators with Stan. Their most celebrated collaboration appeared in *Physical Review Letters* and is a citation classic in their field.[4] In that important paper the trio presented the CFO (after Cohen, Fritzsche and Ovshinsky) model which guided subsequent work in amorphous semiconductor science. According to Hellmut Fritzsche, in *R&A*,

> *...Stan's intuition and deep understanding of the roles of different elements in his materials were ingenious. That more than our painstaking experiments determined our progress and led to specific material compositions for fast switching, for memory action and soon for optical phase-change memories... Stan's laboratories had become a Mecca for many of us from Stanford, Harvard, MIT, Penn State and Chicago. Stan attracted the best and we had exciting brainstorming sessions at the big round table with Stan and kept up with the latest ideas and experiments...To witness Stan's fertile mind at work was a truly deep experience that taught me how to get to the depth of difficult problems...*

One of Stan's closest friends and collaborators, David Adler, from MIT, wrote the following in his Introduction to Stan's 1991 book of collected papers, entitled *Disordered Materials—Science and Technology, Selected Papers by Stanford R. Ovshinsky*, edited by David Adler, Brian Schwartz, and Marvin Silver:[5]

> *... Stanford R. Ovshinsky, a self-taught genius who was previously known in scientific circles primarily for his contributions to automation and neurophysiology, began working in the field in 1955, when almost all physicists believed that amorphous semiconductors could not even exist. Ovshinsky studied the high-field properties of a large number of these materials, and between 1958 and 1961 discovered and developed the two types of reversible switching phenomena which now bear his name. He not only investigated the switching behavior in detail and proposed a*

*wide number of potential applications, but he also developed the
chemical and metallurgical basis for choosing the composition of
the materials in order to optimize the desired characteristics, proposed mechanisms for the origin of the phenomena, and reached
important conclusions about the physical nature of the materials
at equilibrium and their electronic nonequilibrium properties...*

Stan himself, in simplifying the role of disorder, explains it thus:

*The key to amorphicity/disorder is that it offers many degrees
of freedom for atomic design, while very good crystalline materials
are very rigid in that they have repeating atoms which severely
constrain the addition or removal of elements without destroying
the electronic or chemical mechanisms for which the crystals are
designed.*

*Such crystals, for example in a semiconductor, can only have
additions of parts per million of an alien atom. This is called doping and these extremely slight additions change the character of,
for example, the silicon crystal so that it has become the basis of the
whole transistor industry.*

*Not only do we use our principles to make completely amor-
phous materials without crystallinity, but also mixed materials,
even crystalline, that we can use to intervene in the material and
do atomic engineering and synthesize countless new materials with
unique electronic, physical and chemical mechanisms, opening up
a whole new area of opportunity to advance materials science in a
very major manner.*

One can see now that a material's surface composition can be far
more important than scientists had previously thought. Furthermore,
engineering special orbital relationships between various atoms that
have different internal configurations than were being used by clas-
sical materials scientists is key—especially being able to accomplish
this in what is now called "nanoscale," although Stan called it "working at the quantum limits of a material."

Ovshinsky and his colleagues have been doing nanostructure science since the 1950s. They introduced chemists and materials science
engineers to the significance of lone pair electrons (first described by
Mark Kastner of MIT), coordinate bonding, the novel chemistry of
defects, and the like. These characteristics of amorphous science allow for the atomic engineering of materials to obtain desired characteristics that never before existed. For example, ECD has atomically
engineered a metal hydride powder that can incorporate hydrogen

into its atomic structure; is desorbed at relatively low temperatures; possesses good kinetics (can be refueled quickly); is tolerant of a large number of absorption-desorption cycles; and so forth. [See Chapter 9.]

Creating such a material using only conventional crystalline materials has not been a promising avenue. But with their extensive knowledge of the principles of disordered materials, ECD scientists routinely perform such "miracles." Indeed, Ovshinsky's principles state that anytime and anyplace one can get positional, compositional, or translational disorder, even in crystalline material (especially as one enters the nanostructure range), it allows atomic engineering to synthesize many kinds of materials, and provide important new mechanisms (electrical, chemical, structural) that were prohibited by the tyranny of the crystalline lattice.

Disordered and amorphous materials stand our knowledge of catalysts on its head. About 25 years ago, at a Gordon conference, Stan claimed that catalytic sites on disordered catalysts of very small dimensions are more numerous than on crystalline materials. Furthermore, he said that these sites are responsive to atomic and orbital engineering, since one could get the smallest nanoparticles to form multi-element materials with added new dimensions of bonding and anti-bonding orbitals.

The conventional wisdom at the time held that clean surfaces were necessary for catalytic reaction sites. History has not been kind to Stan's doubters. Using his new ideas about disordered catalysts, Stan modified transition and rare earth metal alloys to increase the density of hydrogen storage sites and to speed up the necessary catalytic surface reactions. Stan's key idea here was to employ steric and atomic engineering with the d- and f-orbitals of transition and rare earth elements to control the electronic density and generate new hydrogen storage sites. This is accomplished by controlling the total interactive sites in the material achieving needed new configurations. It is important to note that Stan was the first to grasp the principle (that later became known as nanostructures) that very small particles or thin films may have the same chemical elements but they are bonded or anti-bonded very differently in surfaces than in bulk.

Stan has shown Table 6-1[6], on the following page, for many years as he spoke about nanostructures and the vital role amorphicity and disorder play in permitting new physics, chemistry, electronic mechanisms, etc. As a modern example, in 1992 an important patent on the use of nanoparticles for multi-junction photovoltaics was issued. This patent follows up Stan's work on amorphous materials which was begun in the 1950s. Several layers of his photovoltaics have been nanocrystalline since the beginning.

Since he was the first to describe intermediate order (and with his colleagues proved it existed), Stan had outlined the means for getting intermediate order and nanocrystallites by utilizing a simple rule: Make amorphous materials as close as possible to the crystalline state (or make a crystalline material as close as possible to the amorphous state) and then one can have intermediate order and/or nanocrystals. A sure way (in silicon) to make nanocrystals is with the controlled use of fluorine. Stan had shown years ago that adding fluorine to carbon could make micro- or nanocrystals of diamonds.

Table 6-1

ROLE OF DISORDER

- Disorder provides the degrees of freedom to design local order/environments

- Results in a Total Interactive Environment (TIE) with a distribution/ spectrum of bonding/non-binding sites

- Many new synthetic materials

- New physical, electronic and chemical mechanisms

- Amorphous = thin film large areas

SMALL PARTICLES HAVE UNIQUE PROPERTIES THAT BRIDGE THE GAP BETWEEN CRYSTALLINE AND AMORPHOUS SOLIDS

- Small geometry gives rise to new physics

- 50 Angstrom particles are "mostly surface" — gives rise to new topologies and unusual bonding configurations

- 21% of all atoms in a 50 Angstrom particle are on the surface and ~ 40% are within one atom of the surface

- Compositional disorder in multi-element nano-alloys is large in small particles... e.g. in a 50 Angstrom particle, each element in a 10 element alloy will show 3% variation in concentration just due to statistics

- Quantum confinement effects are apparent

- Band structure effects are disturbed

The practical consequences of Stan's novel treatment of catalysts are staggering. He developed truly innovative electrode pairs for nickel-metal hydride batteries that now outperform all other propulsion batteries, and are now in use for all hybrid, electric, and fuel cell vehicles. [See Chapter 8.]

Stan's approaches have resulted in breakthroughs in the atomic engineering of disordered materials. But he is far more than a creative materials scientist. He is also a creative industrialist. He invents the materials, the products, and the production technology. His production processes are directly related to the physics and chemistry which are embodied in new products such as the Ovonic solar cells.

A number of years ago, various labs demonstrated amorphous silicon cells on glass plates which were not much bigger than the point of a pen. When they went into production with larger areas, they used batch processing on heavy breakable glass. But Stan had a better idea—a much bigger and better idea. He said, "We can produce solar devices by the mile, as one prints a newspaper—some cells being less than 100 angstroms in size." Thus, astonishingly early, when the solar cells indeed were very small, Stan envisioned and planned such production by the mile with a roll-to-roll machine on a flexible substrate with multi-junctions to capture more of the sun's spectrum and with materials which were much more efficient. His use of fluorine to make nanocrystalline layers was a most important innovation and gave him an enormous competitive edge. All had assumed such cells would be strung together in series to form solar arrays, as is still the case with crystalline photovoltaic cells. [See Chapter 7.]

Stan chose not to use paper or glass as the solar cell's backing but instead uses flexible substrates like thin sheets of plastic or stainless steel. These substrates proceed through chambers, as layer after layer of atomically engineered amorphous silicon (each layer 100 times thinner than a sheet of newspaper) is deposited one upon another. The layers are atomically engineered to absorb light from different parts of the light spectrum. Once through the machine, the cells are sometimes cut into shingles. Instead of covering a roof with "regular" shingles, one can now install an "electricity plant" of shingles for the roof which provides protection from the elements and looks like any traditionally shingled roof. Other solar cell configurations are available for standing seam metal roofs. They are not heavy or breakable and are aesthetically pleasing.

The current Ovonic photovoltaic production machine is the 8th generation of this line and is longer than a football field. Stan credits a splendid machine building team, and Herb Ovshinsky, his brother, who continues to play a key role in developing detailed designs of the continuous roll-to-roll machines. He emphasizes the true team effort of the engineers, scientists, and production personnel whose talent, dedication and commitment have done so much to make Ovonic photovoltaics manufacturing and operation so successful.

To say that Stan has built a better mousetrap is to lie by understatement. Some day when you are in the Auburn Hills, Michigan area, stop by the United Solar Ovonic Corporation plant. Who knows? If you are uncommonly lucky, someone might treat you to a tour of "the mother of all mousetraps."

Now to the information side of ECD's businesses, the opposite of the energy side of the same coin. Stan considers information to be encoded energy, and uses the same principles for both. Computer chips based upon amorphous and nonvolatile phase change materials, instead of the well-known crystalline transistors and other conventional devices, could well rule the future of the computer industry.

In 1999, Stan, through ECD, formed Ovonyx with Tyler Lowrey, former Vice-Chairman and Chief Technical Officer of Micron Technologies, to further commercialize his inventions in the information field, particularly Ovonic Universal Memory (OUM) technology. In February, 2000, Ovonyx and Intel entered into a collaboration and royalty-bearing license to jointly develop and commercialize OUM technology. Agreements with other chip production giants like STMicroelectronics, BAE Systems, Elpida, and others were quickly inked. There are many companies that have entered the field now, like IBM and Samsung. Others are joining the field, and in due course will become licensees. What are these chip giants so excited about?

OUM is a robust, high speed, nonvolatile memory that promises large advantages over, for example, widely-used FLASH memory (in cell phones, digital cameras, PDAs, etc.). These advantages include: 1) reduced cost per bit; 2) lower power requirements; 3) low voltage; 4) wide temperature range; 5) high scalability; 6) high speed; 7) nonvolatility; 8) multiple-bit storage per cell; and 9) radiation hardness. OUM also has advantages over other memory types such as DRAM, embedded applications, SRAM, and others.

The disordered world has opened a cornucopia of exciting possibilities in the materials science realm. The Ovonic threshold switch and the Ovonic three terminal replacement of conventional transistors are smaller, faster, and carry 50-times the current. As the semiconductor people say, "they scale"—which a transistor does not. And the ultimate computer is the Ovonic Cognitive Computer. [See Chapter 11.] Stan and ECD have led the charge with amorphous and disordered materials and products for over 45 years. And yet, it looks like the best is still to come in this exciting domain.

Science: Pure and Applied

Brian Schwartz is a condensed matter physicist at CUNY who has been active in the theory of disordered and amorphous materials over the years. Like many other scientists, he first heard of Stan from reading the front page of *The New York Times*, business and technology magazines. In the mid-1960s, Schwartz arrived at MIT as a researcher, first at the National Magnet Laboratory and later as a faculty member of the physics department. As he describes,

...these were vigorous and heady days for science and scientists, especially in the field of physics. The post-Sputnik American emphasis and encouragement of science and engineering had resulted in the commitment of significant new resources to science with a concomitant increase in research opportunities and engineering applications for materials science. As examples, the post-war discovery of the transistor was being used in electronic systems and miniaturized through integrated circuitry; the theory of superconductivity and the discovery of high-field type II materials enabled high-field superconducting magnets which changed the nature of high energy physics and found its way into medicine via the development of MRI techniques and the associated magnet systems. Having entered physics prior to the Sputnik impulse, I was one of the new young scientists riding the wave. During the "golden" decade of the 1960s, the addition of large numbers of young scientists to the research enterprise led to many important discoveries in basic and applied science. The young scientists complimented the much smaller group of more senior scientists, many of whom had contributed to the war effort of the United States in the Manhattan project or in other technologies such as the development of radar.

At MIT, Harvard and the greater Boston area there was a group of young theorists in the field of Solid State Physics (now Condensed Matter Physics) who would meet periodically over lunch and at colloquia and seminars... Through Dave Adler's

scientific collaboration with Stan Ovshinsky, I eventually got to
meet Stan and began a long and fruitful relationship. I got to
know many of the researchers at ECD... Throughout the 1970s I
had informal and periodic encounters with Stan and ECD.

In the 1980s...ECD continued to make progress especially in
the area of amorphous materials as applied to photovoltaic materi-
als, and switching and memory devices. The company ECD had
grown and was beginning to get recognition from the energy com-
munity. After signing a contract with BP for a significant research
and development program especially in photovoltaics, I had the
opportunity to become a regular consultant to ECD with specific
tasks in the areas of materials research, especially superconductors
(and later high temperature superconductors)...

Brian also served as the Director of the Institute for Amorphous
Studies, which was founded in 1982 in Bloomfield Hills, Michigan,
to promote the understanding of amorphous materials and their application. The Institute sponsored a lecture/seminar series, as well as
a book series in conjunction with Plenum Press. Between 1985 and
1991, nine books were published in the series to disseminate the best
research in the field of amorphous materials.

One of the Institute's early brochures provided the following
overview:[7]

New materials and their understanding have always been the
basis for advances in civilization. Historians and anthropologists
have often categorized ages of humankind, such as the Stone Age,
the Bronze Age, and the Iron Age, by the introduction of tools and
techniques created by inventive uses of new materials. As we prepare
for the 21st century, new synthetic materials based on freedom from
crystalline constraints are emerging. These disordered, or amor-
phous, materials will be central to the solution of humankind's
problems in energy, communications, and information processing,
and the basis for many new materials needed for our changing
industrial society...

Stanford Ovshinsky and his colleagues at Energy Conversion
Devices have provided the key principles for the understanding
of amorphous materials. They discovered that amorphous mate-
rials can exhibit certain unique properties that have never been
observed in crystalline materials. It is now clear that structures
free from crystalline constraints represent tremendous advances in
flexibility.

The principles that they developed for understanding the properties of amorphous structures transcend materials science and are relevant to contemporary problems in physics, chemistry, and biology, including neurophysiology, the origins of life, and cosmology. Such concepts as phase transformations, supercooling, freezing in of defects, nucleation, and broken symmetry are becoming the common language for researchers in these frontier areas of science. Amorphous materials can be a catalyst for the transformation of crystalline thought into new and liberating paradigms for understanding the physical world...

[I]t is the ability to synthesize a myriad of new materials with new and unique physical, chemical, and electronic properties which makes amorphous materials so exciting both for their scientific value and their technological potential. The ability to engineer such materials results from the elimination of the restrictions of the crystalline lattice. The freedom to place atoms in three-dimensional space that this affords is the great potential of amorphous materials...

It is rather amazing that amorphous materials were classified as liquids for so long, especially since most of the solids we encounter in everyday experience are amorphous rather than crystalline. These include glass, plastics, rubber, and leather. Glass has many attributes: it is transparent, noncorrosive, inexpensive, and can be decorative. It is relatively dense and quite breakable. Plastics are now designed for a whole array of different uses. Both glasses and plastics are used in what we now call "passive" applications, e.g., packaging. With the rise of the electronics industry, there has been an intense effort in the design of "active" materials, those which generate or conduct and control electricity under certain circumstances. It perhaps came as a surprise to many scientists that amorphous materials exhibit the same gamut of electronic properties as crystals—they can be magnetic, transparent or opaque, insulating, semiconducting, metallic, or even superconducting...

There are many applications for active amorphous solids, just as there are increasing applications for passive amorphous materials. In the active area, amorphous materials are used for a wide spectrum of devices such as switches, memories and transistors, optical memories, photoreceptors, copying drums, television pick-up tubes, etc. In recent years, efficient, low-cost photovoltaic devices based on amorphous semiconductors have been developed, including solar cells for power generation and light-activated cells for consumer electronics (e.g., hand calculators). Amorphous materials will soon revolutionize the microelectronics and information processing markets, finding unique applications in large-area electronics, flat-screen displays, erasable video disks, optical data storage, and a host of other areas. Amorphous switching devices, having played a crucial catalytic role in the development of nonvolatile programmable memories, should soon make their mark in computer control and telecommunications applications. In addition, x-ray mirrors, thermoelectric devices, and batteries employing amorphous and disordered materials have been developed. It is clear that this long-neglected class of solids is on the threshold of becoming the most important class.

Stan is an applied researcher, as his hydrogen loop represents a thoroughly practical solution to many of society's energy problems in the twenty-first century. However, right from the start, Stan has also taken pains to conduct research that has high theoretical import. Stan has more than 300 published articles and papers, some in the finest physics and materials science journals in the world. His published papers range from neurophysiology to cosmology. Appendix 12 presents a partial list of Stan Ovshinsky's scientific journal articles, book chapters and conference papers. Clearly Stan has bridged the theoretical-applied chasm in science in a most productive manner.

Sir Nevill Mott, Stan and Max Powell

The CFO Model authors in 2005 (Morrel Cohen, Hellmut Fritzsche and Stan)

Subhendu Guha, Secretary of Energy Samuel Bodman, Iris, Stan, and Bob Stempel at United Solar Ovonic

Chapter 7

Photovoltaics

One very vivid memory I have is in Stan's and Iris' home with a number of key employees, where Stan outlined his concept to manufacture photovoltaic cells in a revolutionary way like newsprint or photographic film. For those who have witnessed first hand the miracle of production of photovoltaic cells from our existing production equipment, it may not seem as impossible as it did to us, but in the late 1970s when "large area cells" were measured in centimeters, Stan's concept was beyond revolutionary—beyond comprehension. Nearly everyone in the group was skeptical that it would ever work. ECD, under Stan's leadership, has built many generations of roll-to-roll photovoltaic production machines culminating in the latest 30-megawatt plant that has earned the acclaim of people throughout the world. Observing Stan over the years, I have learned that when he tells me something is important, I don't have to understand it but can count on his vision and intuition.

Nancy Bacon
Senior Vice-President, ECD

Recall that in the hydrogen loop, presented in Figure 1-1, photons (light) are emitted by the sun and through photovoltaics produce electricity. The electricity can go directly to a battery or be used to electrolyze water. The hydrogen from the water then gets stored in ECD's solid hydrogen storage units. Finally, the hydrogen can be used either to power an internal combustion engine or a fuel cell. Stan has made a seminal contribution to the science at every step of the hydrogen loop. The next four chapters will discuss his work in each of these areas from photovoltaics to fuel cells, followed by a

83

chapter on ECD's information technologies. Every attempt will be made to have these chapters be as simple and understandable as possible. More scientifically advanced readers are directed to the book's Appendices, where more in-depth and technically sophisticated papers on the various topics by Stanford Ovshinksy and his colleagues are offered.

Photovoltaics was an interest area for individual researchers and hobbyists for most of the twentieth century. With the OPEC oil embargo, the 1970s saw the first serious efforts to make photovoltaics a sustained energy generation industry. However, with the return to cheap oil prices, photovoltaics languished as an industry. From 1977 on, ECD, under Stan's direction, made numerous generations, each larger than the last, of its Ovonic multi-layered, thin film amorphous photovoltaic processor, utilizing its continuous web production methods which he had first pioneered in the Ovonic thin films he had used in the information field. As ECD made alliances and raised money, it was always toward his goal of having photovoltaics be competitive to fossil fuels, a world changing event.

All other approaches of significance were with batch process single band gap, single- or poly-crystalline material, hundreds of microns thick compared to Stan's half micron multi-band gap amorphous materials which utilized the full spectrum of the sun's available light. ECD is now reaping the benefits of having made a radical departure from the conventional crystalline approach.

The Science

Here's my understanding of photovoltaics (PV). First, an overview of crystalline silicon photovoltaic production technologies and products, then a look at Ovshinsky's amorphous, thin film photovoltaic cells. Most photovoltaic cells are made of refined silicon, which has been plentiful and is a good conductor of electricity. Research papers often say that silicon photovoltaic cells are "grown." What this means is that first a large amount of refined silicon is melted (at around 1250° C.), and then a small seed crystal is put into the melt and slowly pulled out. The liquid silicon attaches to the seed crystal as it is drawn out in a regular, crystallizing pattern that eventually forms a cylinder called a silicon ingot. That is what is done to "grow" a silicon crystal.

Once you have the ingot, it is first sliced into thin round wafers. Then, to make the wafer a solar cell, some small impurities must be put into the silicon wafers in order to make a so-called p-n junction. Why is a silicon p-n junction necessary?

A solar cell works when light falls onto the silicon crystal and an electron is excited by the energy in the light. The electron goes from a lower energy position (leaving behind a hole) to a higher energy position. This creates what is called an electron-hole pair, which consists of a positive and a negative charge. But in order for a solar cell to work, these positive and negative charges must be separated. The internal field of the p-n junction serves as the separation mechanism. These separated charges want to come back together, and the physicist allows that to occur through an external wire—a wire that connects the two sides of the junction. Of course, electrons moving through a wire is electricity.

There have been two advantages to this crystalline silicon solar cell approach: 1) the use of silicon is a very mature scientific field because of the many years of work with semiconductors, transistors, integrated circuits and the like, which are all made of silicon; and 2) silicon is abundant in nature (sand is oxidized silicon). However, in 2006, as solar cell production has significantly increased, the demand is exceeding the supply of refined silicon, thus increasing its cost.

The basic challenge for the crystalline silicon industry is cost. It takes a long time to grow the crystal. It is an energy intensive process because a lot of energy is used to heat the silicon to a very high temperature. Because of the way the ingot is sliced into wafers, a lot of material is lost, which adds to the cost. After junctions are imbedded into the cells, a large number of solar cells must be wired and connected to one another to form a solar panel. These processes are also costly. Another problem with silicon crystals is that they are very brittle and break easily. In order to protect the solar cell from the external environment, a glass sheet is placed over the array of cells. This adds both unwanted additional costs and weight. So cost, weight, and breakage represent crystalline silicon's Achilles' heels. Furthermore, the crystalline lattice has lattice mismatch with different crystals so it is impractical to be made as a triple-junction.

There are still other technical problems with crystalline solar cells. For example, if some leaves or a shadow covers a single (usually 6 inches in diameter) solar cell in a much larger array, the current produced by the entire array is reduced dramatically. This is because the individual solar cells are linked in series, and the current produced is limited by the cell producing the lowest current. Also, because of all the energy required to melt the silicon at the beginning of the "growing" process, the energy payback of crystalline silicon solar cells is estimated to range from four to seven years (rather than approximately seventeen months for the Ovonic amorphous silicon-germanium alloy cells).

Now that we know the strengths and weaknesses of the crystalline silicon industry's production process, let's turn to Ovshinsky's ECD amorphous, thin film photovoltaic cells. The first advantage of a thin film approach to depositing silicon on any substrate is a tremendous savings in material costs. While complex in practice, ECD's silicon deposition process is simple in concept. Essentially, a gas such as silane and/or germane is decomposed into silicon or germanium and hydrogen [Flourine is used for some critical layers.] with the silicon/germanium depositing on a stainless steel substrate and the hydrogen being pumped away. This occurs in a vacuum chamber, with the decomposition energized by a "glow discharge" created by very high frequency alternating voltages applied between parallel metal plates.

So now ECD has a very thin film on a substrate, instead of a sliced crystal, as its photovoltaic cell. Even though nine similar layers are deposited over one-another to create an advanced "triple-junction" photovoltaic cell, the total thickness is less than one-half micron (a "micron" is one-millionth of a meter) whereas the best crystalline cells must be about 200 microns thick, as thinner cells break too easily. Thus ECD's material costs are significantly lower.

The crystalline photovoltaic cell has a very regular pattern of atoms throughout the solar cell, while ECD's thin film has an amorphous atomic structure—that is, the atoms are deposited on the substrate in a random pattern. To make a very complex topic very simple, suffice it to say that there are some quantum mechanical truths that reveal that light is absorbed much more efficiently by a randomly ordered pattern of atoms than by a regular pattern (as in the crystalline solar cells). Thus, amorphous silicon can be easily deposited onto a substrate by a glow-discharge method to produce an efficient absorber of light energy that employs very little material.

Recall that with crystalline silicon cells, the junctions are created in a planned manner. With amorphous silicon cells, the atoms and the carriers of the light energy, the electrons and the holes, are randomly distributed. These random patterns produce many defects in the amorphous silicon. These defects gobble up the electrons and holes. Thus, while you've created the electrons and holes, you cannot easily get electricity from the thin film. So the challenge for ECD researchers was: How do you reduce the number of defects in the thin film solar material? Basically, you compensate for the defects by adding hydrogen/fluorine gas during the deposition process. This reduces the number of defects, and you can then obtain a good level of efficiency in the thin film. ECD's successful approach from the beginning was that it was able to reduce the defects in the thin film solar material.

Why are thin film, amorphous photovoltaic cells so unique? Ovshinsky said that amorphous materials can be stacked, layer upon layer, quite efficiently. Because of the random pattern of atoms, thin film is a very forgiving material. Thus, ECD developed its triple-junction thin film approach. Rather than having only one solar cell junction, there are three layers of materials, (two of them containing germanium) stacked one on top of another that create three junctions instead of one. This advantageous situation is not true for crystalline solar cells. If you have a single crystal silicon cell and you place it on top of a single crystal germanium cell, you will get a pretty defective interface. This is because the silicon has a certain lattice constant (i.e., the distance between the atoms). Germanium has a different lattice constant. Thus, if you attempt to grow one cell on top of another you get a lattice mismatch.

However, rather than having only one layer of solar cells in their arrays, ECD continuously lays down three layers of cells, one on top of the other, which do not appear as distinct layers (since they are inherently a part of the solid material), but as a solid. Therefore, in the solid there are three junctions instead of one. Further, each cell is atomically attuned to a different part of the light spectrum. The top cell is made of amorphous silicon alloy only, which captures the blue part of the light spectrum. The middle cell gets about 10% germanium added, which captures the green light. In the bottom cell, there is about 40% germanium, which captures the red light. This triple-junction structure is why ECD's photovoltaic cells capture energy from a broader range of the light spectrum than do crystalline cells.

Recall that standard photovoltaic cells work well under sunny conditions, but they deliver almost nothing on cloudy days. Similarly, under perfect operating conditions, traditional photovoltaic cells deliver energy well. However, should a shadow or some leaves fall on a crystalline photovoltaic array and completely cover one cell in the array's series of cells, the entire series will not produce electricity.

ECD's photovoltaic cells are not restricted by these limitations. It is important to consider the real-world effectiveness of a photovoltaic system in delivering electricity under the far-from-perfect conditions that present themselves in our daily lives. We should consider not only what percentage of light energy a particular system can extract under laboratory conditions (e.g. 9%, 12%), but also what amount of electricity is produced under real-world conditions. This former figure is kin to an automobile's EPA estimates of city and highway mileages; the latter is kin to your actual mileage achieved under real-world conditions. Which is more important to you, a car with a good mileage *estimate* or a car that *gets* good mileage?

In a study by Michael Schmela comparing nine types of photovoltaic cells, ECD's amorphous multi-junction photovoltaic cells produced much more total energy (which is what you pay for) than the eight other types of solar cells.[1] Similar real world results are reported in other studies conducted in Germany and in California.[2] Appendix 3, entitled "The Material Basis of Efficiency and Stability in Amorphous Photovoltaics," provides further discussion of the materials Stan has developed to capture energy from sunlight.

Machine Building

David E. Brown profiled "thirty-five inventors who helped to shape the modern world" for a book entitled *Inventing Modern America: From the Microwave to the Mouse*.[3] Here Stan rubbed shoulders with Henry Ford (assembly line), Steve Wozniak (personal computer), Wilson Greatbatch (implantable cardiac pacemakers), and their like. Stan was chosen for his pioneering work in amorphous photovoltaics and the fundamental changes that came from his introducing multi-junction, roll-to-roll, continuous web production machines (previously mentioned in Chapter 6) that made solar cells by the mile, and therefore could lead to making photovoltaics competitive to fossil fuels in producing electricity. Appendix 4, entitled "25/30MW Ovonic Roll-To-Roll PV Manufacturing Machines," includes pictures and descriptions of this remarkable machine.

Stan, who always was a scientist, started out his inventive career as a machinist, tool maker, and machine builder, all based on his inventive talents. He introduced new physics into metal cutting and new servo-mechanistic controls into a very old-fashioned industry. For example, his Benjamin automatic center drive machine (named after his father) was used in the automotive industry. Also, when the

Korean War started, the New Britain Machine Company manufactured his center-drive machines that produced steel cartridge cases many times faster than any existing machine. He always used new physics to make an entirely different machine tool than anyone had ever considered before with orders of magnitude improvements over conventional machines.

Stan was interested in building new industries and his aim even in those days was not to make incremental improvements to existing products but to create important new products that the world needed. For example, Stan felt that the automotive industry should not be using hydraulic power steering wherein the faster an auto went, the more dangerous the power steering was. In the early '50s he was director of research in the Amgears Division of the Hupp Corporation in Detroit, an automotive supplier which originally was the manufacturer of the Huppmobile. There Stan invented electric power steering. His servo-mechanistic power steering sensed the road and gave just enough (but no more) assist sufficient to meet the needs of driving under any conditions. He felt that the automotive industry could benefit from the use of low-cost sensors rather than relying on the strictly mechanical approaches that were utilized at the time. This was a very prescient approach to auto steering.

As Stan continued his work at ECD as a scientist and businessman, he never lost his love for machines and inventions. Most companies purchase machines and materials, which then enable them to produce their products. In contrast, Stan invents the new materials to build new products, he invents the products, and then he invents the production technology—all of which are based on his approach to amorphous and disordered materials. Thus, under Stan's leadership, the ECD teams design and build the production machines that will be required to manufacture their novel products (e.g., photovoltaic cells, nickel-metal hydride electrodes and batteries, solid hydrogen storage powders). The procedures and machines are developed, and the production processes necessary to create the new products are initiated and then debugged. Therefore, ECD actually creates new industries.

As mentioned in Chapter 1, demand for ECD's photovoltaic cells has been sufficiently high to warrant a doubling of its solar capacity, and in 2005, ECD made the decision to build a second 25/30 MW photovoltaic machine near the original Auburn Hills United Solar Ovonic plant. ECD owns 100% of United Solar Ovonic. The company is currently considering building new plants in the U.S., Europe, and Asia thereby again multiplying its solar capacity.

Stan feels that his greatest invention is building the teams of talented, creative and committed colleagues who then collaboratively become part of his inventive approach. He recognizes the latent abilities of his co-workers, and helps them to actualize their potential and flourish professionally. Looking at his patents, it is obvious that he includes as co-inventors all those who contribute. To Stan, the collegiality and collaboration needed to make great strides is a critical part of ECD's culture.

Stan leads ECD's machine building group which has been responsible for building many generations of machines. Their track record is truly amazing, and they can look forward to playing an even greater role in the future. Similar is the talent and leadership in all of the scientific and technical groups of ECD (for example, hydrogen, batteries, information). One is hard pressed to identify another company that spans the range of activities from materials creation to product sales as does ECD. Unique in the breadth and ambition of its work, ECD's objective is to put the twin pillars of our global economy, energy and information, on new foundations.

Ribbon cutting for 5 MW Ovonic photovoltaic processor at
United Solar Ovonic which preceded the 25/30 MW one below

The 8th generation 25/30 MW annual capacity photovoltaic
manufacturing machine using ECD Ovonics' proprietary continuous
roll-to-roll solar cell deposition process that was originated by Stan and
developed with his ECD colleagues.

Bob Stempel and Stan surrounded by Ovonic NiMH EV-1 electric vehicle batteries. Ovonic NiMH batteries enable the electric and hybrid vehicle industry.

Chapter 8

Batteries

One: Out of clutter, find simplicity. Two: From discord, find harmony. Three: In the middle of difficulty lies opportunity.

Albert Einstein

There are two basic types (or families) of batteries. A *primary* battery is a one-time use battery. Energy is stored in the form of chemical energy. When the chemicals react they produce electricity, and that process cannot be reversed. There are several types of primary consumer batteries: zinc-carbon, magnesium dioxide, and some of the lithium-based batteries. The so-called Coppertop battery, the Nine Lives battery, and so forth are all examples of primary batteries. In *rechargeable* batteries, or secondary batteries, electrons are also stored as chemical energy. As with primary batteries, when the reactants react, they change their form and release an electron to the external circuitry. However, unlike primary batteries, which are not rechargeable, with secondary batteries one is able to replenish the electronic storage through recharging.

Based on Stan's principles, ECD has developed a family of Ovonic rechargeable nickel-metal hydride batteries (NiMH) ranging from ubiquitous consumer batteries to the large batteries that have enabled the electric and hybrid vehicle industry. The consumer batteries are very popular and are licensed throughout the world for use in a variety of small electronic devices, including laptop computers, cellular telephones, and medical equipment. ECD is involved in a joint venture in China to produce Ovonic nickel-metal hydride consumer cylindrical batteries. The Ovonic Battery Company and the Machine Building Division of ECD designed and built the factory that produces these batteries. Furthermore, the Ovonic nickel-metal hydride propulsion batteries are used for all commercial electric and hybrid vehicles, and are manufactured by COBASYS, a 50-50 joint venture with Chevron.

Up until the late 1970s, there were only two principal types of commercially available rechargeable propulsion batteries. One was a lead-acid battery, which had been around for more than 150 years. The other was a nickel-cadmium battery, which had been around for about 100 years. In the early 1970s, we had an oil crisis that was brought about by the oil cartel, OPEC. The crisis spawned a big push towards developing a new generation of batteries for electric vehicles. Doing so, it was believed, would enhance the energy security of our country, and make it the world leader in the electric propulsion field.

These new generation batteries involved difficult technical challenges. In a rechargeable propulsion battery, one needs to optimize: the amount of energy stored in a given weight and volume; the amount of power that can be drawn over a short period of time; how long the battery lasts; how many times one can recharge the battery; how safe the used materials are from both an environmental standpoint as well as a manufacturing standpoint; how economically available the needed materials are, and so forth. One wouldn't make a battery using expensive materials like platinum or palladium. One wouldn't want to make a battery using cadmium or arsenic or other dangerous substances. One can't have a battery that has very high energy density but is very poor in power density, or one that is good in both domains but very expensive to manufacture.

Stan and ECD were chosen by the United States Advanced Battery Consortium (USABC) to develop their Ovonic nickel-metal hydride battery for the electric and hybrid vehicles envisioned by the automobile industry to be their future. Said J. Michael Davis, Assistant Secretary of Conservation and Renewable Energy,[1]

> *...Ovonic is a small company whose expertise and innovation can help sustain the nation's technological leadership...Depending upon size and type of vehicle, this battery could provide two to three times the vehicle range of current battery technology. Nickel-metal hydride batteries also hold the promise of meeting USABC's goals for an environmentally-friendly power source—from development to disposal...*

This original Consortium contract was the first time that the Big Three domestic automakers worked jointly with the government on a research project, and ECD was chosen for the project over about 60 other companies.

The advantages of the Ovonic NiMH battery technology come from both its composition and environmental soundness. The battery is composed of two electrodes. The negative electrode is a multi-component atomically engineered hydride alloy, consisting of transition and rare earth elements and, as Stan's patents say, "of f- and d- orbital elements." The positive electrode is nickel hydroxide which shows some very interesting reversible phase change physics. The electrolyte is good old potassium hydroxide, an excellent conductor. The NiMH battery uses a starved electrolyte technology that is sealed and maintenance free. All components of the battery are 100% recyclable.

What makes these batteries so unique is that, unlike any other battery that is tremendously constrained by its simple electrode materials and the chemistry and physics that go with it, Stan's principles of disorder permit many degrees of freedom for placing multiple atoms (by design) which results in the ability to continuously improve the battery in both power and energy density. This is what is meant by atomic engineering. Indeed, it is orbital engineering—since some of the negative electrodes can be composed of as many as ten or eleven different elements. The materials are a planned system of catalysts, a spectrum of hydrogen binding sites, and so forth.

ECD's proprietary Ovonic NiMH secondary batteries have become important since they were able to "solve" all of the challenges elaborated above. As was said earlier, all of the hybrid electric, pure electric, and fuel cell automobiles in production employ NiMH propulsion batteries. Appendix 5, entitled "A Nickel-Metal Hydride Battery for Electric Vehicles," provides a more detailed description.

Very early, by 1960, Ovshinsky had already invented a high energy density, exceptionally high power lithium battery. This was many years before lithium became used in commercial battery manufacturing. Lithium technologies have come a long way since that time. They have very good energy density, but poorer power density. In addition, lithium is a troublesome material to handle because it is very flammable and difficult to contain, especially when it is used in large quantities, which is what you would have to do for propulsion batteries.

The only lithium rechargeable system that is commercially available today is lithium-ion. It still suffers from the safety issue. Hewlett Packard recently recalled thousands of lithium ion batteries due to melting. What happens if your car is in an accident, or if you pierce the battery with something, and the lithium gets exposed to air? Work is currently in progress to make lithium more stable by putting coatings on it, or changing the electrolyte. The fact is, however, that this approach is fighting an uphill battle against the chemistry. Because such improvements might eventually prevent dangerous events from taking place, there is still much activity in this area. However, a recent article in *Business Week* (April, 2005) on current strides in battery technology states,

> *...Engineers from Tokyo to Detroit are working on solutions, including lithium ion batteries, which have greater power density and cheaper raw materials. But for now, lithium batteries are too expensive to make—and they can't handle the shocks of a moving vehicle. Says John German, American Honda Motor's manager for environmental and energy analysis: "Lithium ion is 10 years [away from] volume production"...*

In summary, the auto industry has found a solution to its propulsion battery needs that enables hybrid vehicles, and that solution is Ovonic nickel-metal hydride batteries. Stan Ovshinsky invented, and with his team developed, these batteries to the point that they now are manufacturable at acceptable costs, and can be continuously improved to satisfy the growing needs of hybrid auto manufacturers. Ford Motor Company produced the first hybrid vehicle built in North America, and ECD receives battery royalties from Sanyo, which produced Ford's battery using ECD's technology.

The stream of propulsion battery orders to COBASYS (the 50-50 joint venture with Chevron) has also now begun. As described in Chapter 1, on August 29, 2005, COBASYS announced that it received battery pack purchase orders from customers for upcoming hybrid electric vehicle (HEV) production programs. These battery systems will be "plug and play," fully integrated solutions, manufactured and assembled by COBASYS at its large Springboro, Ohio facility. The joint venture also has a very large and talented engineering department in Lake Orion, Michigan. ECD provided the basis of its group with many young engineers whom Stan calls his "young tigers."

In late 2005, Azure Dynamics employed NiMH batteries in all demonstration vehicles it produced. Finally, on January 9, 2006, COBASYS announced that it will provide battery systems for GM's Saturn VUE Green Line SUV which will be available to consumers in the summer of 2006. This represents the first auto line of many on which GM and COBASYS will collaborate.

On November 14, 2005, Stan Ovshinsky received *The Economist's* Innovation Award for "Energy and the Environment." This award celebrates the achievements and innovations of individuals who have positively transformed global business. The 2005 award was given to Stan for his pioneering work in the development of the high-powered NiMH battery.

Stan's Creation of the NiMH Batteries

Conventional lead-acid and NiCd batteries have been in use for over one hundred years. In inventing his fundamentally new batteries, what Stan did was to utilize his great physical intuition and his insightful knowledge of the Periodic Table to atomically engineer the materials using the degrees of freedom in disordered materials and achieving new electronic, chemical and physical mechanisms. As Brian Schwartz, a condensed matter physicist, noted: "Stan is the man who speaks with the elements."

To him the Periodic Table is not just one table, for when he adds new combinations of elements, he visualizes the Periodic Table going on and on (as the combinations are almost infinite). With this approach, Stan founded a new area of science and technology that is still producing great advances. That explains why Stan still calls his disordered and amorphous field a new and young science, and why a scientist like Nevill Mott could say that Stan's work was completely new, for it was in the direct opposite direction from where solid state physics was going. Solid state physics then dealt with ordered (crystalline) materials. Disorder then was considered a *defect*, and it was assumed that there could be no possible use for such "schmutz" (dirty) materials.

Stan has used compositional, positional, and translational disorder across the board to invent not only new synthetic materials but also new important mechanisms. Thus we have new batteries, photovoltaics, hydrogen storage, catalysts, fuel cells and information devices that now include his Ovonic cognitive computer, a new paradigm in computation. In Stan's NiMH batteries, the electrodes were able to store and release hydrogen in the electrodes themselves, not just perform electro-chemical tasks as they did in conventional batteries. This was a revolutionary feat in the field of catalytic chemistry. Prior to Stan, catalysts were to be clean-surfaced, polished, and purified to improve their performance—or so the world of materials science thought.

At a Gordon conference in 1978, Stan, in his talk, discussed how catalysis in the solid state was based on wrong assumptions. He felt that what are now called nanomaterials, based upon the freedom provided by disorder which permits atomic engineering in the angstrom range, would open a whole new field of catalysis based upon the new physics of disordered materials. The reaction of the other conference attendees was not positive. The conference chairman characterized Stan's ideas as "completely untenable." It was a thoroughly upsetting experience for both Stan and Iris. However, soon afterwards many of the people attending the meeting were working in the area of disordered and amorphous catalysts, including the conference chairman.

This example highlights an important aspect of scientific discourse. In time, as Stan produced the data that supported his claims, and as other scientists replicated his findings in their own laboratories, Stan's so-called "completely untenable" ideas moved to "accepted wisdom." In my opinion, this is why science works as well as it does, and highlights the importance of Stan's (slightly modified) aphorism, "(Only) in God do we trust—everyone else (scientists) must show data."

The Role of Luck in Science and Partnerships

"Stan," I asked, "hasn't anyone ever said, 'I want to help you because you're doing the right thing'?"

"I've always tried to be a constructive resource to the system, not destructive to anyone else's work or product. And there were various people who helped us at various times. One person who helped us and made a big difference was Thornton Bradshaw. He was a brilliant person, an unusual talent, and the President and COO of ARCO. He had an eminent career. In addition to directing ARCO, he later ran RCA and the MacArthur Foundation.

"The story actually begins at a fledgling photovoltaic meeting in Colorado in 1978. I was the second of three main speakers. The first person basically said, 'Here are the problems now facing us.' I presented data showing that these problems were being solved. The third fellow went on talking about all of the problems again as if he hadn't paid any attention to my talk.

"I left the room and a person who identified himself as Dick Blieden, a senior scientist from ARCO (who years later joined ECD) followed me saying, 'We've got to talk!' I said, 'Fine, but I'm rushing home to get to a family event. Come visit me at ECD, and see for yourself,' never really expecting to meet him again. Well, he came and we received a contract of $1.5 million from ARCO.

"But the real story is about the ARCO COO—Thornton Bradshaw—who was a major figure in a group in Aspen, Colorado, the Aspen Institute of Humanistic Studies, that discussed important environmental and societal problems. Bradshaw was concerned about making a real difference in society by helping to address and solve global problems. He came to see us and brought along Jack Conway (whom I had known from his labor days as a leader of the UAW) and their wives. Bradshaw said, 'I know from my people that you are working on some extremely important societal problems utilizing your science and technology. I believe in you. How much do you need?'"

"You couldn't possibly..." Stan replied.

"No!" Bradshaw countered, "We're out to solve the problems with energy. I'm doing this because I believe you are the person who can solve the problems that are so important to the world's future. How much money do you need to make a difference?"

"Twenty-five to thirty million dollars," Stan replied.

"Okay," Bradshaw said, "I'll give it to you. I'll make my lawyers get it done in a month, and we won't interfere with your work or have you reviewed. We'll just leave you alone and let you do what you feel is necessary that can contribute to solving the energy problems. But I've got to tell you, you shouldn't expect to have any relationship with my company after three years, because I won't be there." And although his lawyers had to sleep at their desks to do it, they got it done in that month!

Stan was able to make huge strides by laying the foundations for Ovonic batteries, photovoltaics, hydrogen storage, fuel cells and catalysis. As Bradshaw had predicted, when the three year contract was completed, there was no further relationship between ARCO and ECD. ARCO got bought out shortly thereafter. For Stan, however, it was a great once-in-a-lifetime experience. He didn't have to fight to get money to develop his vision of how to solve the energy problems that face us, and he was not constrained by "jumping through hoops" and the bureaucracy of the normal big company corporate procedures. Stan had enormous respect for Thornton Bradshaw and wished there were more like him. It made Stan very happy when Bradshaw expressed his great appreciation for Stan's accomplishments.

Another high point of luck that Stan describes was when Bob Stempel joined him and Iris, propelling the company forward to build the new automotive industry that Stan envisioned from batteries to hydrogen. Stan, Iris and Bob share the same vision of building this new automotive industry based upon hybrid electric cars, hydrogen and fuel cells. Bob's help in keeping ECD's early culture alive has allowed ECD to continue living up to its potential. According to Stan, this unique culture of ECD has been the foundation of the creative support and contributions of what he calls ECD's "wonderful group of colleagues and collaborators."[2]

Stan lecturing in Japan in 1978 and 1986

Ovonic hydrogen hybrid being filled up from
an Ovonic hydrogen dispenser

Rosa Young, Stan and Iris in front of
mobile Ovonic hydrogen refueling station

Chapter 9

Hydrogen Storage

*It's our intention to lead the way to a hydrogen economy.
Our metal hydride storage systems offer a cost-effective,
safe, and efficient means of transporting the energy
necessary for vehicles of the future.*

Bob Stempel
Chairman and CEO, ECD

I hate to be pessimistic, but our country's energy policies have put us in a very dangerous predicament. The United States currently consumes 20.5 million barrels of oil each day. A staggering 63% of that daily total is imported. Finally, domestic oil production has declined each year since the early 1970s. In 2004, domestic production declined by 3.8% in one year. Our government describes 2004's rate of decline as "accelerating." We are now in a terrible situation for global oil supplies, in part, because countries like China and India are increasing their consumption of oil and natural gas at staggering rates. All of this cries out for the United States to move to a hydrogen economy as soon as is humanly possible. At present we have gasoline powered internal combustion engines and gasoline-electric hybrid cars. We could work toward using hydrogen in hydrogen fuel cell vehicles, as well as using hydrogen in internal combustion engines, proving that, as Stan likes to proclaim, "anything that burns can be replaced with hydrogen." And we could have a cleaner and safer world as a result.[1]

A recent (January 10, 2005) statement by Bill Reinert, Toyota's national manager of the Advanced Technology group, claimed that "without breakthroughs that reduce the cost of the fuel cell stacks and hydrogen-storage systems, fuel cell vehicles won't be ready for mass production until 2030 at the earliest." If his claim holds up, I fear that it could have catastrophic consequences for our country. But,

I believe that Stan and ECD have the breakthroughs that Reinert asked for already in hand. Thus, Mr. Reinert's statement might need to be modified.

Before going into the science behind Stan's solution to the hydrogen storage problem, I need to make two points. First, the recent, dramatic increases in the number of hybrid vehicles sold will ameliorate somewhat the troubling trends in world oil supplies noted above. In this regard, because of their dominance in the hybrid car industry, Toyota deserves the lion's share of the praise for the sudden popularity of gasoline-electric hybrid vehicles. Second, the hydrogen economy need not be held up by problems encountered in conventional fuel cell development. As mentioned in Chapter 1, ECD retrofitted a Toyota Prius to run on hydrogen. The internal combustion engine burned hydrogen, the ultimate fuel. The Ovonic NiMH batteries were part of the system, and the Ovonic solid-state hydrogen storage cylinders provided the fuel. In other words, the all-hydrogen hybrid produced much less pollution than even the gasoline hybrid Prius, and no CO_2 climate changing gases at all. Another amazing (and unexpected) point is that its mileage was the same as the gasoline hybrid. Having driven it, I can assure you that it represents a nice, crucial part of the solution to the world's oil problems.

Any internal combustion engine can be modified to operate with hydrogen as the fuel and clean water as the only by-product. We ought to begin building the infrastructure of the hydrogen economy long before the time when fuel cells might be ready for mass production in automobiles at reasonable costs. For example, by utilizing the unused nighttime electric capacity of utilities, one can produce hydrogen at reasonable prices by the electolysis of water. Electricity from Ovonic solar cells inherently breaks apart water to produce hydrogen in this manner. In fact, any other source of renewable energy, such as hydroelectric or wind power, could also be used to generate hydrogen by electrolysis. In Arizona, for example, hydrogen is now being profitably produced by a utility and is selling at about the same price as diesel.

The value of contributions such as the gasoline-electric hybrid vehicles and the use of internal combustion engines to operate with hydrogen in reducing our dependence on oil deserves to be acknowledged. This is exactly why Stan and Iris laid out a complete hydrogen loop strategy and why there are now hydrogen hybrid vehicles enabled by the Ovonic nickel-metal hydride batteries and utilizing the Ovonic solid hydrides. They use a conventional internal combustion engine to burn the hydrogen and, most importantly, they prove that gasoline is not needed to run an automobile, and that the vehicle can not only be run on hydrogen, but that its mileage in equivalent gallons of gasoline is the same—startling the entire vehicular and fuel industries. It also shows that one need not fight wars over oil! And that one can eliminate carbon dioxide, the major global warming gas. The transportation sector is responsible for 75% of carbon dioxide. Hydrogen hybrid vehicles not only have no carbon dioxide, but have orders of magnitude less pollution than the very low emission levels of a gasoline Prius.

They have also shown with their Ovonic solid hydrides that the infrastructure problem can be solved through their safe economic storage of hydrogen both in fueling stations and in vehicles. ECD built the world's first solid hydride hydrogen fueling station that certainly challenges the argument that one has to spend trillions of dollars for a new hydrogen infrastructure. [See picture on page 102.] What is now needed is to have these transformative advances put into production just as the gasoline hybrid is becoming a leading segment of the automotive industry.

The Science of Solid Hydrogen Storage

There are currently three solutions to hydrogen storage: gas, liquid, and solid. One can easily put hydrogen into a container as a gas. Unfortunately, the space requirements are astronomical for a container that holds enough hydrogen at atmospheric pressure (15 psi) to go, for example, 300 miles in an automobile. Thus, very high pressures (e.g., 5000 psi, 10,000 psi) are required to contain an adequate supply of hydrogen in a reasonable space. Several problems emerge from such high pressure solutions. First, it eats up energy to generate such pressures. Second, losses of hydrogen through leakages increase with higher pressures. Third, the thick-walled metal container that can withstand high pressures becomes rather heavy. Finally, from a user's perspective, who would want to risk a serious traffic accident with a 10,000 psi heavy metal hydrogen container in one's automobile?

A similar set of problems emerges when one tries to store hydrogen as a liquid. Liquid hydrogen must be stored cryogenically at -253° Celsius and it is very dangerous to handle. The costs in energy and in money to liquefy hydrogen are substantial, and considerable amounts of hydrogen are lost over time due to unavoidable boil-off of the liquid hydrogen. Also, safety concerns are present in a serious accident.

Because these problems with gaseous and liquid storage of hydrogen were well known, Stan and his colleagues created a nanostructure, disordered catalytic material to store hydrogen as part of a solid. Two important technical problems needed to be overcome. First, the H_2 molecule needed to be split into two hydrogen atoms. Stan created an amorphous catalytic material whose atomic structure was capable of slicing the H_2 molecule into two hydrogen atoms. Once split, the second problem emerges. What kind of material includes spaces in its atomic structure that will accept and bond hydrogen atoms into its voids? Further, the bonding cannot be too strong, since it is necessary to easily release (simply by mild heating) the hydrogen atoms in order to supply a steady stream of hydrogen gas to the internal combustion engine or to the fuel cell.

For years, Stan and his team had been dealing with the storage and release of hydrogen in the electrodes of his nickel-metal hydride batteries. Thus, they brought an enormous amount of experience to the challenge of solid hydrogen storage. As with the Ovonic battery, ECD does not utilize just several elements to store hydrogen; Stan and his collaborators developed a *range* of materials that possessed differing characteristics. For example, if space and weight are not problems in a particular application (such as for electricity load leveling) then a relatively heavy, metal hydride solution at low pressure could be used. If space and rapid kinetics are required (as in an automotive application) one would want to store materials that operate at low pressure (e.g., anywhere from 0 to 3600 psi rather than the 10,000 psi of gaseous hydrogen). Thus, one can atomically design an array of materials and specifically design formulations that best fit one's needs.

Ovonic Hydrogen Storage Systems describes its technology in the following manner: Its proprietary Ovonic metal hydrides are alloys formulated using unique atomic engineering principles developed by Stan. They absorb hydrogen gas, much as a sponge absorbs water. Figure 9-1[2] depicts these relationships.

Here's how it works. When hydrogen molecules from the hydrogen gas come into contact with the surface of the metal hydride alloy, they separate into atomic hydrogen and bond with the metal alloy.

This concentration of atomic hydrogen in the solid (Phase 1) increases as the pressure in the hydrogen gas increases until the critical "plateau pressure" is reached. At this point, the hydrogen is absorbed

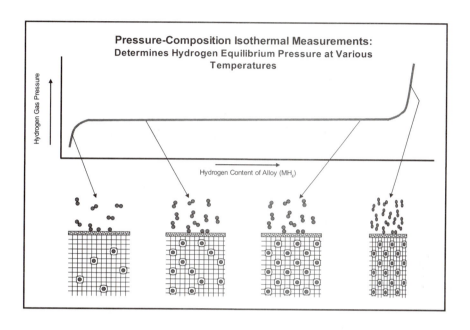

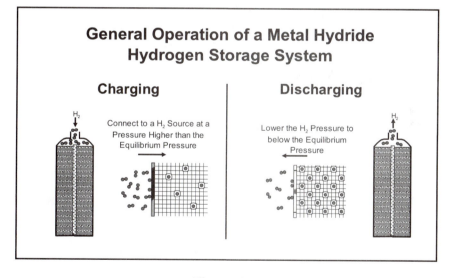

Figure 9-1

and reversibly bonded into the alloy making it a hydride which is hydrogen bonded in the solid alloy. When this happens, the pressure of hydrogen in Phase 1 no longer increases until the hydride in Phase 2 occupies the entire volume of the storage material. Once full capacity is reached, hydrogen pressure in the gas increases again (Phase 3). To release the hydrogen from the storage material, the ambient gas pressure of hydrogen is simply lowered to a value under the plateau.

When the metal hydrides absorb hydrogen, they release heat. Conversely, when they absorb heat (from engine exhaust or ambient air, for example), the alloys release hydrogen. ECD also utilizes these mechanisms for building its solid-state hydrogen compressor.

ECD lists a number of ways in which its solid hydrogen storage solutions offer important advantages to conventional hydrogen storage solutions:

1. Safety. ECD's metal hydride devices are safer than conventional methods for storing liquid and compressed hydrogen because the hydrogen chemically bonds with the metal, is stored at relatively low pressures and limits discharge in the event of puncture.

2. Scalability. Due to its modular design, ECD's storage vessels can supply fuel for any size hydrogen-based application—small or large, vehicular, portable, on-board or stationary.

3. Flexibility. With simple modifications, internal combustion engines, or fuel cells, can be fueled by these storage devices.

4. Compact/low pressure. These tanks and canisters can provide high volumetric storage densities without the use of expensive high-pressure compressors.

5. Reversibility. These storage devices can be discharged and recharged with speed, efficiency and control.

6. Long life. ECD's hydrogen canisters are robust and are designed to have a long service life. The same can be said of the Ovonic nickel-metal hydride batteries.

7. Easy handling. These storage devices hold more hydrogen per weight and volume than compressed hydrogen cylinders, readily accept hydrogen from reformers, electrolyzers and other sources, and can be used safely in more applications than liquid hydrogen.

A more detailed discussion of solid hydrogen storage can be found in Appendix 6, entitled "A Hydrogen ICE Vehicle Powered by Ovonic Metal Hydride Storage."

Building the Infrastructure of the Hydrogen Economy

In 2006, we are witnessing the beginning of the hydrogen economy. While oil peak and pollution concerns, along with the serious problems of climate change and wars over oil, virtually assure that the hydrogen economy will develop, two questions about this transition now remain unanswered: How quickly will the change come about? and What materials and systems will the infrastructure employ? The first question is difficult to address, as the answer depends as much on unknowable, geopolitical events—such as the political fates of OPEC members like Saudi Arabia, Venezuela, and Iraq—as it depends on technological breakthroughs.

Conversely, the dimensions of the second question—what materials and systems will make up the hydrogen economy's infrastructure—depend on whether the perspective one takes is a reflection of our current infrastructure system or a new idea for an infrastructure system unique to the characteristics of the hydrogen economy. Because the standard solution expressed by the government, oil companies, and auto manufacturers sees the change as a modification of the current crude oil/gasoline infrastructure, it closely resembles this present infrastructure. ECD's solutions are different from the consensus views currently being expressed. Take, for example, the question of how hydrogen will be produced, transported, stored, carried and converted to mechanical energy in automobiles. First, a broad overview of this modified current infrastructure, then a broad overview of ECD's vision will be presented.

In the current infrastructure, the key to the oil economy is to go where the oil is: Saudi Arabia, the North Sea, Venezuela, Russia, and so forth. The comparable key to producing hydrogen is the availability of cheap energy which could come from off-peak power plants, photovoltaics, nuclear reactors, geothermal energy, tides energy, wind energy, and the like. So large hydrogen production plants might spring up near Niagara Falls (hydroelectric), Iceland (geothermal), the East Coast of the United States (tides), western Kansas (wind turbine), anywhere that the sun shines (photovoltaics), and so forth. And of course even nuclear plants can produce large amounts of hydrogen.

The world is replete with wasted energy. Ovonic nickel-metal hydride batteries utilize the wasted thermal energy of braking to provide electricity to recharge and therefore add many extra miles to the gallon. Very importantly, utilities waste a lot of energy by running, as they must, at night. Using the cheap wasted electricity to electrolyze water and generate hydrogen is a classic example of how one can turn a loss into profit without increasing pollution or climate change gases. Waste energy can be turned into useful energy, a fact that seems not to be understood by those who think that one is thus increasing pollution when in fact one is decreasing it.

In the current infrastructure, carrying crude oil to refineries can involve oil tankers and pipelines while transporting refined gasoline to service stations usually involves gasoline trucks. Utilizing this present infrastructure model, hydrogen produced in Iceland would require large hydrogen tankers; hydrogen from western Kansas might make use of existing natural gas pipelines; and hydrogen produced via wind or tides off the East Coast might be trucked to hydrogen dispensing stations nearby. Once at the hydrogen service station, the fuel would be stored in tanks and dispensed via pumps into autos. Even in this standard infrastructure system, however, Ovonic solid hydride storage could be utilized. Standard trucks, trains, or boats could simply be filled with Ovonic solid hydrides wherein the hydrogen is chemically bonded to the hydrides. Furthermore, both in the service station tanks and in the autos themselves, the hydrogen could be stored in one of ECD's Ovonic hydrides.

The differences in ECD's vision of the hydrogen infrastructure flow directly from the hydrogen loop depicted in Figure 1-1. All that is required is energy (supplied by the sun), water (usually supplied by the local government, or by pumping water from the local aquifer), and an efficient system for dissociating oxygen from hydrogen in the water (which ECD has developed). Thus, photovoltaic collectors on the roof, awnings and/or pump coverings could generate the energy to produce the hydrogen on site. Should more hydrogen be required than the solar energy can produce, service stations have access to natural gas which can serve as a backup source of hydrogen. However, given the cheap PV electricity expected in the future, hydrogen from natural gas would be more expensive to produce and the byproduct CO_2 would result. Thus, early in the transition to the hydrogen economy, hydrogen can be produced at the hydrogen fueling station itself, as well as at nearby hydrogen producing substations from which the hydrogen can be distributed.

The hydrogen could easily be stored in Ovonic solid hydrides at low pressures anywhere in the service station or substations. It doesn't leak and, since it is so safe, it doesn't need to be underground. The transfer of hydrogen to autos, which would also have solid hydride

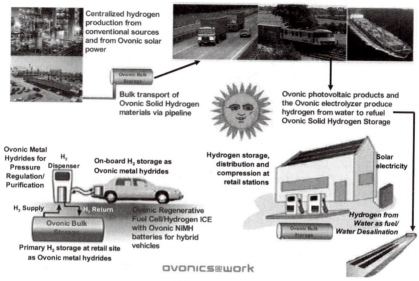

Ovonic™ Solid Hydrogen Systems Make the Hydrogen Economy Possible: the Practical Solutions for the Hydrogen Infrastructure

Figure 9-2

storage tanks, is facilitated by an ingenious thermal management system that ECD has already created. Figure 9-2[3] presents some of the ways that Ovonic solid hydrogen storage could be used in the hydrogen infrastructure.

ECD has put together a system that service station owners should love. There is a one-time cost of developing the service station's infrastructure (install photovoltaic cells and hydrogen storage). The electricity from the photovoltaic cells disassociates water and the hydrogen is sold to owners of automobiles. Unlike gasoline, the hydrogen that service station owners sell is a free gift of the sun. It's there, it's yours, it's free. And this system can use existing service stations. In fact, given the availability of photovoltaic cells and hydrogen storage, other structures such as auto parking lots could become hydrogen service stations—using photovoltaic electricity from PV shades covering the lots. Even individual homes could also become a significant source of hydrogen fuel.

The need to totally replace the existing infrastructure has been greatly overstated by opponents of the hydrogen economy. Perhaps the fact that the system, as envisioned by ECD, cuts out the most costly aspect of our present hydrocarbon system—the fuel itself, and the resulting dependency on oil companies—explains some of the opposition. However, energy companies (e.g., BP-Amoco, Chevron) could be producing new jobs by embracing aspects of the hydrogen economy. For example, the development and manufacturing of new kinds of hydrogen tanks or hydrogen dispensers, as well as the development of foundries that make the hydride materials, etc. represent viable opportunities for prescient energy companies.

A final, interesting application of solid hydrogen storage materials involves the United States military. Hydrogen continually gains greater use in battlefield situations. ECD equipped a flat bed trailer truck to make and transport hydrogen. [See picture on page 102.] Because of its transport versatility, the truck can deliver hydrogen to soldiers on the battlefield. U.S. Tank Army Command (TACOM) was very congratulatory of this accomplishment.

Akron Wasn't Built in a Day

Stan tells me that the mayor of Akron, Ohio, Don Plusquellic, is an extraordinarily talented person who surrounds himself with others like himself—committed, dedicated, true public servants. He has been until recently the head of the U.S. Conference of Mayors and was previously named the United States Mayor of the Year. Jeff Wilhite works as the Mayor's assistant. Stan admiringly says that Jeff is the best organizer he has ever met, is tremendously effective and is highly motivated to build Akron to its former glory.

Stan and Iris say that since they have been going to Akron they have been amazed at the civic-mindedness and wonderful skills of the local government. The entire Akron community has been warm and welcoming to the Ovshinskys and their ECD team. I was interested in getting the "Akronites" reactions to Stan's and Iris' January, 2005, trip to Akron, so I called Jeff. He was very excited, and we had a long talk about Stan, Iris and ECD. During the conversation, he made the following interesting points.

"Several years ago, we tried to put solar panels on the National Inventors Hall of Fame building here in Akron. That project didn't work out, but in checking out solar panels, I discovered Stan and Iris Ovshinsky. Meeting them had a huge impact on me. Seeing Stan's hydrogen loop made me think I had actually seen the future. I thought, 'Why not Akron?' Let's get into the hydrogen business.

"I'm the kind of guy who thinks that lightning can strike in the same place three times ..."

"Three?" I interrupted. "What were the first two strikes?"

"Canals were first," Jeff continued excitedly, "then about one hundred years ago, we became the rubber capitol of the world. I'm hoping the hydrogen economy will be Akron's third bolt of lightening."

"What part of the hydrogen loop will Akron bite off?" I probed.

"Solid hydrogen storage," Jeff explained. "We'll make and test the canisters that will hold Stan's powders. We've got some land for them already, and the city bought some adjoining land so that we'll be ready when the need to expand comes. Clean, high paying jobs in an expanding business domain."

"That's great," I responded.

Then Jeff continued, "I've been a public servant all my life. This is the sort of initiative that can impact and improve the lives of so many citizens. You endure a million frustrations in this job for the chance to make the kind of a difference in the life of a city that producing hydrogen canisters might bring about. This is the filet mignon of public service..."

Three days later, at lunch with Stan, I found out that Jeff's plans for canisters was only the beginning. I had wanted to get Stan's vision of ECD's partnership with the city of Akron, "Tell me, Stan, will anything come of the Akron connection?"

"Oh yes, we've made rapid progress with them. They've made generous offers of land and water ..."

"Water?" I interrupted. "Why do you need water?"

"Our plans for them are actually much bigger than just testing. They originally wanted us to do R & D work there. We told them we wanted to set up test sites for solid hydrogen storage units. But once we've done that, if we go into full production in Akron, we can make Akron the "Saudi Arabia equivalent" of the world..."

"What does that have to do with water, Stan?" I asked.

With an impish gleam in his eyes, Stan continued, "Years ago, Akron needed lots of water for the manufacture of rubber. But they are no longer in that business. When I asked about water they said, 'We've got all the water you need.' Next, I'll talk with their electric utilities and note that they're now only using about 50-60% of the electricity they produce. They sell very little of their off-peak electricity, but they have to keep the generating plant machines running. Soon I'll say to them, 'You want to make some extra money with your wasted (unused) electricity?' Electricity plus water gets you..."

"Hydrogen!" I whispered in amazement.

"The same is true of their garbage dumps," Stan continued. "They can use the garbage as a biofuel to produce electricity or they can siphon off the natural gas to use as a feedstock to produce hydrogen..."

"Akron will be the Riyadh of the Rust Belt," I stammered. "That's remarkable!"

"In its own way," Stan continued. "And they'll make money from their unused electricity, have more room in their landfills, and create a stream of clean, high valued, high paying jobs. Their tax base will increase. And more specifically, it will be a working example of what needs to be, and can be, accomplished throughout the United States..."

Stan's voice trailed away as he attacked his desert of raspberries, and I realized that there are more pleasant surprises out there for Jeff, as Stan's vision for Akron becomes part of its very real future.

Reception in Japan including Professor Kenichi Fukui, Nobelist,
and his wife next to former U.S. ambassador to Japan,
Edwin Reischauer and his wife Haru, both ECD board members

Bob Stempel, Stan and Iris in front of the Periodic Table

Chapter 10

Fuel Cell Applications for Automobiles

The problem with a battery is that it runs out of reactants and is slow to recharge. Supposing we could continually refresh the high energy hydrogen molecules, and continually supply air to the oxidant—the battery becomes a fuel cell...

Alastair Livesey
The 2nd Annual Ovshinsky
Science Symposium for Young People

The first significant fuel cell market will undoubtedly be for stationary (as opposed to automotive) applications. This market will be dominated by units in the range of 0.5 – 10kW of electric power. These small units now supply primary and/or back up power for banks, schools, hospitals, and other institutions. Soon they will appear in individual homes. Although this market is extremely small currently, it is growing rapidly, and many companies are working to develop products that will be significant in the stationary fuel cell market.

In the automotive domain, historically, Ballard Power's PEM fuel cell has been the leader. PEM is short for "proton exchange membrane," which indicates a different mode of operation than other types of fuel cells (e.g., SOFC: Solid Oxide Fuel Cell, ORFC: Ovonic Regenerative Fuel Cell).

The fuel for all fuel cells is hydrogen, although in some cases the hydrogen is derived from methane, kerosene, biofuel, propane, etc. The hydrogen atom contains one proton and one electron. Pure hydrogen is fed into a PEM fuel cell where it encounters a proton exchange membrane. Using precise electricity gradients, the proton moves through the membrane while the electron is prohibited from crossing the membrane. Free electrons enter a wire which loops around the membrane and eventually these electrons are reunited with free protons which also combine with free oxygen to form water (H_2O). It is the free electrons flowing through the wire (i.e., electricity) that are used to power an electric motor which converts the electricity into rotational motion (i.e., torque) to propel an automobile. Hydrogen in—electricity (the desired product) and water out. A pretty simple process, wouldn't you agree? The process works through chemical reactions alone. Because there is no burning of hydrocarbons when H_2 is the energy source, there are no pollutants or greenhouse gases produced.

ECD's Ovonic Regenerative Fuel Cell (ORFC) works in a different way. ECD's fuel cell encases two electrodes separated by a potassium hydroxide solution. One electrode (i.e., the H_2 electrode) is made of disordered alloys (i.e., metal hydrides). The second is made up of metals/metal oxides (acting as a catalyst that is capable of oxygen reduction). Hydrogen's proton is dissociated from its electron in the anode (negative electrode) of the Ovonic fuel cell. The proton migrates across the potassium hydroxide solution while the electron exits the anode via a wire as electricity. When the electron finally ends up at the cathode, it helps in the reduction of oxygen by producing hydroxyl ions. These ions become part of the electrolyte. The electricity is used to propel an automobile and the electrons are delivered (by wire) to the cathode (which is made of a different Ovonic material than the anode). At the cathode, protons are reunited with electrons which (in the presence of oxygen) combine to form water, the only waste product. Hydrogen in—electricity and water out. Stan's hydrogen loop is a water to water cycle. To this point, the PEM and Ovonic fuel cells achieve the same end result—converting hydrogen into electricity. However, there are important differences between the two fuel cells.

First, cost is always a prominent concern in a business. The most expensive components of PEM fuel cells are costly platinum catalysts, proprietary polymer membranes, and expensive graphite conductive plates. The Ovonic fuel cell avoids all three of these costly components and, in doing so, provides the best opportunity to meet challenging fuel cell cost targets.

Second, in propulsion applications, an energy storage functionality to utilize regenerative braking energy is essential to meet efficiency targets. In PEM fuel cells, either heavy batteries or other short term energy storage devices (e.g., ultra capacitors) are required. The

Ovonic fuel cell itself accepts regenerative braking as hydrogen can be stored in the Ovonic fuel cell's electrodes. The Ovonic fuel cell system requires no battery or ultra capacitor, and thereby substantially reduces weight, cost and complexity.

Third, when one starts a PEM automobile, there will be a slight delay (perhaps 10 to 20 seconds) before there is sufficient electricity available to run the car. This is because hydrogen must be obtained from the storage system (first delay) before the fuel cell can begin its work of producing electricity (second delay). This delay is in contrast to gasoline powered internal combustion engines which start almost as soon as one turns the ignition key. Because hydrogen is stored in the Ovonic fuel cell's electrodes, it gives instant start-up, similar to the internal combustion engine powered automobile, but unlike the PEM fuel cell.

Fourth, PEM fuel cells' efficiencies decline in cold temperatures. The energy storage functionality of the Ovonic fuel cell technology imparts excellent low-temperature performance, as well as the ability to operate even during an interruption in the hydrogen fuel supply. In contrast, in the PEM, water retained in the membrane will freeze at low temperatures, rendering the membrane non-operable. Similarly, any interruption in the flow of hydrogen to the PEM will stop the car. The Ovonic fuel cell, however, can tolerate interruptions by using the hydrogen stored in its electrodes.

All of these advantages spell trouble for the PEM fuel cell—especially in automotive applications. While ECD entered into partnerships for the Ovonic fuel cell in the past, ECD now (in 2006) owns 100% of its fuel cell technology. For those readers seeking greater technical detail, Appendix 7 provides a more thorough description of ECD's revolutionary fuel cell, entitled "The Ovonic Regenerative Fuel Cell, A Fundamentally New Approach."

Current Status of the Ovonic Fuel Cell

As this book goes to press, the Ovonic Fuel Cell Division has working prototypes of its fuel cell. These prototypes can provide energy for consumer uses, including replacing a battery. To achieve the size of a fuel cell that might run an automobile, most probably a hybrid, requires the packaging of an increased number of cells to form a stack. To date, all of the components have been hand manufactured to demonstrate viability. Now it is necessary to design and produce them for high volume manufacturing. Thus, the next year (through 2006) will be consumed by work that will increase the manufacturability of the components in order to shrink the cost of ECD's automotive fuel cell.

Stan loves to say, "In God we trust, everyone else must show data." So we will now review data on the Ovonic fuel cell (circa mid-2005). Figure 10-1[1] (top) depicts the basic structure of an Ovonic fuel cell. Each cell is about the size of a CD case, and an automotive fuel cell comes from the connecting of approximately one hundred of these cells in series (See Figure 10-1, bottom).

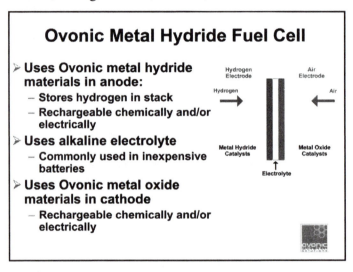

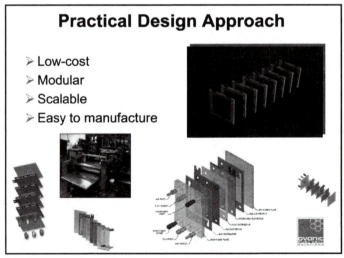

Figure 10-1

Figure 10-2[2] offers two different pictures of the Ovonic fuel cell's instant start capability. The top panel shows that it goes to 100% power instantly. The bottom panel shows how long the Ovonic fuel cell can run without any hydrogen being supplied under several levels of current. Figure 10-3[3] (top) presents data on the low temperature operation of the Ovonic fuel cell.

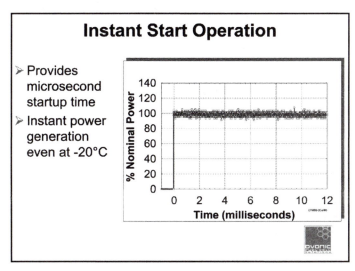

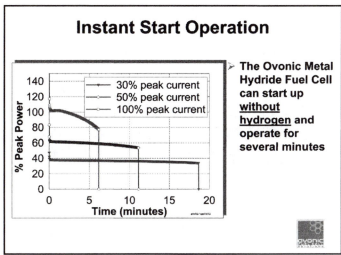

Figure 10-2

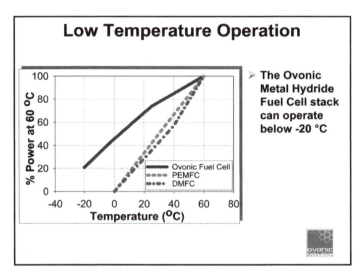

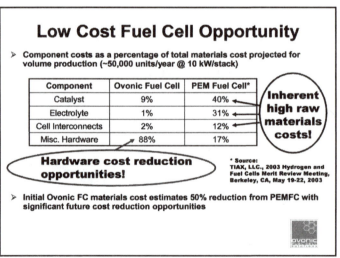

Figure 10-3

Finally, there is optimism at ECD regarding the next year's work on manufacturability and cost reduction issues for the Ovonic fuel cell. Figure 10-3 (bottom) depicts the cost breakdown for the Ovonic fuel cell versus the PEM fuel cell. One can see that for the PEM, 83% of its costs are tied up in inherent high raw material costs, leaving only 17% of fuel cell costs to be reduced by further research and manufacturing modifications. In contrast, the Ovonic fuel cell's cost might be reduced substantially through further research and manufacturing modifications. A full 88% of the Ovonic fuel cell's costs fall into this category, while only 12% of its costs are tied up in the cost of its basic components. Thus, these are good grounds for hope that the next year's work will produce dramatic reductions in the cost of the Ovonic fuel cell, providing a cost-effective fuel cell that can be used for many purposes, including automotive use. Stan has also come up with a novel approach with his electrodes that has the potential to raise the real efficiency of a fuel cell from about 40% to approximately 80% or more.

Photovoltaic cells and fuel cells are ECD's two energy generation processes. Both technologies produce electricity but each has a different power source—light for photovoltaics and hydrogen for fuel cells. On February 23, 2005, *EV World* noted,

> *Every hybrid electric car manufactured today relies exclusively on the Ovshinskys' NiMH battery chemistry. Their thin film solar cell discoveries make it possible to literally print miles of plastic film that turns the sun's light into pollution-free electricity. And someday hydrogen fuel cell vehicles from bicycles to motor scooters to cars and buses may store their "fuel" in metal "sponges" pioneered by the Ovshinskys.*

The first rewritable optical disk

Chapter 11

Information Technologies

...and a year and a day after he signed his noncompetition agreement with Micron, Tyler Lowrey showed up on our doorstep.

Bob Stempel
Chairman and CEO, ECD

When one reads early annual reports of the company (circa 1970) it is clear that the memory and switching properties of glassy compounds were prominent in ECD's thinking. Here's how the 1970 ECD annual report described "Ovonics: ECD's Science and Technology."[1]

> *Over a decade ago Stanford R. Ovshinsky became interested in the switching and memory processes of the human nervous system.*
>
> *In a continuing quest for effective models of how the nervous system transmits, orders and stores information he turned to the glassy—or "amorphous"—compounds of certain elements. Founding ECD, he developed theories and models of unique switching action in amorphous materials.*
>
> *Aided by his wife, Dr. Iris M. Ovshinsky, a biochemist, Dr. Hellmut Fritzsche, a Professor of Physics at the University of Chicago, and other prominent consultants, Stanford Ovshinsky studied this relatively unexplored area of solid-state physics and developed the technology that would put it to commercial use.*
>
> *We call the science and technology of these glassy compounds, as disclosed by the inventions of Ovshinsky and his group, "Ovonics."*

125

Three concepts basic to Ovonics

A working knowledge of Ovonics involves an understanding of three basic concepts: (1) amorphous materials, (2) thin films, and (3) response to various forms of energy.

1. Amorphous materials

A glass is an "amorphous" or disordered substance, lacking the regular crystalline structure of most chemical elements and compounds. Ordinary window glass consists principally of compounds of silicon but there are hundreds—even thousands—of other kinds of glasses.

Some elements—as, for example, oxygen, sulphur, selenium, and tellurium—are capable of linking up with other neighboring elements in the Periodic Table, such as arsenic, germanium and silicon, to form highly complex glasses with unusual properties. It was these glasses that Ovshinsky used to develop the unusual effects forming the basis for Ovonics.

By melting and mixing different proportions of amorphous materials, all of which are readily available commercially, it is possible to achieve a virtually limitless range of glasses, with widely different physical and chemical characteristics. At Energy Conversion Devices, we typically combine two, three, four, or even five of these materials, according to predetermined specifications, to achieve the properties we are seeking in the resulting Ovonic compound.

2. Thin films

Ovonic compounds display their useful properties to best advantage when they are arrayed as very thin layers or films. At Energy Conversion Devices we achieve these thin films, for example, by vaporizing the amorphous mixture under carefully controlled conditions and condensing the vapor as a film on a supporting base, known as a substrate. Substrates can be either rigid or flexible. Those used at ECD include glass plates, metal drums, silicon wafers and mylar film. The thin film of Ovonic material which we deposit on them may be as little as 1/100,000-in. in thickness. The equipment we use in this operation consists of standard, commercially available units. The accumulated processing techniques for performing this work in a production sense are called thin film technology and many of these techniques as applied to amorphous materials have been developed at ECD.

3. *Response to various forms of energy*

Two different fundamental changes may be produced in a variety of amorphous materials, in each case designed to produce the result desired:

1. a change—that can be reversed—in the atomic structure of the amorphous material that produces machine-detectable and/or human-readable characteristics of many types (the Ovonic memory effect).

2. a temporary electronic change in the amorphous material that allows it to serve as a switch (the Ovonic threshold effect).

These changes are effected by the application of energy in a variety of forms and are accompanied by very distinct changes in various properties of the materials. In the threshold switch we use primarily the electrical properties. An Ovonic memory material can retain its information without sustaining energy and at the same time have important changes in its non-electrical properties, such as optical and mechanical. Some of the forms in which energy may be applied to alter a memory material are light—from a laser, from a lamp (including a flashlamp) or from sunlight—heat, electricity and stress. Two or more of these forms may be applied simultaneously.

It is our potential to change and control various properties of the materials to make them into useful products that is the real cornerstone of the commercial development of Ovonics.

These, then, are the basic concepts of Ovonics. At Energy Conversion Devices we work with a relatively small number of elements which, in combination, provide a large group of materials with which to work. The materials we use are in thin film form—the thickness of the film as well as the nature of the Ovonic compound having a critical bearing on the characteristics achieved. We apply forms of energy, singly or in combination, to these amorphous materials to achieve properties that are useful in commercial applications.

The Current Status of the Information Technologies

"Bob remembers that incorrectly," Tyler interjected, as I repeated the Stempel quote that began this chapter. "I was tied up for 18 months, not a year. I visited ECD one day after my eighteen months were up."

"Oh, I see," I said. "How did you know about OUM?"

"Well, I was CTO (Chief Technology Officer) at Micron Technologies in Boise, Idaho. In a position like that, everybody-and-his-brother has the next great technology idea and wants some time to show it to you. I had a working policy that I'd give everybody an hour—but no longer than that. Most of those hours were complete wastes of time..."

"But not ECD's hour?" I asked.

Tyler smiled impishly and said, "No, ECD's hour wasn't a waste of time. As I remember it, four guys came out—Stan, Wally, and some other guys. I can't remember exactly who the others were. They told me what they had and brought their stuff to demonstrate right there in my lab. I was very interested. I actually pitched OUM to the Micron people but—long story short—they passed on it. I kind of remembered it as 'the one that got away!'

"Many years later, I did well in my separation from Micron, so I didn't really need another job. During my eighteen month vacation I asked myself the question, 'What would be a fun and important thing to do in my next job?'"

"What else did you do in the eighteen months?"

"Worked on fluorescent light bulbs."

"What!? You're kidding!"

"No. Actually, I did it for a friend."

"So, Tyler," I concluded, "has your present job been fun and important?"

Tyler smiled and said, "Yep. That hour with Stan and the others while I was at Micron was time very well spent."

Stan is very enthused over Tyler. Their partnership is extremely close, as is their camaraderie. Stan said that he is, without question, "one of the most brilliant and effective people I know."

OUM (Ovonic Universal Memory)

The technology with the greatest long-term financial potential is probably OUM. The advantages of phase change memory over the incumbent silicon chips are quite impressive. ECD's intellectual property in this domain (consisting of numerous patents) is now held by a company, Ovonyx, a joint venture formed to commercially exploit phase change memory, with Tyler Lowrey as CEO and Intel Corporation as an investor and technical partner. In ECD's organizational structure (Figure 5-3), phase change activities fall under the purview of the Ovonic Information Group.

OUM is ECD's replacement for conventional silicon memory types such as Flash, DRAM, SRAM, embedded memory and the like. Revenues in these markets currently total to approximately $140 billion/year. OUM has numerous advantages over the traditional memory types. While this chapter will explain two of OUM's advantages, for a more advanced discussion, readers should consult Appendix 8, entitled "Characteristics of OUM Phase Change Materials and Devices for High Density Nonvolatile Commodity and Embedded Memory Applications."

Any computer memory device must be able to be included in an electric circuit in either of two states. These states ("on" or "off") must then be easily distinguishable. OUM is an alternative (to silicon memories) two-state device, as a material's amorphous state is easily distinguished from its crystalline state. Stan's Ovonic memory switch makes it easy to reverse from one state to another. Thus it has the potential to replace standard memory technologies. What are OUM's advantages?

The first advantage is that it is nonvolatile, whereas many other memory types are volatile. Each morning when I arrive at work, I turn on the electricity for my computer. It takes my computer 4 minutes and 51 seconds to reboot. This is because each memory chip "forgets" where it was the day before (whether in an "on" or "off" state) when the electricity was turned off. Thus, it needs to run a complex restart program before it is ready to respond to my commands. Since OUM is a nonvolatile memory, when the electricity for an Ovonic computer is turned off, each OUM memory cell remains in its last state (i.e., amorphous or crystalline). When the electricity is next turned on (e.g., the next morning, or 50 years later) the Ovonic computer is instantly right where it was when last used. Thus, there is no need to reboot the computer. This advantage also becomes significant when information needs to be stored for long time periods and then recovered.

Further, OUM requires little energy; is easily read; can be manufactured easily; is easily embedded, and so forth. But perhaps its single most compelling advantage is that it scales, while traditional memory types do not. This is exceedingly important because of Moore's Law.

Moore's Law (named after Intel's co-founder Gordon Moore) claims that microprocessors' capacities will double every 18 months. The law has held up reasonably well since it was first stated in 1975. While many factors have produced the effect described in Moore's

Law, undoubtedly the largest part was due to the miniaturization of computer chips (i.e., their scalability). The computing potential that formerly required a roomful of memory chips, now rests comfortably inside a thin laptop computer. Unfortunately, silicon chips possess physical limits to their size that are due to practical limits of voltage and manufacturability, as well as to quantum mechanical realities. While the limits vary from one memory type to another, they are generally in the 60 nm to 90 nm range. OUM's performance, on the other hand, improves as it shrinks in size. OUM scales nicely.

Central Analytical Lab

As you examine ECD's structure in Figure 5-3, the Machine Shop and General Engineering Support are found on the top, left hand side. On the top, right hand side, you find the Central Analytical Lab, and the Wafer Lab and Clean Room. These support services and facilities are important, multi-functional components of the ECD organization. As OUM nears production, the Clean Room and Wafer Lab become ever more important. Partners and licensees are quick to commission studies to be conducted in the Analytical Lab. Thus, like the Machine Shop, the Analytical Lab, headed by the highly talented and respected Ben Chao, furthers ECD's research efforts while, from time to time, returning a profit to ECD.

The Ovonic Cognitive Computer

This is one of ECD's newest ideas, and yet oldest work. It is a "machine" that completes Stan's and Iris' earliest interests in the different types of "thinking" that occur in traditional computers versus the way that human brains think. In 1955, after reading Stan's paper, "The Nerve Impulse,"[2] Ernest Gardner, Professor of Anatomy at Wayne University's School of Medicine and later president of the Medical School, invited Stan to do research at Wayne Medical School. Stan continued his experiments on neurophysiology there. Since the mid-1950s, this has been a continuous area of development for Stan and Iris.

The Cognitive Computer is based upon OUM memory cells as well as other Ovonic devices, and it represents a fundamentally different approach to a thinking machine. As is the human brain, the Cognitive Computer is capable of multi-level (as opposed to binary) storage of information and is capable of massive parallel processing. It is based upon amorphous materials. This is in sharp contrast to traditional binary, sequential, silicon information processing machines.

All current computers are based upon the von Neumann paradigm, which demands that all information be reduced to binary logic ("yes" or "no"). This condition can be met in electrical circuits by electricity being "on" or "off." All that is required is that one have two distinguishable states—with OUM it is the "amorphous" or "crystalline" states of the memory material. However, there actually are degrees of order designed in the Ovonic material that provide many more states than in the conventional binary switch. It is these multi-level capabilities that permit the Ovonic phase change device to be an almost perfect analog of neuronal and synaptic activity. So when using the Ovonic cognitive computing device, the machine can "think" in, for example, base 10 (as we do in our arithmetic system) rather than in base 2 (binary) as the von Neumann computers do.

In the von Neumann paradigm, everything is done sequentially— one step at a time. Very ingenious things have been done over the years to compensate for this sequential condition, such as pipelining, parallelism, etc. Parallelism is accomplished via architecture, or software; it is not intrinsic to the system in a von Neumann machine. The human brain, however, is massively parallel in its functioning. Neurons possess multiple connections to other neurons. Further, these neurons possess plasticity—that is, experience can strengthen or weaken the connections between neurons.

Ovonic cognitive devices, in contrast to von Neumann computers, possess elements of functionality that parallel the brain. The various connections communicate with each other in a manner very much like biological neurons and their synapses. Further, both the human brain and the Ovonic Cognitive Computer are massively and interactively parallel. Finally, and extremely important, both the human brain and the Ovonic Cognitive Computer possess adaptability, that is, the plasticity absolutely necessary for learning and intelligence. One other difference between traditional computers and the Ovonic Cognitive Computer is that, rather than silicon, the cognitive computer employs thin films of disordered materials, whose functions depend upon their local order.

Beyond this rather spartan overview of the Cognitive Computer, things quickly become very technical and complex. For those interested in this deeper level of sophistication, Appendix 9, entitled "A

New Information Paradigm—The Cognitive Computer," might be the next logical step.

Finally, the Ovonic Cognitive Computer will continuously evolve as years go by, thus its economic potential appears to be almost limitless. A recent quote by Bill Gates forcefully makes this point: "If you invent a breakthrough in artificial intelligence so machines can learn, that is worth 10 Microsofts."[3]

Rewritable CDs and DVDs

All rewritable CDs and DVDs use Stan's phase change technologies. Information is stored on light-sensitive phase change material. Reprogramming is accomplished through a laser beam that simply writes over the original material. Thus, there is no need for separate erase and rewrite steps.

ECD and GE have a joint venture and strategic alliance in the rewritable DVD field. ECD can scale down to some very small dimensions that are required by the laser technology called Blu Ray, and in fact are only limited by the wave length of the light. This area is growing rapidly.

ECD originated liquid crystal displays, and ECD's technology is present in thin displays on computers, television screens, etc. The Ovonic phase change devices became ubiquitous in industry when Stan licensed all of the major companies in the world. Historically, ECD has licensed its display, CD, and DVD domains, and since the 1970s, fees have come from licensing, not production. The attendant monies helped support ECD's research and operations over the last few decades. Programs such as these have played important roles in furthering research and development in all of ECD's product domains.

Few people know that ECD originated the thin film liquid crystal display industry. In fact, when Stan was in Ford Hospital in 1989, he completed licensing negotiations with Samsung, which resulted in Samsung becoming one of the largest companies in the LCD field. In 1981, Sharp had entered into a joint venture and licensed amorphous photovoltaics from ECD. This work with amorphous materials had trained Sharp personnel so that they could work with amorphous transistors that controlled LCDs, and the leaders of LCD development at Sharp came out of that original group. Amorphous transistors that utilized mechanisms similar to crystalline transistors were developed by ECD.

Stan was unhappy with the above approach, and so he expanded his thinking on the Ovonic switch (a two terminal device) into a three terminal device, which he worked on for many years. The three terminal device has the following advantages: 1) it is much smaller than a conventional transistor; 2) it is much faster (in fact it is so fast that the speed has never been measured); 3) it carries 50 times the current of the best transistors; 4) this thin film device is much cheaper to produce; and finally, 5) using industry accelerated testing procedures, its extrapolated lifetime is (at least) a staggering 10^{23} cycles. This work on the Ovonic three terminal threshold switch has been seminal in Stan's strategic planning for the development of an all thin film computer, whether binary or cognitive.

The conventional transistor was of great importance, and gave birth to a trillion dollar/year information industry. It allowed for the computer industry, the semiconductor industry, etc. The three terminal threshold switch, because of its unique scientific principles, positions ECD to lead the way toward the unusual and promising electronic instruments that the future holds in store.

Again looking to the future, organic light-emitting diodes (OLEDs)—plastic materials that emit light and could replace conventional lighting devices—hold great promise. ECD and GE have a partnership wherein GE provides plastic materials while ECD contributes thin films. The resulting OLEDs are manufactured using ECD's roll-to-roll machines. The first such machines are now being built. Concepts like OLEDs can be important additions to ECD's information technology portfolio, as are OUM and the Ovonic Cognitive Computer. David Strand, a much appreciated and fast-rising manager, is in charge of the optical and information areas of ECD's work. Without a doubt, the Ovonic information area has shown that the semiconductor and computer industries are now building their future on the work that Stan pioneered many years ago, and we are witnessing the establishment of a whole new approach to the storage of information. Appendix 10, entitled "Why Chalcogenides are Ideal Materials for Ovshinsky's Ovonic Threshold and Memory Devices," provides further elaboration of the materials basis for Ovshinsky's information technologies.

Part III

The Big Picture

In ECD conference room mid-1970s.
(Above) *Seated* - Professors David Adler, MIT, Bill Paul, Harvard, Mel Shaw, Wayne State, Ted Davis, Bristol University, Stan, Sir Nevill Mott, Cambridge University. *Standing* - J.T. Chen, Wayne State, Marc Kastner, MIT, Arthur Bienenstock, Stanford, Hellmut Fritzsche, U of Chicago and ECD group.
(Below) *From top left* - Professors Arthur Bienenstock, Heinz Henisch, Penn State, Hellmut Fritzsche, Stan, Marc Kastner, Bill Paul and Mel Shaw.

Chapter 12

The Complex World of Science

My approach to science is that man made disciplines, nature did not. Therefore, there is potential for discovery for those who will utilize all of science.

Stan Ovshinsky

One of the collection of inscriptions from outstanding scientists and engineers that graces the entrance hall of the Sony Research Center.

Evelyn Fox-Keller wrote a wonderful biography of the Nobel Laureate biologist Barbara McClintock entitled, *A Feeling for the Organism.*[1] One of Keller's themes was that McClintock's decision to stick with genetic studies of corn rather than shift to research on Drosophila (fruit flies), as did virtually all research geneticists at the advent of the microbiological revolution, rendered her an outsider to her own field. Decades later, McClintock's work unexpectedly took center stage in genetics and eventually earned her the Nobel prize. Fox-Keller has this to say about McClintock's life story,[2]

It might be tempting to read this history as a tale of dedication rewarded after years of neglect—of prejudice or indifference eventually routed by courage and truth. But the actual story is both more complex and more illuminating. It is a story about the nature of scientific knowledge, and of the tangled web of individual and group dynamics that define its growth.

A new idea, a new conception, is born in the privacy of one man's or one woman's dreams. But for that conception to become part of the body of scientific theory, it must be acknowledged by the society of which the individual is a member. In turn, the collective effort provides the ground out of which new ideas grow. Scientific knowledge as a whole grows out of the interaction—sometimes complex, always subtle—between individual creativity and communal validation. But sometimes that interaction miscarries, and an estrangement occurs between individual and community. Usually, in such a case, the scientist loses credibility. But should that not happen, or, even better, should it happen and then be reversed, we have a special opportunity to understand the meaning of dissent in science.

Take a moment to think of our solar system as a metaphor. If the field of genetics is composed of insiders who are close to the sun (e.g., Mercury, Venus, Earth, Mars), then Barbara McClintock was like the planet Pluto for the bulk of her scientific career. In this model, where would we locate Stan Ovshinsky? He'd be a planet in some other galaxy—many light-years away from our sun. Thus, Barbara McClintock was an outsider, but only in a relative sense. Next to Stan Ovshinsky, she looks like a complete insider (e.g., a Ph.D. in genetics from Cornell University; a job at Cold Spring Harbor through the Rockefeller Foundation; election to the National Academy of Sciences). However, rather than seeing Stan as a complete outsider to the world of materials science, my informants see Stan as the sun in the science of disordered and amorphous materials. Interestingly, I believe that Stan Ovshinsky's life tells us a great deal—some good, some bad—about science as practiced in the last half of the twentieth century.

Science is a difficult career in which to gain credit for one's work. Most scientists see themselves as "outsiders" to a group of "insiders" who are associated with a cadre of elite institutions (e.g., Harvard, Stanford, Oxford, MIT). One can easily elicit stories of how difficult it is for an outsider to crack the club of insiders. As was true of Stan's efforts over the years against the companies allied to the burning of hydrocarbons, his status as a far-far-outsider must have made his struggles with the scientific establishment virtually intolerable.

In this patently uneven battle with the scientific establishment, Stan had some very important allies. First and most importantly, Stan happened to be right about the enormous importance of disordered and amorphous materials for the twenty-first century. In science, there are perhaps a thousand wrong ideas for every important, right idea.

What if amorphous materials had not held the answers to several problems raised by the hydrogen economy and for the future of information technologies (such as memory chips, CDs, DVDs)?

If amorphous materials did not provide solid answers to important questions, neither you nor I would have even heard of Stan Ovshinsky. And ECD would have gone bankrupt decades ago.

Second, ECD's scientific interests and Stan's interests went hand-in-hand. To be able to guide an R & D firm's research agenda in directions you choose is a luxury that precious few scientists enjoy. Of course, this privilege made enormous demands upon Stan also. Raising money to fund research has been a lifelong, onerous challenge for Stan and ECD. Because the company was a publicly-held firm, company forms, stockholders' letters, SEC requirements, shareholder conference calls, etc. have compromised the opportunity to devote long hours of uninterrupted work that often characterize productive scientific research and writing.

Third, Stan possessed an array of personal characteristics (from genius through creativity) recognized by brilliant scientists. This enabled him to collaborate with some of the scientific giants of the twentieth century. When Iris sent Stan's collected papers to Nobel Laureate Isidor I. Rabi in the early 1980s, Rabi responded with a note that read:

> *Thank you for sending me a copy of Stan's collected papers. They are indeed stunning and monumental. I have watched their growth since a very long time ago.*
>
> *I have two complaints. One, the picture does not do him justice (he is not all that starry eyed) and two, you should have been included as a guardian angel of Athena hovering overhead.*

What other high school graduate would be up to the challenge of publishing with great scientists? Stan has been recognized by the leading scientists of the world and has published with most of the eminent scientists he has attracted to his field, working and/or coauthoring articles with Sir Nevill F. Mott (Cambridge, Nobel Laureate), David Adler (MIT), Hellmut Fritzsche (University of Chicago), Arthur Bienenstock (Stanford), Heinz Henisch (Penn State), Karl Böer (Delaware), Morrel Cohen (University of Chicago), David Turnbull (Harvard), Isidor I. Rabi (Columbia, Nobel Laureate) Linus Pauling (Cal Tech, Nobel Laureate), Kenichi Fukui (Kyoto University, Nobel Laureate), and many, many more.

Stan has long enjoyed the wonderful support of Iris Ovshinsky and their colleagues at ECD. As mentioned before, he is particularly proud of the culture that he's established that's enabled ECD to grow and bring out the potential that lies in so many people. With colleagues such as these, even seemingly impossible problems became solvable. As noted earlier in this book, Stan has also had input and support from an eminent and unusual Board of Directors who have believed ECD's goals were vitally important to the world. [See page 160.]

What does the Stan Ovshinsky story tell us about science at the dawn of the third millennium of our common experience? It reinforces Evelyn Fox-Keller's points about outsiders having a rougher row to hoe than do insiders. Personal tendencies, like Barbara McClintock's desire for solitude and her need to work alone, helped her to remain productive for decades while genetics moved away from the study of corn toward microbiological questions. Stan Ovshinsky, on the other hand, was self-confident, fearless, inspiring and persistently enthusiastic. His self-confidence and his fearlessness allowed him to work productively with scientists who were far better credentialed than he. His ability to inspire and his enthusiasm served him well in his seemingly endless efforts to raise money to support his research.

But the Stan Ovshinsky story is actually a positive testament to science. Very few insiders can boast a roster of colleagues and collaborators as eminent as Stan's. At least once during the second half of the twentieth century, a distant outsider has achieved great success as a scientist. Therefore, the shop of science is not completely closed to outsiders.

Although many in the scientific establishment are only impressed by traditional credentials, perhaps great scientists do resonate to great ideas—no matter who offers them. It reminds me of Martin Luther King's prescient quote from his *I Have a Dream* speech,[3] "I look forward to a day when my children will be judged, not by the color of their skin, but by the content of their character." Stan found a way to get past the small minds in materials science, physics and inorganic chemistry in order to interact with the great minds. Quite a scientific achievement for a planet from a distant galaxy.

Genius in Science

In my search for parallels to Stan among the geniuses of modern science, Evelyn Fox-Keller's biography of Barbara McClintock, *A Feeling for the Organism*, was especially helpful. Over many years of intense study of the genetics of corn, Barbara developed an intimate feeling for "her organism." While always difficult to explain to others, Barbara often cited her understanding of corn genetics as fundamental to her solution to the many problems that she encountered. Every scientist must rely on his/her intuition when solving novel problems.

Fox-Keller's thoughts on McClintock's brand of genius are instructive,[4]

> *To some extent the stories she tells to illustrate the meaning of "understanding" recall what might be called the "naturalist" tradition—a tradition that in most parts of biology had long been replaced by the experimental tradition, but traces of which nevertheless still survived in the mid-1930s. McClintock was able to incorporate and integrate these traces into an otherwise thoroughly experimental stance. No scientist ever develops in a vacuum, but it is difficult to find any direct intellectual influences that can be held responsible for this element in her thought. Rather, it would seem that she came to this amalgam in her own highly individualistic way, dictated more by internal forces than by external ones. The stories themselves reflect this...*
>
> *The nature of insight in science, as elsewhere, is notoriously elusive. And almost all great scientists—those who learn to cultivate insight—learn also to respect its mysterious workings. It is here that their rationality finds it own limits. In defying rational explanation, the process of creative insight inspires awe in those who experience it. They come to know, trust, and value it.*
>
> *"When you suddenly see the problem, something happens that you have the answer—before you are able to put it into words. It is all done subconsciously. This has happened too many times to me, and I know when to take it seriously. I'm so absolutely sure. I don't talk about it, I don't have to tell anybody about it, I'm just **sure** that is it."*

I think it is telling that Fox-Keller places McClintock's "brand" of understanding in the naturalist tradition of the 19th century. I believe that Stan possesses a similar "feel for the disordered and amorphous world." Remember his description as, "the man who speaks with the elements." He just knows the ways of the amorphous surfaces of materials, the strange relationships of lone pair electrons, and the like. You and I can only understand glimpses of that world. We see it "as through a glass darkly."

Recall my skepticism earlier when Stan reported that he knew what he wanted and needed to make the Ovonic threshold switch and the Ovonic memory switch work, and that he knew why they would work and what they could do. When I told Hellmut Fritzsche of Stan's unusual claim, he replied, "Stan sees the world of amorphous materials differently than we do. He possesses so much more experience with those materials that he feels they are 'his' materials. And while one may not patent 'acts of nature' like amorphous materials, Stan certainly uses them to solve societal problems as if he owned them."

Stan loves the humor of others—especially when the joke is about "his" world. As you now know, the surfaces of matter are by nature disordered. Imagine Stan's delight upon reading the Nobel laureate physicist Wolfgang Pauli's statement about disorder, "God created the solids, the devil their surfaces." How very strange to find someone conversant in the languages of both the gods and the devils.

From left to right: Rosa Young, Sir Nevill Mott, Stan, Iris, David Adler,
Hellmut Fritzsche, Jeff Yang, Subhendu Guha, Ron Citkowski,
Prem Nath and Marv Siskind at Old Plant 1 on Maple Road, Troy, MI.

ECD's hydrogen powered hybrid auto

Chapter 13

The Future is Now

Scientific American Frontiers: It sounds like every idea you have, people would say "It can't be done," or "that will take way too long."
Iris: That is absolutely true.
Scientific American Frontiers: What do you take from that, and how do you use it?
Stan: Well, I use it philosophically. What we do has never been considered as possible, or people tried and failed, either one. We get basic patents. We use that time of incredulousness or skepticism, which is natural, on something that is dramatically different. And then we don't allow the criticism to do anything but spur us on. It goes with our belief that you don't talk about it, or wave your hands... We always build it to show that it works. And when that does it, that shifts the debate pattern. It's very difficult for somebody to say it isn't going to work when you're driving around in a car with it.

There was no hydrogen loop before Stan Ovshinsky drew it. No one was working on an integrated whole. And this is important. Working on one aspect of the hydrogen loop, for example fuel cells, is necessary, but not sufficient, because you need the *complete* operating system realistically. Here's a research report that came across my desk in July, 2005.[1]

After announcing General Electric's company-wide push into so-called green technologies in May, Jeffrey Immelt, the company's CEO, stressed that the move is not part of some save-the-planet idealism.

Rather, he said, 'GE's Ecomagination initiative is driven by profit, plain, and simple. With oil at $55 [a barrel], you have to root for me', the Financial Times quoted him as adding.

This is perhaps the highest profile example of why next-generation energy companies—those that generate power with little or no environmental impact—are likely to provide investors a long-tailed secular growth opportunity, according to Greg Curhan, managing director at Merriman, Curhan & Ford. The San Francisco-based investment bank, which specializes in fast-growing companies, foresees compound annual growth of about 24 percent over the next decade for companies that produce green technologies, like solar-photovoltaics, hybrid electric vehicles and hydrogen fuel cells.

Why Go Green?

Rising oil prices have brought energy efficiency to the fore, and green energy technology tends to be very efficient. Brion Tanous, a process engineer who worked on the space shuttle's fuel cells and now tracks next-generation energy for Merriman, points out that coal-fired power plants generate electricity at 34 percent efficiency and internal combustion engines at 15 percent. By contrast fuel cells—battery-like devices, which produce electricity, generate zero pollution and are 100 percent silent—are between 60 percent and 80 percent efficient.

It's telling that even the oil-heavy American Stock Exchange has given a nod to the rising importance of green energy, introducing the PowerShares WilderHill Clean Energy Index in March.

Consumers, too, are warming to the green technologies—particularly in cars. According to automobile researcher R. L. Polk, there were 83,000 hybrid vehicles on the road in 2004—81 percent more than in 2003. Toyota recently increased the production rate of the Prius, its hybrid-electric, to 180,000 vehicles per year, and Honda now offers three hybrids. Hybrids combine a gasoline engine and electric motor and represent a critical transition phase to a yet-cleaner future of fuel cell vehicles, of which there are still few (only about 400) at present. Still, Tanous notes, hybrid technology is about 75 percent transferable to fuel cell vehicles.

You're only replacing the gas engine with a fuel cell, he said. All of the electrical propulsion used in the hybrid, i.e., electric motors and the digital power management, gets used in the fuel cell vehicle.

For this reason, fuel cell transition technologies are a key growth area. Another is solar cells, which are photovoltaic (PV) cells made of semiconductor materials that produce electricity. According to the U.S. Department of Energy, costs of solar technology have declined by 80 percent over the past two decades, while the PV market has grown over 30 percent each of the past five years, claims Clean Edge research. A bill pending in California (The Million Solar Roofs bill, SB 1) proffers 10 years of incentives to stimulate the installation of solar energy systems in a state that is already the world's third-largest market for solar power, behind Japan and Germany...

Energy Conversion Devices offers a portfolio of clean energy technologies and participates in two rapidly growing markets, photovoltaics, a 30 percent CAGR segment, and hybrid vehicles, a 39 percent CAGR segment. The company owns Uni-Solar, [United Solar Ovonic] which provides thin film amorphous silicon solar cells for roofing and has grown by 70 percent over the past year. Uni-Solar is selling everything it makes and has $80 million worth of back-orders.

Energy Conversion is also set to sell nickel-metal hydride (NiMH) battery packs into the rapidly growing hybrid market through its 50 percent ownership of COBASYS (Chevron Texaco Ovonic Battery Systems). Tanous, whose firm does banking for Energy Conversion, sees potential to dominate the hybrid-electric battery market, though the firm has ample competition from Panasonic and Sanyo. [Author: Fortunately this competition is not so. Both Panasonic and Sanyo are licensees of Ovonic Battery Company.]

A third business is Ovonic Unified [Universal] Memory (OUM), a technology designed to replace flash memory that is supported by STMicroelectronics and Intel and 41.7 percent owned by Energy Conversion. Though Jefferies Group analyst Jeffrey Bencik points out that Energy Conversion is not yet profitable and believes shares are fully valued at present, Tanous is nonetheless bullish. Energy Conversion expanded its revenue by 8 percent in the most recent quarter, but still lost 39 cents per share. Management is shooting for sustained profitability by July 2006.

The analyst offers this "sum of the parts" valuation: In photovoltaics, comparable company Evergreen Solar trades between three to five times sales on enterprise value. If you apply that here, you get $10 per share, he says. The battery business is based on a royalty stream from Sanyo and other licensees and worth $20 to $30 per share.

> *The third piece of the pie is OUM technology, a wild card that could be worth anywhere from $10 to $30. Do the math, Tanous urges, and you get to the mid-$40's without any trouble.*
>
> *A compelling argument, if one that requires some forward thinking and faith.*

In discussing the report with Stan, I said, "I was so pleased to see that ECD is the largest (by market capitalization) of the next generation energy companies mentioned. I think that's because Ballard is only into PEM fuel cells, while Quantum is about high pressure hydrogen storage, but ECD is about the *total* hydrogen loop—about four separate products that address what eventually will become markets that are in the hundreds of billions of dollars in sales. Also, it's always nice to be grouped with the likes of GE."

"No one ever thinks of GE as a bunch of wild-eyed, ecologist-dreamers," Stan mused. "They are a completely hard-headed, profit-oriented business."

As GE targets revenue from Clean Energy Technology at over $20 billion by 2010, Jeff Immelt, GE CEO, told *Business Week*, "This is a time period where environmental improvement is going to lead toward profitability. This is not a hobby to make people feel good."

"You know, George," Stan continued, "we are part of a worldwide economic system with many forms of capitalism. The predominant structure, no matter what the evolving system, is the ability for business to be profitable. And contrary to what some might believe, a good way to be profitable is to build the new industries that provide answers to the world's needs. For example, the Ovonic NiMH battery enabled hybrid vehicles, which will be the new automotive industry. The old one suffers from a lack of profitability; the new one can be very profitable. It is the same for every industry that we have formed. They are all based on the acknowledgement and belief that the profit system is absolutely necessary, but is also connected with what is necessary for society.

"The unbridled struggle for profitability for its own sake is unfortunate. Profit is an integral part of the larger successful use of talent to build new industries—not just an end in itself. What is important is the ability to have the funds to achieve the growth of these new industries, which, of course, involves how profitable they can become. But they are profitable in other senses besides the return to the shareholders. They bring prosperity to the people who work. They bring products that are necessary to solve problems of our world economy. And they can make for a more peaceful world. What's wrong with that concept of profit? In my opinion, there's not only nothing wrong with it, it is a preferred way of thinking about how you can have happy shareholders and build new businesses that become the resources of the world's population to reach out beyond the levels of poverty and achieve sustainability. For more than sixty years, I've been about *Science* that creates new *Industries* that produce *High Quality Jobs*, where workers will continue their life-long *Education*.

"At this point we *have* solutions. We need to let the solutions that are already here get priority to be built. To change the world for the better, we need industrialists, inventors and businessmen with the most advanced science and technology, and with sufficient funding to make it happen. I'm trying to be an effective problem solver. I do build the factories if I have the money. That's what I believe in. That's what I do. And not only are we now a major company with the products that we are producing, we also have the strategies for how to grow and be one of the major companies *globally*."

There was silence for a long time before Stan added, "...and that's why it's important to note that my hydrogen loop creates *five* new industries—not four."

I was perplexed. "Photovoltaics, batteries, hydrogen storage, and fuel cells. That's four. What am I missing?"

"Machine building," Stan began. "ECD is a factory for factories. Build enough factories, and pretty soon you have an industry. In the case of photovoltaics, that industry is now about $7-8 billion. But as we reduce costs and begin to compete with fossil fuels, it will be a world-wide revolution. That's a trillion dollar per year business."

I was thinking out loud, "So ECD has multiple profit streams from its manufacturing activities (for example from wholly owned United Solar Ovonic), from joint ventures and strategic business alliances, from licensing, and from machine building. It's like taking more than three bites from one pie. And companies are willing to sign these deals?"

"There's a lot of real interest out there," Stan said with a grin. "It's a win-win situation. We leverage our huge investment in the technology and profit from our intellectual property, as we should. Those who join us, for example, in partnership, also reap good profit on their investment."

"And the machine building group can construct several plants at a time?"

"I come from the machine tool industry. Once you perfect the machines, they can be produced in a constant stream. But don't lose sight of the bigger picture, George. We'll probably do the same thing with fuel cells, solid hydrogen storage, and other products as well. Remember, ECD is a factory for factories. Build enough factories and soon you're creating new industries. Science, New Industries, High Quality Jobs, and Education to solve real world energy problems…"

"Better world," I said softly. "You are creating a better world."

Stan just smiled a smile that shouted, " That's always been my intention."

I thought back to the quote by Daniel Davidow and Elihu Nemiroff, *R&A*,

> *Vision. A rare quality, possessed by few, envied by all. What gave Stan the unique powers of a visionary? If we could answer that question, we would all be standing in line waiting our turn to receive that power. But one thing is certain. Stan Ovshinsky is unique. He combined an innate genius for science with the perceptiveness of a gambler. He merged his quest for knowledge with a natural intuitiveness that would make a fortune teller green with envy. His vision allowed him to see a future that the rest of us had trouble comprehending. For Stan Ovshinsky, looking ahead twenty, thirty, forty years into the future was like writing next week's schedule.*

The Future—Right Now

So much has happened in the decade since I first drove to Troy, Michigan to check out ECD. I saw batteries, photovoltaic cells, solid hydrogen storage, computer chips, DVDs, and much more. Today I see a completely different company than the one I saw ten years ago. The world has changed dramatically. One now sees hybrid automobiles everywhere; the Secretary of Energy now attends the groundbreaking ceremonies for ECD's newest photovoltaic plant; independence from Middle East oil is now a national priority; expensive gasoline ($60+/barrel for oil) and the Peak oil phenomenon are now taken for granted; multiple, devastating weather events each year suggest the strengthening grip of global warming, etc. In short, Stan and Iris were right, and the world has finally come to see our future as ECD has seen it for the last 45 years.

Stan and Iris, with their talented and creative team of colleagues and collaborators, have done what they said they were going to do. They are recognized leaders in the fields of both energy and information, the twin pillars of our global economy. Stan was right in saying that science and technology could contribute solutions for the world; Stan and Iris and ECD are providing those solutions.

It's not surprising that the world is also making its way to ECD's door to dip into its mountain of intellectual property. Valued at zero on the company's books, this intellectual property serves as the basis for a rapidly expanding, broad array of strategic business alliances in photovoltaics, batteries, hydrogen storage, nonvolatile memories, unique switches, cognitive computer chips, and on and on. The decade where the world transitions from the hydrocarbon economy to the hydrogen economy will see ECD go from a small business to a multi-billion dollar industrial giant. Stan, Iris, Bob, Jim Metzger and their inspired team are now the resource they always wanted to be, helping the world to transition to a better future—toward a clean and renewable hydrogen economy.

It's a dream that Stan and Iris have dedicated their lives to fulfill. More importantly, it's now a dream come true.

Stan and Iris at groundbreaking of COBASYS plant in Springboro, Ohio
where Ohio's Governor named the street on which the plant is located
Ovonic Way in their honor.

Chapter 14

Creating a Better World

The best way to make your dreams come true is to wake up.

Paul Valery
French Poet

At some point in time, all of us must ask ourselves some sobering questions—"What is the value of my life? Do I count it as a success or not?" To answer these questions, one must first answer the more fundamental question, "What is success?"

We sometimes joke about this question: "The person who dies with the largest bank account wins;" "The person with the most 'toys' wins;" "The one with the largest, happiest family wins;" "The person who has accumulated the most positive experiences;" "The one with the most power or fame is most successful;" "The most enlightened is the most successful;" and so forth. But we know that such simplistic views of the meaning of "success" can not possibly be correct.

So we consult the wise ones, spiritual leaders, philosophers, poets, and the like. Their definitions of success are typically richer and more plausible. The answer to the question "What is success?" by the poet/philosopher Ralph Waldo Emerson has long intrigued me:[1]

To laugh often and to love much; To win the respect of intelligent people and the affection of children; To earn the appreciation of honest critics and endure the betrayal of false friends; To appreciate beauty; To find the best in others; To leave the world a bit better, whether by a healthy child, a garden patch, or a redeemed social condition; To know even one life has breathed easier because you have lived; That is to have succeeded.

So how do we measure the success of the life of Stan Ovshinsky?

Upon finishing any book, one should ask, "What have I learned?" What do you now understand better because of your hours of dialogue with this volume? Do you understand physics and materials science a bit better? Do you better appreciate the dream of Social Democrats? Do you better understand the forces that oppose disruptive technologies in our society? Do you have a stronger grasp of the coming hydrogen economy? Do you better understand why computers work the way they do? Do you also realize why the computers of tomorrow will be quite different from today's machines? Do you (like me) now stand in even greater awe of true genius? Do you understand disordered materials better? Do you appreciate better how wonderful a marriage of soul mates can be? Do you better understand the demands and rewards of true colleagueship? And finally, do you realize how lucky this world is to have served as home for Stanford R. Ovshinsky?

If you answered "yes" to any of those questions, then you can now see further—into science, industry, love, and the future. And, like me, you can see further because you have been privileged to stand on the shoulders of a genuine giant.

How are we to evaluate Stan's vision of a better and more beautiful world? World-changing dreams must pass an unusual test. They succeed or fail based solely on their ability to inspire us to become better human beings. Does our current management-workers situation detract from Eugene Victor Debs dream? Is the terrible state of contemporary politics a black mark on Thomas Jefferson's vision of a democracy? Can our violent world be an indictment of Mahatma Ghandi's nonviolent vision? Are contemporary strained race relations to be counted against Martin Luther King's dream? Of course not. Current problems testify to our inability to live up to the dreams that remarkable visionaries have held out to us. Stan is one such visionary. Will his dream of a better world be a success? Will you join him in creating a better world?

Ovonic Hydrogen Systems, LLC

Anything that burns can be replaced with Hydrogen

Afterword

Talent hits a target no one else can hit,
Genius hits a target no one else can see.

Arthur Schopenhauer
Philosopher

This book began with the suggestion that ECD and the hydrogen economy were here to stay. Chapter 1 explained how the month of August, 2005, witnessed a cascade of events that convinced many that the hydrogen economy was no longer only possible, but that it had become inevitable. Happily, we didn't have to wait long for ECD's next powerful step. A second sea change at ECD covered the last week of 2005, and the first months of 2006. It marked the commercial birth of OUM. On December 28th ECD announced that Ovonyx, Inc. (its 39.5% owned joint venture) and Samsung Electronics had entered into a long-term license agreement to produce OUM beginning in 2006. Later another announcement read, "Hynix semiconductor has decided to invest heavily in next generation PRAM (OUM), making a move similar to rival Samsung Electronics, which plans to launch volume production of PRAM in the second half of this year"[1] Apparently, the race was on.

Samsung earlier (August 19, 2004, *english.chosun.com*) stated their yearly expectations for PRAM: "The industry expects that PRAM will dominate the memory semiconductor market worth US$46 billion in several years." Since OUM produces royalties for ECD, virtually all OUM royalties become profit. If, instead of "dominating" that market, OUM only takes a 20% share, these royalties to ECD each year will be over $100 million, and would then dwarf the other sources of company profits. Why is the OUM news important for ECD's place in the hydrogen economy?

For more than 45 years, money has been ECD's most important constraint on the commercialization of its hydrogen technologies. Ever increasing OUM royalty streams will neutralize ECD's principal brake on commercialization. For example, $100 million per year could easily build one photovoltaic factory (eventually producing up to 100 MW per year) each year. Such new factories would be wholly owned by United Solar. This would easily make the growth at United

157

Solar Ovonic geometric. Actually, ECD will now possess the ability to be an effective factory of factories, whether these factories produce photovoltaic cells, batteries, solid hydrogen storage systems, CDs, DVDs, fuel cells, or whatever.

On February 16, 2006, ECD announced that its United Solar Ovonic would go from its present 25/30 MW/yr to 300 MW/yr by 2010[2] financed by a stock offering and internal funding.[3] A few hours later, the *Detroit News* announced that President George W. Bush would visit the Auburn Hills United Solar Ovonic plant on February 20, 2006, to deliver a speech on our country's urgent need to develop its solar/hydrogen economy.

Although this book devoted less than a paragraph to Organic Light Emitting Diodes (OLEDs), on February 21, 2006, GE announced that GE and ECD received a contract with NIST (the Commerce Department's National Institute of Standards and Technology) to develop a low-cost, roll-to-roll process for the production of large-area organic electronic devices. NIST based its selection on the innovation, technical risk, potential economic benefits to the nation, and strength of the commercialization plan of the program. This project breaks new ground in the development of large, thin and flexible electronics systems.[4]

Lastly, on March 1, 2006, ECD announced that it had priced its shelf offering of 7,000,000 shares of stock at $49 per share. The offering was greatly oversubscribed, showing extraordinary interest in the company. The approximately $325 million that ECD will receive will be used primarily to expand solar production. This second corner was turned less than six months after turning the hydrogen economy corner in August, 2005.

Footnotes

Foreword

[1]Shakespeare's *Romeo and Juliet* ends with,
For never was a story of more woe
Than this of Juliet and her Romeo

Preface

[1]*On the Shoulders of Giants.* Stephen Hawking, 2002, Philadelphia, Running Press, p. 725.

[2]*The Double Helix.* James D. Watson, 1968, New York: Simon & Schuster.

[3]*Thematic Origins of Scientific Thought: Kepler to Einstein.* Gerald Holton, 1973, Cambridge, MA: Harvard University Press.

Chapter 1

[1]Stan considers information to be encoded energy, and that energy and information are two sides of the same coin and the twin pillars of our global economy.

[2]The plaque states that Stan is an honorary member of the International Association of Machinists and Aerospace Workers "in recognition of many years of adherence to the principles and ideals of the Trade Union Movement, and your fine human spirit."

[3]Stan Ovshinsky received a remarkable gift on the occasion of his 80th birthday. A book entitled *Reminiscences & Appreciations*, which contained the reflections and birthday wishes by dozens of his colleagues, was created. I will use these authors' words often to demonstrate that the characteristics I mention in Stan and Iris also are noticed by many others. These references will be noted as *R&A* plus the author's name. All authors gave permission to have their quotes included herein.

Chapter 2

[1]Ashley, Laura, "Iris and Stanford Ovshinsky." *Stand Up & Celebrate! The Workmen's Circle/Arbeter Ring 2004 Gala Celebration.* (December 6, 2004).

Chapter 3

[1]Stan is quick to acknowledge the many outstanding Directors, which he describes in this way:

In business, Ralph Leach, former Chairman of the Executive Committee of Morgan Guaranty Bank, New York and an architect of the post World War II economic policy of the United States; James Birkenstock, Vice President of IBM to whom Mr. Watson, IBM Chairman and Chief Executive, gave credit for making IBM a computer company; Ray MacDonald, Chairman and Chief Executive of Burroughs Corporation when it was a leading computer company; Robert R. Johnson, Vice President of Engineering at Burroughs; Florence Metz, former Project Manager for Business and Strategic Planning, Inland Steel; Jack T. Conway, a member of the cabinets of Presidents Johnson and Kennedy; Richard H. Cummings, Vice-Chairman, National Bank of Detroit; Momoko Ito, who became President of Japan ECD, had multifaceted talents and yet she could focus like a laser to achieve solutions to very serious business problems. This was always done in her own way. As Stan often said to her, one does not teach a bird how to sing. Her contributions were so many and varied that Stan called her ECD's vice-president of intangibles who, as if by magic, produced the most tangible results; Umberto Colombo, Chairman of the Scientific Councils of ENI, former Chairman of ENEA, member of the cabinet of the Italian Government and head of Science and Technology for the European Community and a wonderful advisor to Stan; Walter McCarthy, Chairman and CEO of Detroit Edison; Arthur Seder, Chairman and CEO of American Natural Resources Co.; James Trebilcott, Vice President, American Natural Resources Co.; Takashi Kojima, Senior Executive of Canon Corp.; Nancy Bacon, formerly of Touche Ross, who became Senior Vice President and Director, and a long time talented and important contributor to ECD, especially in her achievements in finance and governmental affairs.

In science, Nobelist I.I. Rabi, "grey eminence of American science," world leader of the scientific community and President Eisenhower's science advisor and head of the U.S. Atomic Energy Commission was one of the first. Robert R. Wilson, founder of the Fermi Lab and past president of the American Physical Society; Hellmut Fritzsche, 10-year chairman of University of Chicago, Department of Physics and Stan's closest scientific collaborator and an internationally recognized leader in the field of amorphous and disordered materials; Stanley K. Stynes, Dean of the College of Engineering, Wayne State University.

In public affairs, Douglas Fraser, former President of the UAW; former U.S. Ambassador to Japan, Edwin O. Reischauer and Haru Matsukata Reischauer, his wife, a great talent in her own right.

[2]Morgenson, Gretchen, "Explaining (or not) Why the Boss is Paid So Much: Looking at Chief Executive Pay Expressed as a Multiple of the Employee Average Pay at that Company for 2003." *The New York Times* (January 25, 2004, Section 3: Money and Business).

Chapter 4

[1]Colin J. Campbell, and Jean H. Laherrére. "The End of Cheap Oil." *Scientific American,* March, 1998.

[2]Colin J. Campbell and Jean H. Laherrére. "The End of Cheap Oil." *Scientific American,* March, 1998.

[3]*The Hydrogen Economy.* Jeremy Rifkin, 2002, New York: Penguin.

[4]*Beyond the Limits.* Donella H. Meadows, Dennis L. Meadows, & Jorgen Randers, 1992, White River Junction, VT: Chelsea Green Co.

[5]Hal Varian, "What Will Happen If We Tax Gasoline Like Europeans Do?" *The New York Times,* October 19, 2000, C2.

Chapter 5

[1]*Collapse: How Societies Choose To Fail* or *Succeed.* Jared Diamond, 2005, New York: Penguin.

[2]*The Population Explosion.* Paul Ehrlich and Ann Ehrlich, 1990, New York: Simon and Schuster.

[3]*The Population Explosion.* Paul Ehrlich and Ann Ehrlich, 1990, New York: Simon and Schuster.

[4]Lenssen, N. "Providing Energy in Developing Countries." In L. R. Brown (Ed.) *State of the World* (1993). New York: Norton.

[5]*www. ovonic.com*

[6]*Giants of Enterprise.* Richard Tedlow, 2001, New York: Harper Business.

Chapter 6

[1]Stevens, William K., "Glassy Electronic Device May Surpass Transistor." *The New York Times* (November 11, 1968, Pages 1 & 42).

[2]Stanford Ovshinksy. "Reversible Electrical Switching Phenomena in Disordered Structures." *Physical Review Letters,* November, 1968.

[3]*www.ovonic.com*

[4]M.H. Cohen, H. Fritzsche and S.R. Ovshinksky. "Simple Band Model for Amorphous Semiconducting Alloys." *Physical Review Letters*, May, 1969.

[5]David Adler, Brian Schwartz, and Marvin Silver (Eds.). *Disordered Materials—Science and Technology, Selected Papers by Stanford R. Ovshinsky*, 1991, New York: Plenum Press.

[6]Personal Communication.

[7]David Adler, S.R. Ovshinsky, and Brian Schwartz, "Introduction to the Institute for Amorphous Studies." (pamphlet produced by the Institute for Amorphous Studies, 1985).

Chapter 7

[1]Schmela, M., "In Holland, the Sun Prefers Amorphous Modules." *Photon International*, November, 2000, pp. 10-11.

[2]"A Real-World Examination of PV System Design and Performance." Gregg Allen, Terrence Parker & Ron Swenson, United Solar Ovonic. Paper presented at the 31st Institute of Electrical and Electronics Engineers, Inc. Photovoltaic Specialist Conference and Exhibition, January 3-7, 2005, Lake Buena Vista, Florida.

[3]*Inventing Modern America: From the Microwave to the Mouse.* David E. Brown, 2002, Cambridge, MA: MIT Press.

Chapter 8

[1]ECD Announcement (May 19, 1992). "United States Advanced Battery Consortium Announces First High-Tech Battery Contract With Ovonic Battery Company."

[2]Stan's description of this group is:
   Especially Hellmut Fritzsche, great physicist and closest collaborator of Stan's, Chairman of the Physics Department of the University of Chicago for over ten years and still going strong with his incredible problem solving ability. While known as a great experimentalist, he has been extremely important in the theoretical activities of all the groups and is an indispensable talent as a leader of the amorphous field;
   David Adler, a brilliant physicist,Professor at MIT, until his untimely death at the age of 53, an integral part of Stan's work, an ideal collaborator and a very important part of Stan's and Iris' life. His contributions were of great value;
   Morrel Cohen, an outstanding theoretical physicist at the University of Chicago for many years heading the James Franck Institute and later instrumental in setting up the R&D group at Exxon Corporation. With Hellmut Fritzsche and Stan, wrote

one of the most important and quoted papers, "Simple Band Gap Model for Amorphous Semiconducting Alloys (The CFO Model)." Still contributing his great talents.

Arthur Bienenstock, Professor of Physics, Stanford University, whose work with Stan helped lay some of the structural foundations to the amorphous field. He is also highly recognized for his science policy work, having been a U.S. presidential advisor and soon the president of the American Physical Society

Brian Schwartz, formerly a professor at MIT, is now Vice President for Research and Sponsored Programs and Professor of Physics at the Graduate Center, City University of New York. Brian served as head of our Institute for Amorphous Studies and later became a true impresario of science through his remarkable ability to make physics come alive for the general public. If one wants to have a friend, colleague and collaborator, there is none better.

Marc Kastner, with his insightful chemical approach, Chairman of the Physics Department of MIT, who provided in two words—Lone Pairs—the "missing link" that Stan was spending paragraphs on. Marc, with his fine chemical background and his always pioneering work, made one of the seminal contributions with Hellmut Fritzsche and David Adler—the KAF Model. He is a remarkable scientist with deep intuition and clear understanding.

Special mention should be given to long time far away yet close Romanian colleagues and collaborators Radu Grigorovici—a very early and important worker in the field—and his protégé, Mihai Popescu, who are carrying on the East European tradition of making important contributions to the amorphous field. Our great friend and collaborator, Professor Genie Mytilineou from University of Patras in Greece, who has spent many sabbaticals with us, always making important contributions.

While there are so many more who deserve to be more than mentioned because all made important contributions, most are referred to in at least one of the different appendices.

Collaborating with Stan and having a very special role in the amorphous field are Heinz Henisch, Professor of Physics, Penn State University; Raphael Tsu, formerly of IBM and Professor at North Carolina; John Ross, Professor of Chemistry, Stanford University; William Lipscomb, Harvard Nobelist in chemistry; Joe Doehler, physicist extraordinary, wonderful collaborator; Scott Jones a great talent and again a wonderful collaborator; Masat

Izu who is President of the original photovoltaic group and close collaborator of Stan's, continuing his crucial activities as leader of the incredible machine building group. There are so many people not mentioned in prior references who certainly deserve to be—not only the people that make up the all-star Machine Division, but the outstanding operating heads—Kevin Hoffman and Gary Di-Dio—and their support group at Ovonic Solar; Arun Kumar, our resident electronic genius.

Stan feels that each individual at ECD deserves to be mentioned. Each has his or her special quality and has made contributions that they can be proud of.

Particularly and with great feeling, Stan wants to pay his homage to I.I. Rabi, Nobelist, whose scientific progeny include at least 30 more Nobel Prize winners originating from his work. He remains indelibly part of Stan as an incredible friend and early supporter.

The same can be said of Bob Wilson, builder of the Fermi Lab, whose warm friendship and support, Stan and Iris continue to treasure; Linus Pauling whose support, interest, friendship, collegiality and genius we sorely miss; and of Professor Fukui, Nobelist, Kyoto University, great friend, collaborator about whom Iris said, watching him and Stan discuss was like watching two young people intensely making sense of the universe.

Chapter 9

[1]It is now possible and realistic to utilize hydrogen, the ultimate fuel, to begin replacing fossil fuels since the hydrogen economy has already begun with photovoltaics and hybrid and electric vehicle batteries. This ongoing process will lead to a steep reduction in pollution, climate change gases and wars over oil as well as the building of new industries that will make possible continuous displacement of fossil fuels.

[2]Figure 9-1, taken from Ovonic Hydrogen Storage publicity pamphlet.

[3]Figure 9-2, taken from Ovonic Hydrogen Storage publicity pamphlet.

Chapter 10

[1]Figure 10-1 (top and bottom), taken from Ovonic Fuel Cell publicity pamplet.

[2]Figure 10-2 (top and bottom), taken from Ovonic Fuel Cell publicity pamplet.

[3]Figure 10-3 (top and bottom), taken from Ovonic Fuel Cell publicity pamplet.

Chapter 11

[1]"Ovonics: ECD's Science and Technology." Energy Conversion Devices, Inc., Annual Report Fiscal Year Ended June 30, 1970.

[2]S.R. Ovshinsky, "The Nerve Impulse," Unpublished, 1955.

[3]Bill Gates, *The New York Times*, March 1, 2004.

Chapter 12

[1]*A Feeling for the Organism.* Evelyn Fox-Keller, 1993, San Francisco: Freeman.

[2]*A Feeling for the Organism.* Evelyn Fox-Keller, 1993, San Francisco: Freeman.

[3]King, Martin Luther, "I Have a Dream," speech given in Washington, D.C. August 28, 1963.

[4]*A Feeling for the Organism*, Evelyn Fox-Keller, 1993, San Francisco: Freeman.

Chapter 13

[1]Jefferies & Company, *Report on Energy Conversion Devices* by Jeff W. Bencik, March 11, 2005.

Chapter 14

[1]Ralph Waldo Emerson, 2000, Free Thinkers University at *www. transcendentialists.com/1emerson.html*

Afterword

[1]Hynix Press Release, December, 2005.

[2]ECD Press Release, February 16, 2006.

[3]ECD Press Release, March 7, 2006.

[4]GE Global Research-News-"NIST Contact Win," February 22, 2006.

Appendix 1

Proceedings International Hydrogen Energy Congress and Exhibition IHEC 2005
Istanbul, Turkey, 13-15 July 2005

The Hydrogen Loop – The Means for Making the Hydrogen Economy Realistic

Stanford R. Ovshinsky

Energy Conversion Devices, Inc., 2956 Waterview Drive, Rochester Hills, Michigan 48309 (USA)

ovshinsky@ovonic.com

ABSTRACT

The hydrogen economy has already started with the introduction of the Ovonic nickel metal hydride battery which has enabled the rapid growth of hybrid vehicles. Reversible storage of hydrogen in a solid hydride permits the entire loop of hydrogen generation, storage and utilization, all of which have been placed some time in the future. It is often stated that the hydrogen infrastructure does not exist and cannot be put in place. I will show that the hydrogen economy based upon hydrogen, the ultimate fuel, is practical, realistic and is available near-term to our global society. The crisis regarding global warming, pollution, and wars over oil can be solved, at the same time building much needed basic new industries, providing higher value jobs feeding back on the educational system.

Keywords: Amorphous, battery, disordered, energy, fuel cell, hydrides, hydrogen, Ovonic

1. INTRODUCTION

Hydrogen is called the "ultimate fuel." It is also the ultimate element. It was born in the Big Bang and almost all of known matter is composed of it. Its condensation into a star, our sun, through fusion, provides us the energy and the photons which power our earth and which we can utilize in the form of photovoltaics to break apart water and generate hydrogen as an energy source on earth.

The hydrogen economy is here. It has been initiated by the electric and hybrid vehicles which depend upon it for their operation through nickel metal hydride batteries and hydrogen as a fuel for the internal combustion engine and by outwitting the Carnot cycle for use as a fuel cell.

I will discuss the complete system needed for the hydrogen economy from generation to storage to infrastructure and use. Any one part of this loop is necessary but not sufficient.

Our global economy is based upon energy and the societal needs for a nonpolluting, non-climate change fuel which does not require strategic military defense as does oil. The transition from fossil fuels to hydrogen is of revolutionary import not only for its societal impact but also for the new materials science that it absolutely requires in all of its aspects. New science and new technologies build much needed new industries, which provide not only jobs but also feedback on our educational system.

Recall that the ages of civilization are known by their materials. Truly, the present age will be known by the materials that make up the twin pillars of our global economy – energy and information. Therefore, I will address the new science, technology and atomic engineering of the materials so necessary to make positive, realistic and productive this revolutionary transition of energy from its fossil fuel beginnings to the present.

2. PERSPECTIVE

The hydrogen economy was not predicted to occur until approximately 50 years from now as shown in Fig. 1.

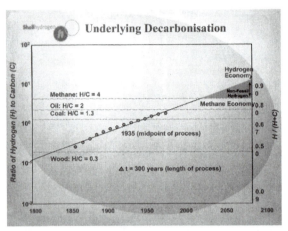

Figure 1

What I will discuss and illustrate is that we have changed this linear progression from millions of years of dependence on fossil fuel by hominids and humans to hydrogen, the ultimate fuel. To put this in perspective, we are decoupling from fossil fuel and coupling to the first particles of the universe, protons, electrons, and photons, born in the Big Bang.

Rather than a discussion of what is needed, what this paper seeks to show is that there are actual concrete solutions to the problems that were barriers to the hydrogen economy.

Figure 2 shows that science and technology created a giant step forward when the electric light bulb was invented by Edison just one year before this cartoon. While the fuels and technology which made steam the driving force of the prior industrial era were revolutionary in nature, the new electrical age still depended for its energy on fossil fuels and increasingly on oil.

"WHAT WILL HE GROW TO?"

This drawing is from an 1881 issue of *Punch* magazine, showing King Steam and King Coal anxiously observing the infant "electricity" and asking: What will he grow to? Many of today's industries, ranging from manufacturing to publishing, are similarly seeking answers regarding the growth of computer technology in the next century. (from *Engineers & Electrons*, IEEE Press, 1984.)

Figure 2

In any case, new science and technology were needed for the achievement of the hydrogen economy which had been put off far into the future by extrapolation.

This was particularly important since petroleum was symbiotic with the developing transportation industry and its internal combustion engine.

What was required was new science and technology, especially expressed in new atomically engineered materials, for generation, usage, transportation and storage. The conventional approaches of high pressure and liquid hydrogen were well known but could not attack the basic problems.

By storing hydrogen reversibly in solids, and solving the problems of storage, kinetics, that is the speed of getting hydrogen in and out, and cycle life, we have been able to achieve a family of hydrides capable of real world applications.

This has been accomplished by our work in disordered and amorphous materials in which the materials are a system composed of a spectrum and density of catalytic and storage sites. This required atomic engineering permitted by the degrees of freedom of disorder where we can use multi-elements and multi-phases and work across the periodic table, not by throwing darts at it, but by following the rules and the scientific base that we have established. In particular, we utilized d- and f-orbital materials for many applications and lighter weight materials chemically modified to achieve the sites required.

This paper is intended to show the results of our approach which has enabled us to advance the hydrogen economy in a seamless energy loop. We have done this by taking a systems approach not only for a family of materials, but for the complete infrastructure, well to wheels, so to speak.

The problems brought about by the increased use of fossil fuel energy, particularly oil, in our social, economic and political institutions are putting pressure on our global society in terms of pollution, climate change[1-2] and the dependence on the military to protect the precious stream of oil.

Fortunately, switching to hydrogen, the ultimate and cleanest fuel can break the great dependence on geographical location of fuel since our hydrogen-fusing sun provides us the photons to break up water. Therefore, the hydrogen economy starts with the sun.

We will show that the science and technology of amorphous materials which we pioneered have resulted in the ability to make thin-film, continuous web, multi-junction material devices that can use the entire spectrum of sunlight resulting in the energy necessary to break up water to generate hydrogen.

3. BACKGROUND

Figures 3 and 4 show Iris and me planning such a systems loop for hydrogen in 1960 in a storefront laboratory in Detroit where we founded Energy Conversion Devices. We sought to build such a loop for one needed to generate, transport, store and utilize hydrogen. In other words, one needed not only to invent the materials, the products and the production technology but to provide a realistic infrastructure that could interface the present one for petroleum.

Figure 3   **Figure 4**

Iris and I founded our company in 1960 (Figs. 3 and 4) to utilize science and technology to solve serious societal problems and build new industries. The most important barrier we had and still have to overcome was not scientific or technological but being classified as a disruptive technology by the very people to whom we were trying to be constructive and a resource to.

4. HYDRIDES

Let us see how we have succeeded. First of all, by inventing the nickel metal hydride battery and introducing solid hydrides in a realistic and cost effective manner, we jump started the hydrogen economy. Almost all electric and hybrid vehicles are enabled by our Ovonic batteries and well over a billion consumer nickel metal hydride batteries were sold last year.

The degrees of design freedom of atomically engineered materials permits us to have not only a simple couple such as lead acid, nickel cadmium, etc. but materials that can be designed and improved both in energy density and in power. The key elements for the batteries are d- and f-orbital materials. Some electrodes have as high as eleven different elements. We do not only atomic engineering but orbital engineering.[3-4]

In brief, our materials approach is a systems one. That is in the same multi-elemental, multi-phase material we have designed new types of highly efficient and non-noble metal catalysts and a spectrum of hydrogen storage sites that can be tailored for energy density and for power.

5. MAKING THE HYDROGEN ECONOMY REALISTIC

Please note in Fig. 5 that the Hydrogen Loop is now shown by actual products.

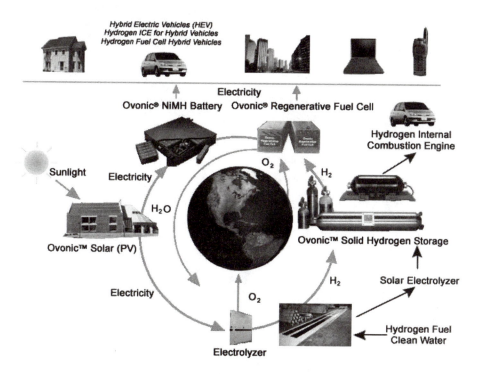

**Figure 5: Making the Hydrogen Economy Possible -
ECD, the Only Company with the Complete Hydrogen Loop**

6. INFRASTRUCTURE

Now for the reality of the infrastructure shown in Fig. 6.　Note how it blends with the existing one without disruption.　We provide a transition from fossil fuels to hydrogen with this approach.

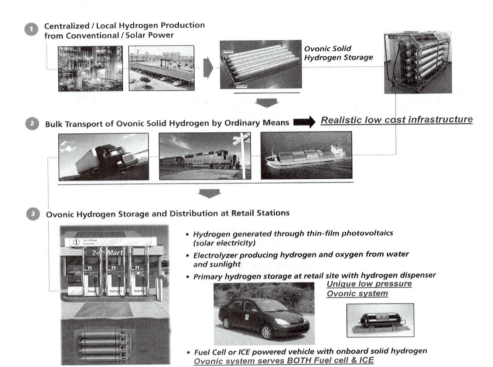

Figure 6:　Ovonic Solid Hydrogen Systems –
Practical Solutions for the Hydrogen Infrastructure

Figure 7 is an old slide showing the electric and hybrid electric vehicles that are powered by our Ovonic nickel metal hydride (NiMH) batteries.

Figure 7

Figure 8

Figure 8 is ECD Ovonic's photovoltaic hydrogen generation and Ovonic all solid hydrogen hybrid ICE vehicle. The Ovonic Uni-Solar thin-film photovoltaic installation on the shelter can be used to generate hydrogen from water.

Figure 9 depicts the Ovonic renewable hydrogen systems. The same system that fuels the ICE vehicle can also fuel the fuel cell.

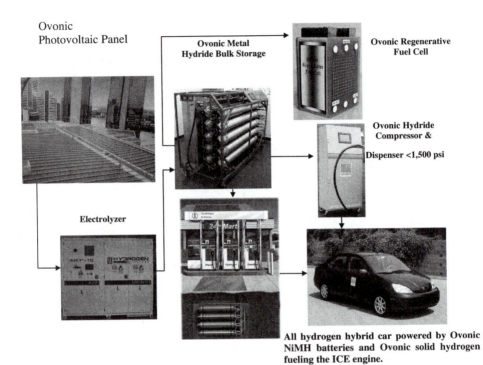

Ovonic Photovoltaic Panel

Ovonic Metal Hydride Bulk Storage

Ovonic Regenerative Fuel Cell

Ovonic Hydride Compressor & Dispenser <1,500 psi

Electrolyzer

All hydrogen hybrid car powered by Ovonic NiMH batteries and Ovonic solid hydrogen fueling the ICE engine.

Figure 9

Figure 10 shows the advantages of our Ovonic Fuel Cell.

Advantages of Ovonic™ Regenerative Fuel Cells
Unique proprietary technology
Atomically engineered, non-noble metal, low cost, and poison-resistant catalyst electrodes
Instant start capability
Absorbs regenerative braking energy
Wide temperature range (-20°C to 100°C)
Higher efficiency (60/80%)
Simple and robust design
Low cost

Figure 10

Figure 11 shows that an Ovonic solid hydrogen ICE hybrid can match a gasoline hybrid in its important parameters. The automotive industry has been committed to the internal combustion engine. Therefore, having a hydrogen burning internal combustion engine, especially in a hybrid form, can provide the transition to the utilization of fuel cells. Indeed, it will probably extend the future for internal combustion engines since there will be a whole family of various kinds of electric/hybrid vehicles. Our approach shows that internal combustion engine burning hydrogen provided by our solid hydrogen storage tank, together with our nickel metal hydride batteries, has the same range as the gasoline ICE hybrid and the present fuel cell prototype cars.

Ovonic Hydrogen ICE Vehicle
EMISSIONS and FUEL ECONOMY-Dynamometer Test

Code: **BOLD**: Hydrogen Ovonic vehicle *ITALICS*: Gasoline vehicle	Tailpipe Emissions, g/mi			
	Hydro-carbons HC	Carbon Monoxide CO	Nitrogen Oxides NOx	Carbon Dioxide CO_2
Gasoline (production configuration)	*0.010*	*0.386*	*0.004*	*222.8*
Calibration, with Current Catalyst	**0.001**	**0.001**	**0.018**	**2.5**
SULEV/PZEV Standard	**0.010**	**1.000**	**0.020**	**N/A**

EPA City Economy	*42.4 MPG Gasoline* **42.3 MPK Hydrogen Ovonic**	NOTE: 1 gallon gasoline has same energy as 1 kg Hydrogen)
EPA Hwy Economy	*45.0 MPG Gasoline* **46.1 MPK Hydrogen Ovonic**	
EPA Combined	**43.9 MPK Hydrogen Ovonic**	Next generation:
55 MPH steady speed	**50.9 MPK Hydrogen Ovonic**	6 Kg ⟹ ~300 mi
Range @ 55 MPH	**137 miles with 2.69 Kg (90%) fill.**	

Figure 11

Most authorities consider that the goal of 250 miles and $3 per kilogram of hydrogen can be reached in 5 years. Some authorities consider as can be seen in Fig. 12 that such a vehicle "isn't likely for many years". The data that I have presented in this paper shows that we can achieve that goal <u>now</u>.

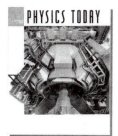

"One of the defining problems that indicates how far research has to progress, said workshop associate chair George Crabtree of Argonne National Laboratory, 'is a system that would store enough hydrogen in a vehicle for a 300-mile trip and be fast enough to allow for acceptable acceleration of the vehicle.'

Such a vehicle isn't likely for many years, . . . Crabtree said..."

Excerpt from article in *Physics Today*, October 2003:
<u>Hydrogen-Based Energy Merits Research</u>

Figure 12

Our approach is to have a family of hydrides for all occasions. They not only operate at room temperature but can be developed for other temperature ranges; for example, Fig. 13 shows how our materials operating at 300°C with 7% storage have solved the problems of storage, kinetics and lifetime.

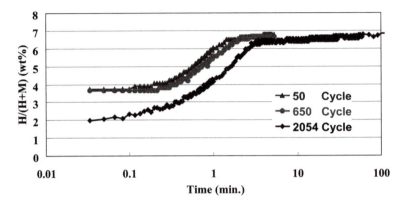

Ideal for onboard storage, provides: 300+ miles, 600,000+ miles life

Figure 13: High Capacity Ovonic Metal Hydride Long Cycle Life

Figure 14 illustrates the special features and benefits of our Ovonic solid hydrogen storage approach.

Special Features	Benefit
• Reversible	Vehicle:
• Safe	• Long Range
• Compact	• Low Fuel Cost
• Tailorable Pressure	• Safe Operation
• Fast Refilling	Stationary:
• Low Pressure Operation	• Small Footprint
• Cold Temperature Start-up	• Directly Refilled from an
• Packaging Flexibility	Electrolyzer or Fuel
• Waste Heat for Desorption	Processor
	Portable:
	• Compact
	• Low Pressure Operation
	• Transportable

Figure 14: Ovonic Metal Hydride Storage Technology

Figure 15 shows low pressure operation and its great advantage in that one can charge at less than 1,500 psi and run the vehicle at approximately 150 psi as against the "normal" 5,000 psi gaseous hydrogen operation that are being used in demonstration vehicles. Low-pressure hydrogen in a solid answers the concerns as to leakage into the atmosphere which can occur when high-pressure gaseous or liquid hydrogen is used.

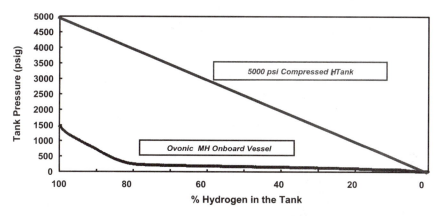

Figure 15: Low Pressure Operation

We started with our hydrogen "burning" sun and we would now like to show how our amorphous triple-junction photovoltaic production is basic to the hydrogen economy and our complete systems loop approach.

7. PHOTOVOLTAICS

Figure 16 is a picture of our 25/30MW annual capacity continuous roll-to-roll triple junction solar cell machine which is capable of producing 9 miles and 6 tons of thin film photovoltaics in a single run.

Fig. 16

The active material is less than one half micron and has eleven layers with three different bandgaps composed of amorphous silicon and amorphous silicon-germanium. The alloys contain both hydrogen and fluorine. Therefore, the full spectrum of the sun can be utilized. Some of these layers are only 100 angstroms and yet we have very high yields. This machine is our 8th generation machine that we have built since the late 1970s. The early machines in the 1980s worked round the clock, seven days a week with very high yields. Nanostructures are something that we have been doing since our first amorphous devices in the 1950s.

Figure 17 shows the rolls ready for processing as well as a finished product.

Figure 17

We would like to cover many of the roofs of the world. That would mean that the hydrogen economy would solve the basic energy problems that bedevil us. Fig. 18 is a typical installation and has aesthetic beauty. Fig. 19 shows our photovoltaic shingles being installed on a school roof. We have them on our own home with our nickel metal hydride batteries for energy storage being charged from our roof.

Figure 18: Jarecki Center - Aquinas College   **Figure 19: Cass Tech Roof - Detroit, Michigan**

Figure 20 shows a roof of an office building in Australia. Figures 21 and 22 show the ease of installation of a membrane roof with adhesive backing.

Figure 20   **Figure 21**   **Figure 22**

There cannot be a global economy without energy. There are two billion people in the world without electricity and many more beneath the poverty level. We feel that we have shown that these are not just something to be mourned but that we can use our hydrogen loop to be the means of providing the energy necessary to make a livable world.

8. CONCLUSION

I hope that I have shown that the ultimate element, hydrogen, should be the source of energy for the new age that will ultimately replace the over a million years of fossil fuel dominance; that the hydrogen age has already started and the people, the global economy and the peace of the world can benefit from this uncoupling of energy from the earth to our universe and that this is being achieved by new science and technology associated with amorphous and disordered materials.

As I said in my 1999 MRS paper, "I believe that I have shown that science and technology can be utilized to build new industries that are responsive to societal problems and needs, providing jobs, educational opportunities and the chance to express the creative urge that has driven humankind since time immemorial. Fig. 23 shows a young woman climbing a mountain barefooted with her future on her back, our photovoltaics, and her future in front of her, her child, bringing our photovoltaics to a village that does not have electricity. There can be no civilization without energy and without knowledge (information). We take this picture as inspiration to continue our work."

Figure 23

9. ACKNOWLEDGEMENTS

I wish to thank all my colleagues and collaborators through the years. The people who make up ECD have contributed their wonderful talents, dedication and commitment to this work. ECD with its unique culture is an example of what human society can be. All of us owe gratitude to Bob Stempel, our partner, the ultimate management person with his knowledge of science and tremendous engineering talents. I and ECD are greatly indebted to Iris who has been my colleague, collaborator, inspiration and the strong bond that has held our company together

REFERENCES

"Disordered Materials: Science and Technology – Selected Papers by Stanford R. Ovshinsky," 2nd Edition, edited by David Adler, Brian B. Schwartz and Marvin Silver, *Institute for Amorphous Studies Series* (Plenum Press, New York, 1991).

Ovshinsky, S. R: Amorphous and Disordered Materials – The Basis of New Industries, Presented at Materials Research Society (MRS), Boston, MA (November 30 – December 4, 1998); *Proceedings,* Mat. Res. Soc. Symp.. 554, 399 (1999); *Bulk Metallic Glasses,* William L. Johnson, Arihisa Inoue and C.T. Liu (Eds.).

Akimoto, H.: Global Air Quality and Pollution, Science, 302, (December 5, 2003), 1716-1719.

Karl, T.R. and Trenberth. K.E.: Modern Global Climate Change, Science 302, (December 5, 2003), 1719-1723.

Appendix 2

AMORPHOUS AND DISORDERED MATERIALS – THE BASIS OF NEW INDUSTRIES

S.R. OVSHINSKY
Energy Conversion Devices, Inc.,
Troy, Michigan 48084

Invited Paper, MRS
Materials Research Society
Boston, MA
Nov. 30 – Dec. 4, 1998

ABSTRACT

As in the past, materials will shape the new century. Dramatic changes are taking place in the fields of energy and information based on new synthetic materials. In energy, the generation of electricity by amorphous silicon alloy thin film photovoltaics; the storage of electricity in nickel metal hydride batteries which are the batteries of choice for electric and hybrid vehicles. In the information field, phase change memories based on a reversible amorphous to crystalline transformation are widely used as optical memories and are the choice for the new rewritable CDs and DVDs. The scientific and technological bases for these three fields that have become the enabling technologies are amorphous and disordered materials. We will discuss how disordered, multielemental, multiphase materials can throw new light upon metallic conductivity in both bulk and thin film materials. We will demonstrate new types of amorphous devices that have the ability to learn and adapt, making possible new concepts for computers.

INTRODUCTION

The great advances in civilization have been based on materials – the Stone Age, the Bronze Age, the Iron Age. The interaction between materials and the industries that have transformed society was the driving force for the Industrial Revolution. The twin pillars of our society today are energy and information. In a deep sense they are opposite sides of the same coin. They both must be generated, stored and transmitted. Information is structured energy that contains intelligence.

I will show how a new scientific approach to materials based upon disorder and local order can enable the development of new pollution free technology which will answer society's urgent needs to reduce its dependence upon uranium and fossil fuels, particularly oil; the latter is a causative factor not only in climate change but a root cause of war. Science and technology which can change the world's dependence on it can create new huge industries so necessary for economic growth. $30 trillion in 30 years for new electricity alone [1]. Furthermore, over 2 billion people in developing countries are without electricity. Electricity is the fundamental requirement of modern life and the common link between energy as an undifferentiated source of power and energy which can be encoded, switched and stored as information.

Devices made of amorphous and disordered materials have become the enabling technology for generating electricity through thin film photovoltaics which can be cost competitive to fossil fuels, for storage of electricity in batteries for electric and hybrid vehicles, ushering in a new, much needed transportation revolution, and high density switching and storage media based on phase change optical and electrical memories, so needed for our information society. Computers which have adaptability, can learn from experience and provide neuronal and synaptic type intelligence, are being made possible by devices described here.

How is it possible that multi-elemental disorder can be the basis for such "revolutionary" possibilities [2] when it is well-known that the great success of the 20th century, the transistor is based upon the periodicity of materials with particular emphasis on one element, silicon? Indeed, with the great success of the transistor based upon the crystal structure of germanium and silicon, we entered the historical era where achieving crystalline perfection over a very large distance became the sine qua non of materials science.

From a materials point of view, the physics that made the transistor possible was based upon the ability to utilize periodicity mathematically which permitted parts per million perturbations of the crystalline lattice by substitutional doping. But right from the beginning, the plague of their disordered surfaces prevented for a decade the fulfillment of the field effect transistor. The disorder of the surface states swamped out the transistor action. Emphasizing again Pauli's statement "God created the solids, the devil their surfaces" [3]. The irony was that the solution that made not only the field effect transistor possible but also the integrated circuit which became the basis for the information age was the utilization of amorphous silicon oxide for photolithography and for the gate oxide.

When I introduced the idea that there was a new world of interesting physics and chemistry in minimizing and removing the constraints of periodicity [4,5], one can understand the resulting consternation of the solid state physicists who had received their Ph.Ds by accepting the dogma of periodicity as being the basis of condensed matter and of the theoretical physicists to whom the control of many elements was as incomprehensible as the conundrum of many-body theory. The change from periodicity to local order permitted atomic engineering of materials in a synthetic manner by opening up new degrees of design freedom. Literally many scores of new materials could be developed and new physical phenomena could be displayed, new products made and new process dependent production technology invented.

Disorder is the common theme in the minimization and lifting of lattice constraints, (what I call the tyranny of the crystalline lattice) which permits the placing of elements in three-dimensional space where they interact in ways that were not previously available. This allowed the use of multi-elements and complex materials including metals where positional, translational and compositional disorder removed the restrictions so that new local order environments [6,7] could be generated which controlled the physical, electronic and chemical properties of the material. Just as the control of conductivity through doping was the Rosetta Stone of understanding and utilizing the transistor, the unusual bonding, orbital configurations and interactions affecting carriers, including ions, are the controlling factors in disordered materials [8-11].

The tools that I utilize for generating these configurations are hydrogen, fluorine, f- and particularly d-orbitals, and nonbonding lone-pair orbitals of the chalcogens. The latter, like the d-orbitals, can be distinguished from their cohesive bonding electrons, freeing them for varied interactions. Even in a sea there are channels and currents affected by topology and climate; in a metallic sea of electrons, we can design paths, control flow and make hospitable environments for incoming ions/protons. Since we are designing new local environments, we also utilize rapid quench technology to make for non-equilibrium configurations and offer a new degree of freedom for the production of unusual local order. Of course, rapid quench and non-equilibrium are associated with vacuum deposition, sputtering and plasma generated materials, in brief, such materials are process dependent.

The understanding of these basic premises became a design tool which we applied universally across the periodic table to build new types of semiconductors, dielectrics and metals. We showed that we can control the density of states in a band/mobility gap affecting conductivity in several ways including chemical modification and the generation of chemically reactive sites [12,13] so as to design, for example, complex, disordered, metallic electrodes of our nickel metal hydride batteries. What we mean by complex is not just that there are many elements, but that we build into a material a chemical, electronic and topological system which performs in the same material various functions such as catalysis, hydrogen diffusion paths, varying density of electrons, acceptor sites for hydrogen, etc. Such a material system in a battery must provide high energy density, power, long life and robustness [14-17].

To put into perspective the principles of disorder, what is required is a metaphor. It is helpful to continue the analogy of the sea. In ancient times, the earliest explorers stayed as close to the shore as possible; there were many things to discover that way – new people, animals, physical environment, things could be strange but understandable. However, to explore the great unknown ocean, they were filled with anxiety for out there was the end of the world and where the dragons lay. Navigational skills were needed to avoid dangerous shoals, utilize favorable currents, etc.

As I pointed out in the 1970s [18-19], amorphous tetrahedral materials to be useful would have to be as close to the four-fold coordination of their crystalline cousins as possible, otherwise, the huge density of states of dangling bonds would prohibit their use. Hydrogen and fluorine were able to act as organizers to assure sufficient four-fold coordination resulting in a low density of states so that the materials could be electronically useful, a necessity for successful photovoltaic products [20,21]. Hydrogen not only capped dangling bonds, but was also valuable as a bridging element providing the connectivity between the silicon atoms and under the proper circumstances assuring enough four-fold coordination. I chose fluorine since it is the superhalogen and provides a much stronger bond and, most importantly, expands the undercoordinated bonds of silicon and germanium so that they can have their full tetrahedral structure. Fluorine also provides useful functions in the plasma and on the surface in the growth of the film. It does its job so well not only in intermediate order but as a preferred element to make microcrystalline tetrahedral materials [22] as well as thin-film diamond-like carbon [23]. It also played a role in making superior superconducting films [24].

The most exciting physics lay in the unexplored ocean that I have been working in since 1955 with our only nautical chart the periodic table and physical intuition our compass. Even though disordered materials could not be easily categorized mathematically, one can constructively design nonequilibrium, nonstoichiometric graded and mixed phase materials to discover new phenomena [8].

In order to follow the exploration process, we will intermingle the relevant scientific and technological approaches with the materials, products, and technologies made possible by utilizing the freedom permitted by disorder to design and atomically engineer local environments.

ENERGY GENERATION –PHOTOVOLTAICS

In photovoltaics, we started our exploration relatively close to the silicon shoreline but had to push further out because contrary to conventional thinking, elemental amorphous silicon had no possible electronic use and therefore required the alloying described above so as to eliminate dangling bonds and yet to retain its four-fold coordination. I felt that it also required new technology befitting its thin film form. Rather than choosing heavy glass as a substrate, we used flexible, thin stainless steel as well as other flexible materials such as kapton.

A historical perspective is needed to show the interaction of science, technology and product. Starting in the late 1970s, we invented the materials, the products and designed and built six generations of production machines utilizing our multi-junction, continuous web technology, the most recent, our 5 MW machine shown in Fig 1. These machines, designed and built at Energy Conversion Devices (ECD), manufacture much needed, simple products using our advanced science and technology and, most importantly, this continuous web approach has shown that it is possible in larger machines to make solar energy cost competitive to conventional fuels. This, of course, would set off an enormous positive change in the use and economics of energy. The plasma physics involved in such a machine makes it possible to discard the power consuming crystal growing methods of crystalline semiconductors and the billion dollar costs now involved in building crystal wafer plants. In crystalline materials, the investment and throughput are linearly coupled, in our amorphous thin film technology, a 4 times increase of capital investment (in the millions of dollars) would yield a 20 times increase in throughput.

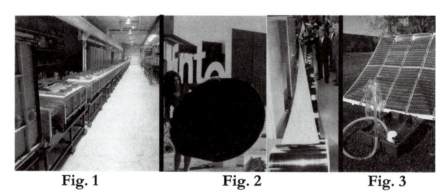

Fig. 1   **Fig. 2**   **Fig. 3**

Fig. 2 shows a 3 inch crystalline wafer (at bottom, center), the state of the art of semiconductors at the time, and what Gordon Moore and Bob Noyes, founders of Intel, utilized as opening humor for their talks, a huge cardboard "wafer", representing what they felt would be the electronic requirements of the 90s. On the right, made in our second generation continuous web machine in 1982 for our joint venture with Sharp Corporation, is the first half mile long, over a foot wide roll of a sophisticated multi-junction thin film semiconductor solar cell continuously deposited on thin, flexible stainless steel. This revolutionary new process was the answer to the fantasy of the cardboard wafer. Obviously the roll could be made much wider and longer. I have called our photovoltaic roll an infinite "crystal".

In order to show the extreme light weight, high energy density potential of our approach, we deposited our films on kapton and demonstrated in 1984 the highest energy density per weight of any kind of solar cell. This is shown in Fig.3 in a water pumping application at that time. These days the same approach is beginning to be utilized for telecommunication, space and satellite applications by Guha, Yang and colleagues[25]. The power density in thin film stainless steel and especially kapton which can store almost 3000 watts per kilogram is so exceptional as to become the solar cell of choice for telecommunication. Just last month, in November 1998, an amorphous silicon solar array was installed on the MIR space station. It was fabricated in Troy, Michigan by United Solar Systems Corp (United Solar), (ECD's joint venture with Canon), and assembled in Russia by Sovlux, ECD's Russian joint venture with Kvant, the developer of the original photovoltaics on MIR, and the Russian Ministry of Atomic Energy.

Fig. 4   **Fig. 5**   **Fig. 6**

Fig. 4 shows shingles made in 1980 [26] providing a new paradigm for energy generation. Paradigm shifting takes time. Figs 5 and 6 are current installations of the shingles and a standing seam roof. These products are gaining widespread approval. Fig 7 shows former Secretary of Energy Pena displaying our solar shingles in 1998.

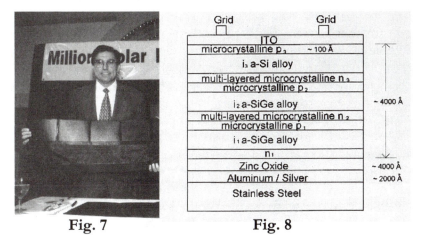

Fig. 7   **Fig. 8**

Fig 8 is a schematic of our triple-junction solar cell showing its multi-layered configuration wherein light can be absorbed in sub-cells with different bandgaps so as to utilize as much of the sun's spectrum as possible. The blue, green and red light is absorbed in layered thin films of amorphous silicon and germanium alloys containing hydrogen/fluorine. ECD and United Solar have all the world's records for efficiency, culminating in the latest world record of 10.5% stable efficiency on a one square foot module and 13% stable efficiency on a .25 square cm cell [27].

Amorphicity is crucial for several reasons. Unlike crystalline tetrahedral materials in which quantum mechanical selection rules make for indirect bandgaps and require layers of 50 to 100 microns in order to absorb the light energy, amorphous materials act as direct band gap materials and therefore the entire triple layer system is less than 1 micron in total thickness. It is important to note that in crystalline materials of different bandgaps, lattice mismatch is a serious problem and therefore such multi-layered structures could not be made in a production manner. In this case, we can see that amorphicity and the physics make possible continuous web production. Amorphous photovoltaics illustrate that when one removes the lattice constraints, atomic engineering can be merged with machine engineering to provide a new, much needed approach to energy generation.

There has been much ongoing work in photovoltaics at ECD since 1977 [28], advancing the science and technology of materials, production processes and new products. At the MRS 1998 Spring Meeting, my collaborators, Guha, Yang and coworkers at United Solar, who have made very significant contributions to our work, gave an excellent review of our recent commercialization progress [29]. The ECD-United Solar team, which also includes Masat Izu, Prem Nath, Steve Hudgens, Joe Doehler, Scott Jones and Herb Ovshinsky among others (the latter the head of ECD's Machine Division which has designed and built our continuous web processors) has through the years made important contributions to our field and has been working on products, production and plasma technology that increase throughput.

From a materials science point of view, we note several points of importance. While amorphous tetrahedral materials are close to the crystalline shoreline in their need for low density of states and substitutional doping, being direct bandgap materials, one can make large area, thin film multi-junction devices by the decomposition of plasmas in a continuous manner. Accomplishing this, we were able to basically alter the way materials could be laid down in a continuous manner, showing the tight coupling in amorphous materials between basic science and advanced technology.

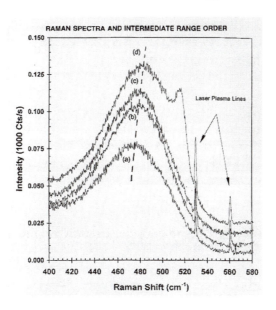

Fig. 9

Illustrating the scientific and technological richness of amorphous materials is the ability to develop intermediate range order in an amorphous matrix as we do in the intrinsic silicon alloy layer of our photovoltaic product [11,30]. (Fig. 9) It is of great interest that quasi one-dimensional ordering is accomplished without introducing grain boundaries that would interfere with electron and hole conductivity. This intermediate state is the signature of the best material. We have shown that fluorine is a great facilitator of intermediate order [31-34] and leads to crystallization. The intermediate order has important implications for the future. It is possible that the carriers have increased mobility due to the intermediate structures and could affect the important parameter of hole mobility in these materials. Microcrystalline materials can also have unique properties that bridge the gap between crystalline and disordered solids. We have incorporated them in our continuous web process by utilizing fluorine [11,21] to make under 120 angstrom micro-crystalline silicon p-layers. When one considers that this is accomplished in a continuous web, very high yield production process, it can be appreciated that atomic engineering and manufacturing are a reality.

ENERGY STORAGE–
NICKEL METAL HYDRIDE BATTERIES

Nickel metal hydride batteries are in a real sense misnamed, for while nickel, by virtue of its filled d-orbital, plays an important catalytic role, there are usually seven or eight other elements that make up the alloy used in the negative electrode; certainly hydrogen is the key component. It is the smallest and simplest atom in the universe (which, by the way, in terms of actual matter is composed of over 90% hydrogen). Therefore, to attain the highest energy storage density not only for batteries but for hydrogen as a fuel is a matter of designing the highest density of reversible hydrogen sites. This can be accomplished by our principles of disorder and local order [11,14-17,35]. From 1960 on, we have demonstrated that hydrogen is not just a future source of energy but a here and now solution that, together with solar energy, offers the ultimate answer to society's need for clean, virtually inexhaustible energy.

Energy technology should be regarded as a system. We have described energy generation. Equally as important is energy storage. Now we must go much further from shore in order to discuss the basis for the materials used for energy storage and later for information which is structured energy and must also be stored.

In the energy storage area, we cannot discern the shoreline, we are in the ocean of many-body theory which has never been adequately understood. I have had a long interest and worked for many years with d-orbital materials [36]. A recent publication sums up present day advanced thinking regarding d-electrons: "d-electron-based systems, in particular, present the combined intrigue of a range of dramatic phenomena, including superconductivity and itinerant ferromagnetism, and the tendency toward inscrutability associated with the fact that key electronic states are often intermediate between the ideals of localization and itineracy which provide the starting points for most theory " [37]. By making multi-elemental, multi-phase d-orbital materials for hydrogen storage in a completely reproducible manner, it is clear that we have been able to understand how to take the mystery out of them and utilize these orbitals in new and unique ways.

We are literally at sea when we discuss metals for they are always described as being composed of a sea of electrons. Why does the sea not swamp out the background provided by local atomic environments? Paradoxically, this is because when we use many, for example, ten, different atoms, particularly those with directional d-orbitals, to make up a material such as the negative electrode in our nickel metal hydride battery, we provide through the disordered state regions of lower electronic density which have a larger probability to overlap with negative hydrogen ions in interstitial sites. To simplify, one can say that it is the s-electrons that provide the sea, the d-electrons sculpt out the channels and receptors. Obviously there is some hybridization possible in many of these materials.

It is in the multielemental f- and particularly the d-orbital material that we introduce a means of delocalizing electrons and still have them represent their parentage. This is where internal topology begins to play an important role in metallic conduction for, as noted, we need channels in the sea of electrons just as we take into account sea level/Fermi level. The different types of atoms provide the interatomic spacings for the hydrogen ions to operate in and the varying electronic density is the steering means for the ions to reach the preferred sites of low electron density. Disordered materials are therefore necessary to provide the spectrum of binding sites. In summary, large interatomic spacing and low energy density make for the optimal binding/storage of negative hydrogen ions. The electron environment surrounding the hydrogen provides the degree of negativity and coulombic repulsion is the steering means. The binding energy provided by the local environment is of such a nature as to assure reversibility so important for the rechargeable battery. While we list characteristics of individual atoms in Fig.10, it is how they act and interact in the alloy that makes for the mechanism that we have described above.

The acceptance of nickel metal hydride batteries has been very rapid. All significant manufacturers of nickel metal hydride batteries are under agreement with ECD and our Ovonic Battery Company (OBC) and over 600 million consumer batteries were sold last year with a 30% per year predicted growth rate. These high production volumes have made for a very low cost battery.

The problems of pollution, climate change and our strategic dependence on oil have provided a global impetus for the use of electric and hybrid electric vehicles [38,39]. The automotive industry has made our nickel metal hydride battery the battery of choice for these vehicles. GM, Toyota, Honda, Hyundai, Ford and Chrysler all have chosen nickel metal hydride batteries. We have a joint venture with GM, GM Ovonic, which manufactures and sells electric vehicle and hybrid electric vehicle batteries to all companies.

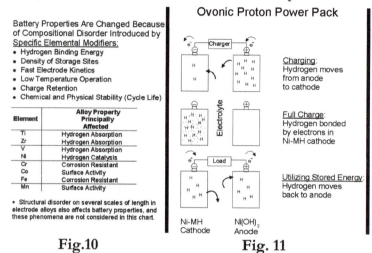

Battery Properties Are Changed Because of Compositional Disorder Introduced by Specific Elemental Modifiers:
- Hydrogen Binding Energy
- Density of Storage Sites
- Fast Electrode Kinetics
- Low Temperature Operation
- Charge Retention
- Chemical and Physical Stability (Cycle Life)

Element	Alloy Property Principally Affected
Ti	Hydrogen Absorption
Zr	Hydrogen Absorption
V	Hydrogen Absorption
Ni	Hydrogen Catalysis
Cr	Corrosion Resistant
Co	Surface Activity
Fe	Corrosion Resistant
Mn	Surface Activity

* Structural disorder on several scales of length in electrode alloys also affects battery properties, and these phenomena are not considered in this chart.

Fig.10

Ovonic Proton Power Pack

Charging:
Hydrogen moves from anode to cathode

Full Charge:
Hydrogen bonded by electrons in Ni-MH cathode

Utilizing Stored Energy:
Hydrogen moves back to anode

Ni-MH Cathode   Ni(OH)$_2$ Anode

Fig. 11

Fig. 12

Fig. 11 shows a very simplified schematic of the nickel metal hydride battery. The battery is based on hydrogen transfer in which hydrogen is shuttled back and forth between the nickel hydroxide and metal hydride without soluble intermediates or complex phase changes. Fig. 12 shows an ingot of our materials as well as our green battery.

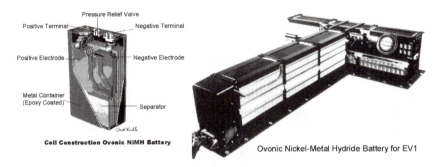

Fig. 13   Fig. 14

Fig. 15

Fig.13 is a cutaway drawing of our NiMH automotive battery illustrating its simplicity. Fig. 14 is a GM EV1 battery pack; Fig. 15 is a photo of the EV1 car whose range is between 160 and over 200 miles, its acceleration is 0 to 60 mph in less than 8 seconds, less than 15 minutes for an over 60% recharge, very robust, environmentally benign, lifetime of the car battery.

Fig. 16 shows James Worden, cofounder of Solectria, having driven his 4 passenger Solectria Sunrise from Boston to New York on the equivalent BTU energy of less than 1 gallon of gas and he

Fig. 16

had 15% energy remaining [40]. Fig. 17 gives world record ranges of EVs using Ovonic NiMH batteries,and Fig. 18 shows the capability of nickel metal hydride to be continuously improved by atomic engineering of the materials.

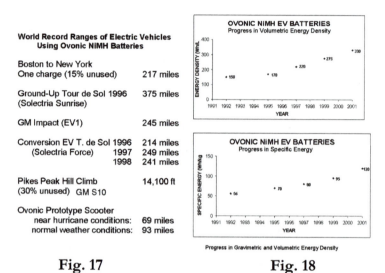

World Record Ranges of Electric Vehicles Using Ovonic NiMH Batteries		
Boston to New York One charge (15% unused)		217 miles
Ground-Up Tour de Sol 1996 (Solectria Sunrise)		375 miles
GM Impact (EV1)		245 miles
Conversion EV T. de Sol 1996 (Solectria Force)	1996	214 miles
	1997	249 miles
	1998	241 miles
Pikes Peak Hill Climb (30% unused) GM S10		14,100 ft
Ovonic Prototype Scooter near hurricane conditions:		69 miles
normal weather conditions:		93 miles

Fig. 17   **Fig. 18**

A gasoline powered GM Geo Metro was tested against the same make and model car rebuilt by Solectria to be an electric vehicle with our Ovonic batteries. In New York City driving, the gasoline car provided an equivalent range of 120 miles compared to the 220 mile equivalent range of the electric vehicle with our batteries [41]. It is quite clear that scientific and technological issues are not what is holding back electric vehicles. Hybrid electric vehicles with our batteries will offer at least 80 miles per gallon in the charge sustaining mode and over 100 miles per gallon in the charge depletion mode.

INFORMATION

Disordered materials depend upon optional bonding configurations of atoms generating various kinds of new orbital relations. While boron and carbon are helpful in this regard, the elements of choice as I have shown for NiMH batteries are f- and d-orbitals. For the information side of our work, we prefer the chalcogenides characterized by Kastner as lone pair materials [42]. We utilize lone pair p-orbitals since they are not only nonbonding but have a spectrum of lone pair interactions that include various new bonding configurations [43-46]. In some respects, they have similarity to the directional d-orbitals, in other respects, they are different, for example, the empty or filled d-orbitals are very localized and do not reach out as far as the lone pair p-orbitals of the chalcogens, where two of the p-orbitals are deep in energy and serve as strong structural bonds responsible for the cohesiveness of the material. The many lone pair interactions are spread in energy throughout the mobility gap. Their similarity to d-orbitals is that neither the lone pairs nor the d-orbitals play a strong role in cohesive bonding but both are available for interesting electronic, optical and chemical interactions. However, their dissimilarity is that the lone pairs being the outer electrons (they are as far out as any valence electrons), can remain free or form weak or strong bonds, covalent or coordinate, depending on the environment. They are as far out as any valence electrons. The d-orbitals, on the other hand, form a narrow but designable band of high density states at the Fermi level and they too can act as receptors in the coordinate bond configuration. A more profound difference is that the divalency of the lone pair chalcogens allows a flexibility of structure which can be controlled by crosslinking so that we can make either an electronic Ovonic threshold switch (OTS) in which the excitation process does not affect bonding (see Fig. 19) or an Ovonic memory switch (OMS) [4] in which the electronic processes initiate structural, that is, reversible phase change. We will concentrate here on the OMS which is now universally utilized in its optical phase change form (see Figs. 20 and 21) [47].

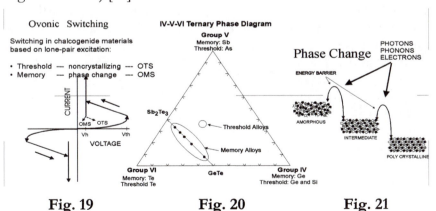

Fig. 19   **Fig. 20**   **Fig. 21**

Phase change rewritable memories have become the basis for the rapidly growing DVD rewritable market which holds so much promise for the future since it is replacing VCRs and CD-ROMs.

The energy necessary for an Ovonic optical memory material to change its atomic configuration is provided by a laser beam which couples to the non-bonding lone pairs so that the electronic energy exceeds a threshold value, causing a high atomic mobility state to occur and a change from the amorphous to the crystalline phase to take place. The same laser, but at different power, is used for recording, erasing and rewriting since the amorphous material can become crystalline again by rapid rearrangement through slight movements of atoms. The different structural phases of the material have different optical constants, so information is stored in the form of regions with different reflectivity. It is particularly favorable to use a phase congruent material for these applications and as we will show, the cycle life for phase change memories is exceptionally long. Electrical phase change memories have gone over 10^{13} cycles when testing was stopped [48,49].

Since Ovonic phase change optical memories are having great commercial success and the markets are growing rapidly, we are now entering the semiconductor memory market with devices using these materials. Conventional semiconductor memories are the basic building blocks of the information age. The data shown in Fig. 22 clearly show that conventional memories can be replaced by Ovonic semiconductor memories since a single plane of our memory can replace DRAM, SRAM and Flash. To indicate the great advantages that our multi-state memory offers in this highly competitive industry, we show a comparison with Intel's multi-level flash memory which was announced as "the Holy Grail" and which they said would have a "revolutionary" impact on the Flash market. (Figs. 23 and 24).

It can be appreciated that the multi-state memory is also a learning device since it adapts its electrical conductivity to the amount of information it receives. In other words, it displays what neurophysiologists refer to as plasticity as the basis for intelligence. We have also developed another version of this thin-film memory which is truly neuronal and synaptic in that it accumulates a number of sub-threshold pulses before it changes state. This device takes advantage of the fact that a small portion of the active volume of the memory will change phase upon application of every

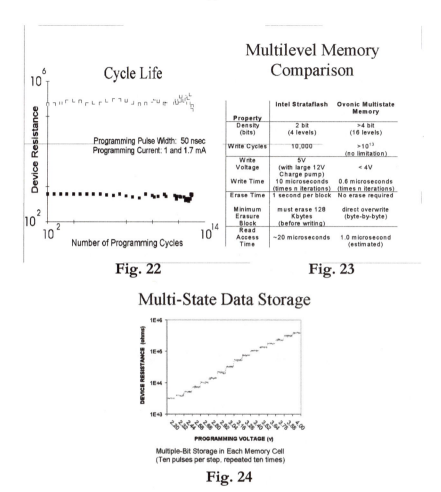

Fig. 22

Multilevel Memory Comparison

Property	Intel Strataflash	Ovonic Multistate Memory
Density (bits)	2 bit (4 levels)	>4 bit (16 levels)
Write Cycles	10,000	>10^{13} (no limitation)
Write Voltage	5V (with large 12V Charge pump)	< 4V
Write Time	10 microseconds (times n iterations)	0.6 microseconds (times n iterations)
Erase Time	1 second per block	No erase required
Minimum Erasure Block	must erase 128 Kbytes (before writing)	direct overwrite (byte-by-byte)
Read Access Time	~20 microseconds	1.0 microsecond (estimated)

Fig. 23

Multi-State Data Storage

Multiple-Bit Storage in Each Memory Cell
(Ten pulses per step, repeated ten times)

Fig. 24

sub-threshold energy pulse. After a specified amount of energy has been deposited, a percolation path is established among the crystallized regions, and a large change in electrical resistance results. The device is reset into its virgin state in the same manner as our other semiconductor memory. This accumulation mode memory device will have important near-term applications in secure, tamper-proof information storage in smart cards and other devices.

What I have in mind for the future is an all thin-film intelligent computer. We have designed all thin-film circuits which can have logic, memory, and adaptive or intelligent memory integrated into a circuit. We have already proven that these devices can be made in three-dimensional and multi-layered circuits, can receive information from various sources, integrate it, remember it and learn from it. This is the basis of a truly cognitive machine, not artificial intelligence as we now know it, nor just a large number of parallel circuits, but a huge density of switching points, receiving and integrating information, in other words, many neurons of different thresholds and frequencies, receiving huge amounts of synaptic information, responding to it and utilizing it [50]. This is what I have wanted to build since 1955; this is what we can build now. I feel that this kind of computer is the computer of the next millenium. Combined with amorphous sensors and displays which we introduced many years ago and which have found widespread use, such a computer could perform tasks which are now beyond the ken of present "dumb" computers. All the various parts have been shown to work and they are all based on amorphous and disordered materials.

CONCLUSION

I believe that I have shown that science and technology can be utilized to build new industries that are responsive to societal problems and needs, providing jobs, educational opportunities and the chance to express the creative urge that has driven humankind since time immemorial. Fig. 25 shows a young woman climbing a mountain barefooted with her future on her back, our photovoltaics, and her future in front of her, her child, bringing our photovoltaics to a village that does not have electricity. There can be no civilization without energy and without knowledge (information). We take this picture as inspiration to continue our work.

Fig. 25

ACKNOWLEDGEMENTS

This work could not have been accomplished without the immense help and loving and fruitful collaboration of Iris Ovshinsky. Amorphous and disordered materials could not have reached its state in science without Hellmut Fritzsche. I am honored to have him as my longest scientific collaborator about whom it can be truly said that he is a giant in our field. Dave Adler's untimely death cut short our warm, close and productive friendship and collaboration. We and the amorphous field owe so much to him. I wish to thank the talented and creative teams of ECD, United Solar, and the Ovonic Battery Company. In the battery group, Subhash Dhar is an inspired multi-talented leader; Mike Fetcenko has made and is making many invaluable, critical contributions, his collaboration with me has been essential to the success of the battery company. Dennis Corrigan is owed thanks by me and the entire EV industry for his essential contributions to EV batteries; Srini Venkatesan has been a mainstay, his finger- and brain- prints are on everything that happens in batteries; Benny Reichman's great creativity has always been deeply appreciated; Art Holland's mechanical contributions have been of great importance in our battery work; John deNeufville's contributions through the years have not only been of great value to us but his latest activities contribute to the development of the amorphous silicon and germanium alloy field; we thank Paul Gifford not only for his battery talents, but for representing us in developing the new industry; particular thanks to our "young tigers" who are literally building this industry from the ground up. Our computer authority, Guy Wicker fits into that category very well. We also wish to thank Krishna Sapru for her early and current valuable work with me on hydrogen storage, batteries and atomic modeling. Our optical memory work would not be possible without the talent, commitment and hard work of Dave Strand; the electrical memory activity is dependent on the innovative talents and motivation of Wally Czubatyj and his group including Sergey Kostylev, Pat Klersy, and Boil Pashmakov; Ben Chao, the head of our analytical laboratory, is a resource beyond comparison to the entire company; Rosa Young is a unique, extraordinarily innovative talent whose important contributions have spanned all of our areas in a remarkable manner; Steve Hudgens has contributed greatly to all areas of our work, his collaboration and advice have been extremely helpful to me and essential to the company. We are indeed fortunate to be working with Bob Stempel, the pioneer and leading figure in electric vehicles, a great engineer, leader and most appreciated partner. I am prouder of the organization and working climate that we have built than of any of my inventions.

REFERENCES

1. The Economist, p, 98, October 2, 1993.
2. U.S. Department of Energy announcement, January 18, 1994.
3. U. Hofer, Science **279**, 190 (Jan. 9, 1998).
4. S.R. Ovshinsky, Phys. Rev. Lett. **21**, 1450 (1968).
5. M.H. Cohen, H. Fritzsche and S.R. Ovshinsky, Phys. Rev. Lett. **22**, 1065 (1969).
6. S.R. Ovshinsky, Rev. Roum. Phys. **26**, 893 (1981).
7. S.R. Ovshinsky and D. Adler, Contemp. Phys. **19**, 109 (1978).
8. S.R. Ovshinsky, in *Physics of Disordered Materials*, edited by D. Adler, H. Fritzsche and S.R. Ovshinsky, (Inst. for Amorphous Studies Series, Plenum Press, New York, 1985) p. 37.
9. S.R. Ovshinsky, J. Non-Cryst. Solids **32**, 17 (1979).
10. S.R. Ovshinsky, in *Insulating and Semiconducting Glasses*, edited by P. Boolchand (World Scientific Press, Singapore, 1999).
11. For further references, see *Disordered Materials: Science and Technology, Selected papers by Stanford R. Ovshinsky*, edited by D. Adler, B.B. Schwartz and M. Silver (Institute for Amorphous Studies Series, Plenum Press, New York, 1991).
12. S.R. Ovshinsky, in *Proc. of the Seventh International Conference on Amorphous and Liquid Semiconductors*, Edinburgh, Scotland, 27 June-1 July, 1977, p. 519.
13. S.R. Ovshinsky, J. of Non-Cryst. Solids **42**, 335 (1980).
14. S.R. Ovshinsky, Presented at 1978 Gordon Research Conference on Catalysis (unpublished).
15. S.R. Ovshinsky, presented in May 1980 at Lake Angelus, MI (unpublished).
16. K. Sapru, B. Reichman, A. Reger and S.R. Ovshinsky, U.S. Pat. No. 4 633 597 (18 Nov. 1986).
17. S.R. Ovshinsky, M.A. Fetcenko and J. Ross, Science **260**, 176 (9 April 1993).

18. S.R. Ovshinsky, in *Proc. of the Sixth International Conference on Amorphous and Liquid Semiconductors*, Leningrad, USSR, 18-24 November 1975, p. 426.
19. S.R. Ovshinsky, in *Proc. of the International Topical Conference on Structure and Excitation of Amorphous Solids*, Williamsburg, Virginia, 24-27 March 1976, p. 31.
20. S.R. Ovshinsky, New Scientist **80** (1131), 674-677 (1978).
21. S.R. Ovshinsky, Solar Energy Mats. and Solar Cells **32**, 443-449 (1994).
22. S.R. Ovshinsky, in *Proc. of the International Ion Engineering Congress, ISIAT '83 & IPAT '83*, Kyoto, 12-16 September 1983, p. 817.
23. S.R. Ovshinsky and J. Flasck, U.S. Patent No. 4 770 940 (13 September 1988).
24. S.R. Ovshinsky and R.T. Young, in *Proc. of the SPIE Symposium on Modeling of Optical Thin Films II*, **1324**, San Diego, California, 12-13 July 1990, p. 32.
25. S. Guha, J. Yang, A. Banerjee, T. Glatfelter, G.J. Vendura, Jr., A. Garcia and M. Kruer, presented at the 2nd World Conference and Exhibition on Photovoltaic Solar Energy Conversion, Vienna, Austria, 6-10 July 1998.
26. J. Glorioso, Energy Management, June/July 1980, p. 45. Shown in 1980 by Stan and Iris Ovshinsky to Domtar, a Canadian roofing company and to Allside, an aluminum siding company of Akron, Ohio.
27. J. Yang, A. Banerjee, K. Lord and S. Guha, presented at the 2nd World Conference and Exhibition on Photovoltaic Solar Energy Conversion, Vienna, Austria, 6-10 July 1998.
28. S.R. Ovshinsky, presentation at the British House of Commons, July 1977.
29. S. Guha, J. Yang, A. Banerjee and S. Sugiyama, presented at the 1998 MRS Spring Meeting, San Francisco, CA, 1998 (invited).
30. D.V. Tsu, B.S. Chao, S.R. Ovshinsky, S. Guha and J. Yang, App. Phys. Lett. **71**, 1317 (1997).
31. R. Tsu, M. Izu, V. Cannella, S.R. Ovshinsky, G-J. Jan and F.H. Pollak, J. Phys. Soc. Japan Suppl. **A49**, 1249 (1980).
32. R. Tsu, M. Izu, V. Cannella, S.R. Ovshinsky and F.H. Pollak, Solid State Comm. **36**, 817 (1981).

33. R. Tsu, S.S. Chao, S.R. Ovshinsky, G-J. Jan and F.H. Pollak, J. de Physique **42**, 269 (1981).
34. R. Tsu, J. Gonzalez-Hernandez, J. Doehler and S.R. Ovshinsky, Solid State Comm. **46**, 79 (1983).
35. M.A. Fetcenko, S.J. Hudgens and S.R. Ovshinsky, Daido Journal (Denki-Seiko) **66** (2) 123-136 (April 1995). (Special Issue Electronics & Functional Materials.)
36. See for ex. 1959 Control Engineering on the Ovitron.
37. P. Kostic, Y. Okada, N.C. Collins, Z. Schlesinger, J.W. Reiner, L. Klein, A. Kapitulnik, T. H. Geballe, and M. R. Beasley, Phys. Rev. Lett. **81**, 2498, (1998).
38. S.R. Ovshinsky and R.C. Stempel, invited presentation at the 13th Electric Vehicle Symposium (EVS-13), Osaka, Japan, 13-16 October 1996.
39. R.C. Stempel, S.R. Ovshinsky, P.R. Gifford and D.A. Corrigan, IEEE Spectrum, November 1998, p. 29.
40. IEEE Spectrum, December 1997, p. 68.
41. 10th Anniversary American Tour de Sol Competition, run in New York City by Northeast Sustainable Energy Association (NESEA), (1998).
42. M. Kastner, Phys. Rev. Lett. **28**, 355 (1972).
43. S.R. Ovshinsky and K. Sapru, in *Proc. of the Fifth International Amorphous and Liquid Semiconductors*, Garmisch-Partenkirchen, Germany (1974), p. 447.
44. S.R. Ovshinsky, Phys. Rev. Lett. **36** (24), 1469-1472 (1976).
45. S.R. Ovshinsky and H. Fritzsche, *IEEE Trans. Elect. Dev.*, **ED-20** (2) 91-105 (1973).
46. M. Kastner, D. Adler and H. Fritzsche, Phys. Rev. Lett. **37**, 1504 (1976).
47. For history and early references, see S. R. Ovshinsky, "Historique du Changement de Phase" in Memoires, Optiques et Systemes, No. 127, Sept. 1994, p. 65; in the *Proc. of the Fifth Annual National Conference on Industrial Research*, Chicago, Illinois, 18-19 September 1969; Journal de Physique **42**, supplement au no. 10 October 1981.
48. S. R. Ovshinsky, presented at the 1997 International Semiconductor Conference, Sinaia, Romania , 1997.

49. S. R. Ovshinsky, presented at High Density Phase Change Optical Memories in Multi-Media Era, 9th Conference for Phase Change Media, Shizuoka, Japan, 1997.
50. S.R. Ovshinsky and I.M. Ovshinsky, Mats. Res. Bull. **5**, 681 (1970).

Appendix 3

The material basis of efficiency and stability in amorphous photovoltaics

Stanford R. Ovshinsky *

Energy Conversion Devices, Troy, MI 48084, USA

Abstract

Amorphous thin film tetrahedrally based alloys have recently achieved an efficiency which permits them in volume production to become competitive to fossil fuels. In this paper, the next stage of development which is to raise stabilized efficiencies to 18% is discussed. It is shown how the scientific and technological problems can be viewed and understood and point to means of solution.

1. Introduction

Amorphous tetrahedrally based alloys have led to recent photovoltaic modules of a one square foot commercial type which reached the 10% stabilized efficiency [1] which has been the holy grail of workers in this field.

The 10% figure has been of vital importance because when such material efficiency is combined with the continuous wide web, triple junction, roll-to-roll production process of a suitable size, for example, a 50 to 100 megawatt machine, it is possible for the first time for solar energy to compete head to head with conventional fossil fuels and nuclear energy at approximately 7 cents per kilowatt hour. The figures used to validate such an assumption are based upon a US government formulation [2].

These advances are of historical importance in the struggle to minimize pollution, to reduce the energy role of depletable fossil fuels, especially oil whose control is a major cause of war, and to create new industries which will generate desperately needed jobs without which social and economic disorder is a given.

It has been shown that proven technology is already available to meet these important objectives (see Fig. 1). Amorphous silicon based alloys are the basis for

Correspondence to: Energy Conversion Devices, 1675 W. Maple Rd., Troy, MI 48084, USA).

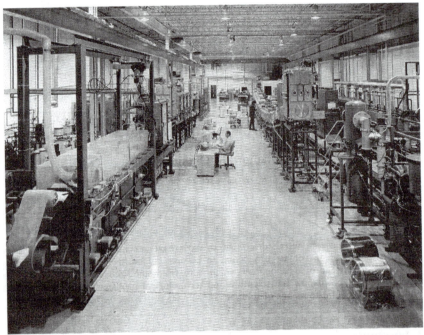

Fig. 1. ECD's fifth generation, continuous web, roll-to-roll, triple (three band gap), photovoltaic production plant in Troy, Michigan. In its initial operation in the US before shipment to its Sovlux joint venture in Russia, it had already achieved world records for efficiency.

the only thin film solar cell technology that has been proven in production and these products have through the years met the test of use. However, rather than resting on our laurels, the author would like to discuss in this paper the strategies that can raise the efficiencies to the 18% stabilized range and beyond. As of now, the small area initial efficiency record is 13.7% which was achieved at our laboratory [3].

The attainment of this next transition step would make photovoltaics ubiquitous and do so much to achieve Bernie Seraphin's vision of freeing the developing world from the ever-deepening energy crisis that envelops it, preventing the achievement of industrial development so necessary for the dignity inherent in a civilized standard of living.

It is fitting that this paper is dedicated to Bernie Seraphin who is an exemplary figure and represents the best part of science. He has made important contributions and at the same time has recognized that science and technology are not value free but have responsibilities to serve our world societal needs. Bernie has done more than anyone to develop scientists from Third World countries so that they can be nucleating agents for change in their native lands as well as to integrate them into the international scientific community. Iris and I remember with great pleasure our visits to Trieste at Abdus Salam's International Centre for Theoretical Physics to address Bernie's meetings. We interacted with scientists from various parts of the world and felt that we influenced their thinking about the possibilities of much desired nonpolluting energy for the building of their countries and introduced them to the scientific and technological potential of amorphous and disordered materials and thin film technology.

2. Amorphous and disordered materials problems

While the advantages of amorphous and disordered materials in the field of photovoltaics are now quite obvious, the remaining problems that have acted as barriers to their further development can be clearly stated. By understanding their physical and chemical causes, one can develop strategies to minimize or indeed eliminate them. For example, the Staebler–Wronski Effect, which concerns itself with the decline of initial efficiency within a period of time, is such a problem. Amorphous materials by nature have a degree of freedom available for relaxation not found in rigid crystalline structures such as crystalline silicon/germanium [4]. Another problem is the high density of states that is generated when germanium is added to silicon to form alloys of lower band gap materials which incorporate hydrogen. The same problem holds true when carbon is added to silicon in the higher bandgap materials.

A triple-junction device of three different bandgaps (altogether no more than one micron thick) is the optimal configuration to utilize the solar spectrum for the highest efficiency. If the density of states can be lowered in the two other layers to the same degree ($5 \times 10^{15}/cm^3$) as the amorphous silicon alloy layer containing silicon, hydrogen and/or fluorine (the author has a great affection for fluorine [4]) and stabilized, then a stable 18% photovoltaic commercial product is assured.

3. Influence of local chemical configurations

The triple band gap device is already being put into production. Here we would like to discuss the basis for new plasma chemistry. Rather than discussing the transient chemical species which are the precursors that become part of the film-making process, we wish to address the basic and fundamental problem which when understood can lead to the generation of the proper chemical species necessary to achieve our goals.

Why should the addition of germanium and/or carbon, which are band controlling elements so necessary in a multijunction, high efficiency device, cause critical limiting problems and if one has an understanding of these factors, are there solutions? The author believes so and discuss here such approaches. From a materials point of view, much work has been based upon a flawed understanding

Table 1
Bond strengths

Bond type	Bond energy (kcal/mole)
Si–Si	53
Si–H	76
Si–F	135
Si–O	190
Ge–Ge	45
Ge–H	69
Ge–F	108
Ge–O	158

of the structural/chemical basis of the semiconducting properties of amorphous tetrahedral materials. The treatment of the Column IV elements, particularly silicon and germanium, had as its basic assumption that in the amorphous state these two elements were equally made tetrahedral in new configurations by the introduction of hydrogen. A glance at Table 1 shows that the silicon–silicon bond is quite weak, the silicon–hydrogen bond is far from optimal and the silicon–fluorine bond is the preferred configuration. When we look at the germanium–germanium bond, we find it to be even weaker than the silicon–silicon bond. The germanium–hydrogen bond is weaker than the silicon–hydrogen bond and again we see that the germanium–fluorine bond is the preferred one.

We can also understand that the stronger bonding elements will compete with the weaker ones in an alloy, for example, hydrogen and fluorine would prefer a silicon mate rather than a germanium one during the conventional deposition process. We can appreciate the perils of an insufficient vacuum which would allow contaminants with strong bonding energies such as oxygen to fill up sites and generate defects that should be available to truly compensating elements such as hydrogen and/or fluorine. Fluorine's small size and particularly its unique extreme electronegativity make it ideal for expanding orbitals, for example, in utilizing the "inert" orbitals (lone pairs) of germanium so as to assure tetrahedral bonding. However, due to its high reactivity, it is difficult to utilize fluorine in the plasma.

Other differences between silicon alloys and alloys containing germanium have to do with the larger size and heaviness of the germanium atom. This not only affects the mobility of the germanium atom on the growing surface, but requires higher temperatures during deposition which increase hydrogen evolution. This lack of surface mobility in films containing amorphous germanium has other negative aspects since there is a higher degree of disorder in the network and a higher porosity in the deposited film. This is a subject which requires greater discussion and a detailed paper is presently being prepared showing how this problem can be minimized [5]. The Staebler–Wronski Effect is intimately tied to weak bond formation and the relaxations available to unoptimally cross-linked amorphous materials [4]. The answer to this effect lies in stronger and more tetrahedrally bonded configurations and denser materials.

When we examine carbon containing alloys, we should assume that it is no easy matter to create tetrahedral materials out of carbon for if this were true, obviously diamond would be quite common. The problem with carbon is simply the beauty of carbon that allows life to exist that it has many different configurations. Forcing it to assume a uniform tetrahedral structure, one has to fight this tendency. I have shown many years ago that fluorine is an element which has the chemical strength to force carbon into a more tetrahedral configuration for density of states is a reflection of the lack of ability to complete tetrahedral bonding in carbon-based materials [6]. The alloying elements chosen to control the band gap play an obvious role but must be chosen with the basic premise in mind of assuring completed four-coordinated bonding sites without introducing unwanted states in the gap.

The problem of completing tetrahedral configurations is less obvious in germanium than in carbon but has basic similarities. It seems so simple. Alloy silicon with germanium, narrow the band gap, add some hydrogen to take care of dangling bonds and the result will be a low band gap tetrahedral material with a low density of states. The basic point here is that, particularly in the amorphous state, there is a tendency for some germanium atoms to assume trivalent and divalent configurations. These, of course, add to the inherent density of states. (By the way, as one goes down to tin, this tendency to some lower coordination becomes even more pronounced.) Many of these configurations are silent defects since germanium has lone pairs and when tetrahedralness is not assured, these lone pairs can be involved in new configurations. Even if their lone pairs are in their more normal, nonbonding state, they still cannot be detected with ESR since they are spin up and spin down configurations [4]. This has been a source of misunderstanding in the semiconductor community which assumes that in these materials, increase of density of states should be associated with conventional dangling bonds.

What we mean by tetrahedral bonding in amorphous materials is often misunderstood. If all silicon or germanium were truly tetrahedrally bonded, we would have crystalline materials and as I have pointed out [7], there is an important factor that must be taken into account which is that unlike, for example, chalcogenide materials, wherein their divalency allows flexible restructuring and completion of local configurations, we must treat amorphous tetrahedral materials in terms of their manufacturing criteria with the same sort of care that one would manufacture crystalline materials, for any deviation from tetrahedralness introduces states in the gap. It is important to note that amorphous tetrahedral materials are process dependent.

The role of hydrogen and fluorine is not only to assure the lack of dangling bonds by completing the tetrahedral structure, but by so doing, silicon/hydrogen/fluorine generate new configurations with differing local geometries than silicon/germanium atoms alone would assume. In fact, amorphous materials of the tetrahedral type are dependent upon deviations from local order [8,9] as periodic materials are affected by perturbations of periodicity. One may look at amorphous silicon alloys as materials in which disorder is minimized yet utilized for the freedom it permits so that local order and total interactive environment around the local order become the important parameters.

An important factor chemically is that one atom does not fit all sizes. The use of hydrogen has been automatically extended to germanium without taking into account the differences in bond strengths. It is by this time well known that unlike the original hope, it is much more difficult to dope amorphous tetrahedral material than crystalline. Doping not only acts substitutionally but can generate additional defects. As the materials are made into forms that have lower and lower density of states, doping efficiency increases. Also, the tendency for intermediate order increases. In my opinion, there is a great future for the semiconducting industry by utilizing intermediate range and nanostrucally ordered materials in devices [10].

4. Influence of speed of deposition

We have discussed local chemical configurations, both bonding and structural. There is another area of topology that is vital to be addressed if one is to achieve optimum materials. Guha, an important contributor to our field, was able to show that the speed of deposition was becoming a barrier to good electronic quality materials by virtue of porosity [11]. Since porosity in conventional plasma deposition techniques is associated with higher speeds of deposition reflected in greater number of defects leading to increased density of states, we must again turn to a structural/chemical solution. That is, we must generate a different type of plasma than is presently being utilized. This requires the control of free radicals [12] in the plasma. We have and are developing proprietary means of achieving this goal which depend upon the understanding of the gas phase environment and the controlling of the elements within that plasma, the electrons, various types of ions and the chemically active neutral species. The author believes very much that the plasma has been less of a "zoo" and more of a "jungle" and in sorting out and controlling the various desired and friendly species, we have a new approach to plasmas as a deposition means which will assure the proper growth kinetics and surface reactions which control the film growth and density as well as generating local structural/chemical configurations which reduce the density of states.

Thin film technology with its ability to do atomic engineering predates the present emphasis on nanostructures. There are many new device possibilities that have been and are being generated by the investigation of amorphicity, disorder and local order. It is important to point out that local order and the localized total interactive environment are materials design parameters which form the path to highly efficient photovoltaics as well as the forerunners to new areas of semiconductor use.

Iris and Stan wish Bernie many more happy birthdays.

References

[1] S. Guha, J. Yang, A. Banerjee, T. Glatfelter, K. Hoffman and X. Xu, 12th NREL PV Program Meeting, Denver, October 1993 (to be published). Initial efficiency of 11.4% on one square foot validated by NREL August 1993. Stabilized efficiency of 10.2% on one square foot validated by NREL December 1993.

[2] G.J. Jones, H.N. Post and M.G. Thomas, 19th IEEE Photovoltaic Specialist Conf., 1987, p. 25.

[3] S. Guha, J. Yang, A. Pawlikiewicz, T. Glatfelter, R. Ross, and S.R. Ovshinsky, Appl. Phys. Lett. 54 (1989) 2330.

[4] S.R. Ovshinsky, in: D. Adler, B.B. Schwartz and M. Silver (Eds.), Disordered Materials: Science and Technology — Selected Papers, 2nd ed. (Institute for Amorphous Studies Series, Plenum, NY, 1991).

[5] S.R. Ovshinsky, R. Young and D. Tsu (to be published).

[6] S.R. Ovshinsky and J. Flasck, US Patent 4-663-183, 5 May 1987.

[7] S.R. Ovshinsky, Proc. 6th Int. Conf. on Amorphous and Liquid Semiconductors, Leningrad, 1975, p. 426.

[8] S.R. Ovshinsky, Proc. 9th Int. Conf. on Amorphous and Liquid Semiconductors, Grenoble, 1981, p. 1095.

[9] S.R. Ovshinsky, Rev. Roum. Phys. 26 (1981) 893.

[10] S.R. Ovshinsky and R. Young, US Patent 5-103-284, 7 April 1992.

[11] S. Guha, J. Yang, S.J. Jones, Y. Chen and D. Williamson, Appl. Phys. Lett. 61 (1992) 1444.

[12] S.R. Ovshinsky, Proc. Int. Ion Engineering Congress, ISIAT '83 and IPAT '83, Kyoto, Japan, 1983, p. 817.

Appendix 4

Presented at PVSEC-15, Shanghai, China, October 10 – 15, 2005

25/30 MW Ovonic Roll-To-Roll PV Manufacturing Machines

Stanford R. Ovshinsky and Masat Izu

Energy Conversion Devices, Inc., 2956 Waterview Drive, Rochester Hills, Michigan 48309; email: mizu@ovonic.com

Abstract: Energy Conversion Devices, Inc. (ECD Ovonics) is building a new a-Si thin film PV plant, which is a clone of the existing 25/30 MW United Solar Ovonic plant with improvements. The plant, which will be built in Auburn Hills, Michigan, for United Solar Ovonic, will be completed and commissioned for production in 2006. The proprietary production machines have been developed, engineered, and constructed by ECD Ovonics' Production Technology and Machine-Building Division (Machine Division). The machines are automated and designed to produce large, flexible rooftop PV modules that use triple-junction triple-bandgap a-Si alloy solar cells produced on stainless steel. When planned improvements are incorporated into the production line, the plant is expected to produce 30 MW PV modules per year with a module efficiency above 9%

Key Words: Amorphous Silicon, Roll-to-Roll PV Manufacturing, Building Integrated PV (BIPV), Flexible PV Modules

1 Introduction

Photovoltaic (PV) energy generation is one of the fastest growing industries in the world. The ECD Ovonics proprietary multi-junction, triple-bandgap, continuous web, thin-film technology is the ultimate solution for PV energy production [1]. ECD Ovonics, through its wholly owned subsidiary, United Solar Ovonic, has set a new standard for PV products. Compared to traditional crystalline PV, ECD Ovonics' thin-film PV can provide more overall energy since its triple-bandgap technology can capture up to 30% more per rated watt. Our proprietary photovoltaics, manufactured by the miles, are:

- lighter,
- more durable, and
- more attractive (Figs. 4-5) than crystalline products.

In addition, our PV products can be produced in high volume from abundant and affordable raw materials. ECD Ovonics' roll-to-roll process is a most cost-effective process for high-volume production [2].

The United Solar Ovonic flexible thin-film photovoltaic material is made on proprietary high-output, football field-sized roll-to-roll machines (Fig. 2) developed by ECD Ovonics' Machine Division. The Machine Division

- has developed, designed, built, installed, started-up, and optimized the latest United Solar Ovonic roll-to-roll PV production plant;
- has over 25 years PV technology experience from R&D and pilot-scale to large-scale automated manufacturing through eight generations of PV production equipment;
- develops, designs, and fabricates production equipment and pilot lines for all ECD technologies: hydrogen, battery, etc.; and
- has been chosen by General Electric to develop roll-to-roll manufacturing for OLED lighting products.

2 Specifications of Machines

Key specifications of the new 25/30 MW United Solar Ovonic PV production plant include:

- Annual Production Capacity: 25 MW (30 MW when fully optimized), or approximately 4 million ft^2/yr.
- Substrate: Rolls of 14 inch wide, 8500 foot long, 5 mil thick stainless steel (Fig. 3).
- Device Structure: Two layers of backreflector, nine layers of a-Si alloys, and a layer of ITO (Fig. 1).
- Real-time in-line device performance monitoring.
- Lamination: Tefzel/EVA polymer encapsulation.

3 Solar Cell Manufacturing Line

The Ovonic production line [3,4,5] includes a :

Roll-to-Roll Deposition Line consisting of a
- Washing Machine,
- Backreflector (BR) Deposition Machine,
- a-Si Alloy Deposition Machine, and an
- ITO Deposition Machine.

The Automated Module Assembly Line, includes a:
- Roll-to-Sheet Cutting Line,
- Cell Line,
- Interconnect Line,
- Lamination Line, and
- Finishing/Testing Line

4 ECD Ovonics Solar Cell Structure

Figure 1 shows the structure of the ECD Ovonics solar cell.

Grid		Grid
Transparent Conductive Oxide		Sputtering
P3	Nanocrystalline Si Alloy	PECVD
I3	a-Si	PECVD
N3	a-Si Alloy	PECVD
P2	Nanocrystalline Si Alloy	PECVD
I2	a-Si/Ge Alloy	PECVD
N2	a-Si Alloy	PECVD
P1	Nanocrystalline Silicon Alloy	PECVD
I1	a-Si/Ge Alloy	PECVD
N1	a-Si Alloy	PECVD
Textured Metal/ZnO Back-reflector		Sputtering
Stainless Steel Substrate		

Fig. 1. Structure of a-Si Solar Cells.

5 Diagnostic Systems for the Roll-To-Roll Machines

The online non-contacting diagnostic systems [6] for the Ovonic roll-to-roll processors are summarized in Table I.

Table I. Diagnostic Systems for 25/30 MW Line.

Processor	Diagnostic System	No.	Measurement
BR	Scatterometer	1	Specular/diffuse reflection
	Reflectometers	2	ZnO thickness
a-Si	Reflectometers	15	Thickness of each n-, i-, and p-layer
	PVCD	4	Component and device electrical properties
ITO	Film Conductivity	1	ITO conductivity
	Reflectometers	5	Film thickness/uniformity
	PVCD	1	Device electrical properties; degree of physical shunts

Fig. 2 .25/30 MW Ovonic Roll-to-Roll PV Manufacturing Machine

Fig 3.   Roll of a-Si solar cell material.

6 Acknowledgements

The authors thank Herb Ovshinsky and his group for many years of contributions in designing and constructing the ECD Ovonics production machines. Also, we would like to express our thanks to Dr. Scott Jones, Dr. Vin Cannella, Dr. Tim Ellison, Dr. Joe Doehler, and Dr. Hellmut Fritzsche along with their collaborators for contributing the design and technical specifications for the machine. We also express our gratitude to Dr. Subhendu Guha, Kevin Hoffman, Gary Didio, Jon Call, and Dr. Prem Nath for their assistance on this project.

Photo courtesy of
Grand Valley State University

Fig. 4. A United Solar Ovonic BIPV roofing system helps power Grand Valley State University's 22,500 ft^2 Michigan Alternative and Renewable Energy Center.

Fig. 5. United Solar Ovonic was chosen to provide a building-integrated photovoltaic roofing system for the Beijing New Capital Museum. *Photo courtesy of Beijing New Capital Museum.*

7 References

[1] S. R. Ovshinsky, *Proceedings of the International PVSEC-1*, 1988, p.577.

[2] M. Izu, S.R. Ovshinsky, SPIE Proc. 407 (1983) **42**.

[3] S. Guha, J. Yang, A. Banerjee, K. Hoffman, S. Sugiyama, S. Call, S.J. Jones, X. Deng, J. Doehler, M. Izu, H.C. Ovshinsky, *Proc. 26th IEEE PV Specialist Conference*, Anaheim, CA, 1997, p.607.

[4] S.R.Ovshinsky, R. Young, W. Czubatyj, X. Deng, Semiconductor with Ordered Clusters, U.S. Patent 5,103,284, April 7, 1992.

[5] S.R. Ovshinsky, S. Guha, C. Yang, X. Deng, S. Jones, Semiconductor Having Large Volume Fration of Intermediate Range Order Material, U.S. Patent 6,087,580, July 11, 2000.

[6] T. Ellison, Proc. 28th IEEE PV Specialist Conference, Anchorage, AK, 2000, p.732.

Appendix 5

Reprint Series
9 April 1993, Volume 260, pp. 176 - 181

SCIENCE

A Nickel Metal Hydride Battery for Electric Vehicles

S. R. Ovshinsky, M. A. Fetcenko, J. Ross

A Nickel Metal Hydride Battery for Electric Vehicles

S. R. Ovshinsky, M. A. Fetcenko, J. Ross

Widespread use of electric vehicles can have significant impact on urban air quality, national energy independence, and international balance of trade. An efficient battery is the key technological element to the development of practical electric vehicles. The science and technology of a nickel metal hydride battery, which stores hydrogen in the solid hydride phase and has high energy density, high power, long life, tolerance to abuse, a wide range of operating temperature, quick-charge capability, and totally sealed maintenance-free operation, is described. A broad range of multi-element metal hydride materials that use structural and compositional disorder on several scales of length has been engineered for use as the negative electrode in this battery. The battery operates at ambient temperature, is made of nontoxic materials, and is recyclable. Demonstration of the manufacturing technology has been achieved.

The interest in electrically powered vehicles extends nearly as far back as interest in vehicles powered by hydrocarbon fuels. Throughout this period, however, there has been a major technological barrier to the development of practical electric vehicles (EVs) that can compete in performance and cost with those that use internal combustion (IC) engines. This barrier has been the lack of an economical battery with sufficient energy density and other essential performance criteria. In this article, we describe the science and technology of a nickel metal hydride (NiMH) battery that will permit future EVs to replace IC-powered vehicles in many applications.

S. R. Ovshinsky and M. A. Fetcenko are at Energy Conversion Devices, Inc., 1675 West Maple Road, Troy, MI 48084. J. Ross is in the Chemistry Department, Stanford University, Palo Alto, CA 94305, and consultant to Energy Conversion Devices, Inc.

Recently, U.S. federal and state governments have been providing an impetus for the development of an EV industry through legislation aimed at increasing national energy independence and reducing the impact of automobile emissions on the environment. California has passed laws that demand that 2% of new cars sold in 1998 be emission-free, and this percentage is slated to grow to 10% by the year 2003; 12 eastern states are planning similar laws. A comprehensive energy bill passed by Congress contains a tax credit for EV buyers. This bill also requires state and federal governments to purchase alternative-fuel fleet vehicles, with the percentage of new, cleaner fuel vehicles growing to 90% by the year 2000. It is expected that EVs will make up an increasing portion of alternative fuel vehicles as the market grows.

There are several important advantages of EVs compared with IC-powered vehicles. First, EVs are emission-free: they produce no pollution during operation. This quality is particularly important in city centers where congested automobile traffic is the primary source of local air pollution. The overall unwanted emissions that result from combustion of fossil fuels for the generation of electricity are also far less per mile of EV travel than the emissions produced directly by a fossil fuel–powered car. This fact, discussed in detail in a study by the Electric Power Research Institute (EPRI) (1), results from the sophisticated emissions controls that can be used economically by large, efficient, central power-generation facilities. Second, the EPRI study also details how the primary energy efficiency of electric transportation can exceed the efficiency of gasoline-powered vehicles in many instances. For example, the study shows that electric-powered commercial fleet vans that are used in urban areas have a significant advantage in energy efficiency over their gasoline-powered counterparts, traveling about 1100 miles per barrel of oil consumed at the power plant compared with 620 miles per barrel of oil refined into gasoline. This difference results primarily from the higher energy efficiency of power plant combustion—approximately twice as high as combustion of gasoline in an IC engine in urban traffic. Third, conversion from cars directly powered by fossil fuel to ones powered by electricity can shift the choice of hydrocarbon fuels that are consumed in the United States from oil to coal and gas. This change could possibly reduce the oil imports and, consequently, reduce the U.S. trade imbalance and the strategic vulnerability of its energy supply. Photovoltaic and other renewable energy sources are also increasingly available to generate pollution-free electricity for EVs.

In response to the need to develop a practical battery for EVs, the U.S. federal government authorized the establishment of the U.S. Advanced Battery Consortium (USABC) in 1990. Under the aegis of the Department of Energy, USABC brings together Chrysler, Ford, General Motors (GM), and EPRI to sponsor research and development of EV batteries. Although energy density is one of the most important requirements for an EV battery system, USABC has identified a number of other battery criteria as necessary for the development of economically viable EVs (Table 1 provides the primary midterm goals of USABC). Ovonic Battery Company (OBC), a subsidiary of Energy Conversion Devices, has received the first contract from USABC toward the continued development and fabrication of the company's proprietary NiMH batteries and has agreed to establish EV battery production facilities.

In this article, we describe the science and technology of the Ovonic NiMH battery, with emphasis on the materials science aspects of the metal hydride (MH) electrode and their effect on battery performance (2). The MH electrode offers an important opportunity for materials engineering and optimization when compared with negative electrodes for other nickel-based battery systems. In these other systems, the negative electrode (Cd, Zn, or Fe) is typically fabricated from relatively pure elemental metals, and the oxidation-reduction reactions associated with battery charge and discharge convert the electrode back and forth between a metal and a metal oxide that is a poor electric conductor. This type of chemical reaction can be undesirable in a practical battery design because of accompanying changes in the physical properties of the electrode. Changes in the

mechanical integrity and surface morphology of the electrode as a result of dissolution and recrystallization and of its reduced electrical conductivity in the oxidized state are sources of many of the performance deficiencies in these systems.

The MH electrode, by contrast, uses a chemical reaction that reversibly incorporates hydrogen into a metal alloy. In this oxidation-reduction reaction both chemical states are metallic, and so electrical conductivity is high in both the charged and discharged states. Furthermore, the small size of the hydrogen atom allows it to enter the metal lattice during formation of the hydride (reduced) state with only about 10% volumetric expansion and without the changes in crystallography associated with oxidation and reduction of the Cd, Zn, or Fe electrodes.

In effect, the MH negative electrode can be regarded as a matrix for the chemical incorporation of the hydrogen atom. In the Ovonic NiMH battery, we have exploited the ability of this matrix to be engineered through the use of multi-element alloys, using compositional and structural disorder to produce materials with desirable battery properties.

Cell Reactions

The NiMH battery, which has a nominal voltage of 1.2 V, stores hydrogen as a reaction product in the solid hydride phase, unlike the nickel-hydrogen battery that stores hydrogen as a high-pressure gas. The negative electrode of a conventional NiMH battery consists of a hydrogen storage material (3–5) that can allow electrochemical storage and release of hydrogen during battery charge and discharge processes. The nickel hydroxide positive electrode (6–9) is electrochemically reversible between $Ni(OH)_2$ and nickel oxyhydroxide, usually

written as NiOOH. At both electrodes, oxidation-reduction reactions take place in an alkaline medium consisting of 30% by weight KOH in water. During charge, the $Ni(OH)_2$ electrode is oxidized and the MH electrode is reduced. As a result, water is separated into hydrogen and hydroxyl ions, with hydrogen reacting with the metal in the negative electrode to form MH. At the positive electrode, the hydroxyl ion reacts with the $Ni(OH)_2$ electrode to form NiOOH. This reaction results in a change in the Ni oxidation state from +2 to +3. The half-cell reactions on charge and discharge of the battery can be written as

$$M + H_2O + e^- \underset{Discharge}{\overset{Charge}{\rightleftarrows}} MH + OH^- \quad (1)$$

$$Ni(OH)_2 + \\ OH^- \underset{Discharge}{\overset{Charge}{\rightleftarrows}} NiOOH + H_2O + e^- \quad (2)$$

As a consequence of reactions 1 and 2, there is no net change in electrolyte quantity or concentration over the charge-discharge cycle. This result contrasts with other alkaline electrolyte systems such as NiCd where water is generated at both electrodes during charge and consumed at both electrodes during discharge. Although transient electrolyte concentration gradients can occur in the NiMH battery, its constant average concentration has the important consequences of good overall performance in gas recombination, kinetics, high- and low-temperature operation, and resistance to cycle-life limitations produced by corrosion and swelling.

Material Requirements

The MH materials used for an NiMH battery electrode must satisfy an extensive list of requirements. Above all, the amount of hydrogen that the MH material can absorb determines the electrochemical storage capacity of the electrode and, consequently, the energy storage capacity of the battery. It is desirable to have high electrode storage capacity that is electrochemically reversible. To ensure reversibility, an important aspect of the MH design is the range of metal-to-hydrogen bond strengths, which must be about 6 to 12 kcal mol^{-1}. If the bond strength is too weak, hydrogen will not react with the alloys and will be evolved as a gas. If the bond strength is too large, the MH electrode is extensively oxidized and does not store hydrogen reversibly.

Even with an optimally adjusted metal-hydrogen bond strength, the problem of electrode oxidation in the MH battery

Table 1. Primary USABC midterm performance goals for the EV battery and actual performance of the current OBC NiMH battery. DOD, depth of discharge.

Property	USABC	OBC
Specific energy (Wh kg^{-1})	80 (100 desired)	80*
Energy density (Wh per liter)	135	215*
Power density (W per liter)	250	470
Specific power (W kg^{-1}) (80% DOD in 30 s)	150 (>200 desired)	175
Cycle life (cycles) (80% DOD)	600	1000
Life (years)	5	10
Environmental operating temperature	−30° to 65°C	−30° to 60°C
Recharge time	<6 hours	15 min (60%) <1 hour (100%)
Self discharge	<15% in 48 hours	<10% in 48 hours
Ultimate projected price (dollars per kWh) (10,000 units at 40 kWh)	<$150	$200

*A specific energy of 80 Wh kg^{-1} and an energy density of 215 Wh per liter have been achieved in a laboratory prototype, with 50-Ah cells under a discharge rate at which the battery energy capacity is exhausted in 3 hours.

remains. The NiMH battery operates in a strongly oxidizing medium composed of a high-concentration alkaline electrolyte. Because many chemical elements react to form oxides in an alkaline electrolyte, it follows that if these elements are used as electrodes, they will oxidize and fail to store hydrogen reversibly. In addition, MH electrodes are typically designed for use in totally sealed batteries where oxygen recombination occurs at their surfaces. In this aggressively oxidizing environment, oxidation and corrosion resistance of MH electrode materials is critical. Because some oxidation at the metal-electrolyte interface is inevitable and because both passivation and corrosion can have adverse effects on battery performance, these unwanted processes must be controlled in a practical NiMH electrode design.

Another consideration in the use of hydride materials in NiMH batteries relates to electrochemical kinetics and transport processes. The power output of the battery depends critically on these processes. During discharge, hydrogen stored in the bulk metal must be brought to the electrode surface by diffusion. The hydrogen must then react with hydroxyl ions at the metal-electrolyte interface. As a consequence, surface properties such as oxide thickness, electrical conductivity, surface porosity and topology, surface area, and degree of catalytic activity affect the rate at which energy can be stored in and removed from the NiMH battery.

For the battery to operate as a sealed system, it must also tolerate the consequences of chemical reactions that occur during cell overcharge and overdischarge. In overcharge, oxygen gas is generated at the $Ni(OH)_2$-positive electrode and must recombine with hydrogen at the MH electrode to form water. In overdischarge, which occurs when a low-capacity cell in a series-connected string is subjected to reverse polarity, hydrogen is generated at the $Ni(OH)_2$ electrode and must be recombined at the surface of the MH electrode to form water. In a sealed system, these gas recombination reactions must occur at sufficient rates to avoid pressure buildup. This condition requires adequate electrode area, a thin electrolyte film, and, for the hydrogen absorption process, catalytic activity at the MH electrode surface to promote rapid dissociation of hydrogen.

Chemical and Structural Disorder in Engineered Materials

The diverse properties required for a superior MH battery electrode can be attained by the engineering of new hydrogen storage materials on the basis of the concepts of structural and compositional disorder (2, 10–13). Compositional and structural disorder is designed into the new MH materials on three different length scales through the use of elemental composition and processing techniques of alloys and electrodes. The length scales over which disorder is created can be designated: local (or atomic), which comprises regions with dimensions up to a few nearest-neighbor atomic distances; intermediate range, which comprises regions typically about 10 to 20 nm and extending up to about 100 nm; and long range, which involves regions with a dimension larger than 100 nm. Disorder on each of these length scales is used to achieve different goals in the engineered alloys.

This approach allows one to consider a range of alloys for electrode materials containing elements that, if used alone, would be unacceptable for thermodynamic reasons, in particular oxidation or corrosion. Among the elements that become available for alloy formation in disordered electrode materials are Li, C, Mg, Al, Si, Ca, Ti, V, Cr, Mn, Fe, Co, Ni, Cu, Y, Zr, Nb, Mo, Sn, La, W, and Re. The list contains elements that can increase the number of hydrogen atoms stored per metal atom (Mg, Ti, V, Zr, Nb, and La). Other elements allow the adjustment of the metal-hydrogen bond strength (V, Mn, and Zr); provide catalytic properties to ensure sufficient charge and discharge reaction rates and gas recombination (Al, Mn, Co, Fe, and Ni); or impart desirable surface properties such as oxidation and corrosion resistance, improved porosity, and electronic and ionic conductivities (Cr, Mo, and W). The wide range of physical and chemical properties that can be produced in these alloys allows the MH battery performance to be optimized.

Compositional and structural disorder on a long-range length scale is used in the bulk of Ovonic MH alloys to give considerably higher hydrogen storage and better kinetics than possible in the conventional MH alloy structures, which are compositionally ordered and crystalline. The processing of disordered alloys can be optimized to produce polycrystalline, compositionally multiphase material. Figure 1 shows a scanning electron micrograph of a representative bulk region of a typical V, Ti, Zr, Ni, and Cr Ovonic MH alloy. Electron backscattering imaging was used to produce visual contrast between regions of the alloy that have different elemental compositions. This material contains five major distinct compositional phases as determined by energy-dispersive x-ray analysis. In addition, it has been determined separately by x-ray diffraction that the alloy contains three crystal structures: body-centered-cubic (bcc), hexagonal, and ^{14}C Laves crystal structures. From synthesis and characterization of separate, individual phases of a particular alloy, we conclude that the bcc structure can react to store large quantities of hydrogen (2.5% by weight) but lacks sufficient catalytic activity to be discharged at the required rates for battery applications. On the other hand, surrounding phases that may store less hydrogen but exhibit greater catalytic activity can effectively "channel" the hydrogen for rapid electrochemical discharge (12).

Intermediate-range structural and chemical disorder plays a number of important roles, primarily at interfaces both within the bulk of the MH electrode and at the electrode-electrolyte interface. Formation of the polycrystalline, compositionally multiphase bulk alloy gives rise to a high density of grain boundaries between com-

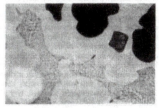

Fig. 1. Scanning electron micrograph of a bulk region of an Ovonic MH battery electrode that shows compositionally and structurally disordered multiphase alloy regions. Scale bar, 10 μm.

Fig. 2. Scanning transmission electron micrograph of the metal-electrolyte interface of an Ovonic MH battery electrode that shows the structure of the engineered multiphase bulk alloy and surface oxide.

positional and structural phases (for example, Fig. 1). The intermediate-range disorder that occurs at the grain boundaries increases surface area, which can greatly increase the density of catalytic sites. At the electrode-electrolyte interface, disorder on a length scale of approximately 10 to 100 nm is created during electrode processing and activation by the exploitation of chemical properties that are traceable to the elemental constituents of the MH alloy. The high-magnification scanning transmission electron micrograph of the electrode-electrolyte interface in Fig. 2 shows the presence of disorder on all three length scales but is particularly useful in illustrating the intermediate-range structural and compositional disorder that occurs in the engineered oxide layer that forms on the Ovonic MH electrode.

The basic Ovonic MH electrode typically contains elements such as V, Ti, Zr, Ni, and Cr. Although the alloy is a system with many characteristics, such as MH bond strength that depend on interactions among the elemental constituents, some alloy properties are influenced by the chemistry of individual components. The primary role of V, Ti, and Zr in the alloy is hydrogen storage. All three elements, rather than just the least expensive (Ti), are used in the alloy for several reasons. Titanium and Zr form thick, dense, passive oxides in alkaline solutions, whereas V forms soluble oxides. These chemical characteristics are used in the preparation of the Ovonic MH electrode during the electrochemical activation step in which soluble oxides are intentionally corroded to produce intermediate-range structural disorder. This change

gives rise to increased electrode surface area and microporosity and thereby increases charge acceptance. Chromium is used to limit the unrestrained corrosion of V and to control the alloy microstructure.

Zirconium contributes the important property of controlled hydrogen embrittlement, which leads to high surface area and, hence, to fast cell reactions. However, because excessive embrittlement can produce mechanical disintegration of the electrode that leads to poor electrical conductivity, high polarization, and low charge-recharge cycle life, one must control this property carefully in designing the electrode alloy.

Nickel serves several functions in the alloy. First, NiH has a weak bond strength. The bond strengths of elemental Ti, Zr, and V with hydrogen are too high for electrochemical applications. However, formation of alloys from these elements in various concentrations with Ni allows control of the alloy bond strength as was discussed earlier. Second, Ni is a catalyst for dissociation of H_2 and subsequent absorption of atomic H into the alloy. Third, Ni is resistant to oxidation. The combination of Ni with Zr, V, and Ti makes the alloy more resistant to oxidation and produces oxide films at the electrode-electrolyte interface that contain regions of metallic Ni. These regions help provide the necessary electrical conductivity and catalytic activity in the oxide film. The interface is characterized by a heterogeneous oxide region (Fig. 2) rather than a sharply defined homogeneous oxide film. We believe that this disordered oxide region is microporous and contains electrically conductive Ni regions that can catalyze the electrochemical discharge reaction (14).

Compositional disorder on the atomic scale is used to increase hydrogen storage capacity and improve catalytic activity

through the incorporation into the MH alloy of elements that generate new chemically active sites. These sites offer an increased variety of hydrogen bonding possibilities and enhanced rates as a result of increased catalysis. Incorporation of elements with multidirectional d orbitals increases the range of stereochemical possibilities for bonding hydrogen, as confirmed by the increased amount of hydrogen absorbed and by increased catalytic activity. These effects also occur to a lesser extent with elements containing f orbitals that extend in still more directions than d orbitals but that are closer to the nucleus of the metal atom and, therefore, are less accessible.

Local compositional disorder is also used to adjust the metal-hydrogen bond strength in the MH alloy. Measurements of equilibrium hydrogen pressure versus MH hydrogen concentration at 30°C are shown in Fig. 3 for a series of multicomponent MH alloys in which the ratio of V to Zr is systematically varied. The equilibrium hydrogen pressure, p, in these measurements is related to the change in Gibbs free energy, ΔG, which occurs for the reaction between gaseous hydrogen and the hydrogen storage alloy to form MH. This value can be written:

$$\Delta G = \Delta H - T\Delta S = RT \ln p \quad (3)$$

Because the entropy term, $T\Delta S$, is small at room temperature compared with the enthalpy change, ΔH largely determines ΔG. Thus, determination of p provides a measure of ΔH, which is related to the metal-hydrogen bond strength. In Fig. 3, variations in the ratio of V to Zr give rise to the observed changes in p for a given hydrogen concentration in the MH alloy. This result indicates that these compositional variations have changed the metal-hydrogen bond strength.

Status of the Ovonic Battery

The storage capacity of current and future Ovonic MH electrodes is shown in Fig. 4, along with the storage capacity of current and improved conventional LaNi₅, or "misch-metal," MH electrodes. The latter materials are frequently referred to as misch metal because they are traditionally made from a mixture of naturally occurring rare-earth elements that can include Ce, La, Nd, and Pr. The data for current electrodes were obtained from electrochemical half-cell measurements of commercial Ovonic and misch-metal battery electrodes, as described in (11). Data for projected misch-metal electrodes are from (15) and are based on electrochemical half-cell measurements of prototype materials. Data for projected Ovonic MH electrodes are based on electrochemical measurements of advanced laboratory thin-film materials.

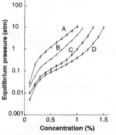

Fig. 3. Equilibrium hydrogen pressure versus hydrogen concentration (percent by weight) at 30°C for a series of Ovonic MH electrode alloys. Data show how variation in alloy composition may be used to control metal-hydrogen bond strength. The MH alloy compositions shown here, expressed as atomic percent, are (**A**) $(V_{21}Ti_{15}Zr_{15}Ni_{31}Cr_6Co_6Fe_6)$, (**B**) $(V_{15}Ti_{15}Zr_{21}Ni_{31}Cr_6Co_6Fe_6)$, (**C**) $(V_{18}Ti_{15}Zr_{18}Ni_{31}Cr_6Co_6Fe_6)$, and (**D**) $(V_{15}Ti_{15}Zr_{20}Ni_{28}Cr_5Co_5Fe_8Mn_6)$.

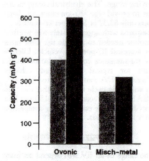

Fig. 4. Comparison of the charge storage capacity of present (shaded bars) and projected (solid bars) Ovonic MH battery and misch-metal (LaNi₅) electrodes.

The USABC contract contains three main program goals: a scale-up from small portable cells (1 to 5 Ah) to large EV cells (50 to 250 Ah), an increase in energy density from 56 to 80 Wh kg^{-1}, and the construction of series-connected battery modules to produce the voltages required for EV propulsion (180 to 320 V). The performance capabilities of the present Ovonic NiMH technology are shown in the second column of Table 1. To a large extent, prototype batteries of several designs and sizes have demonstrated performance characteristics that satisfy or exceed individual USABC midterm goals shown in the first column. Efforts to optimize all performance characteristics within a particular cell design are an ongoing activity. Another program objective, scale-up of cell size, has also been achieved. The ability to manufacture batteries with this technology has been demonstrated by OBC and several of its licensees who have been producing small portable batteries since 1987. Series-connected battery modules up to 40 V have been constructed by OBC and are under test. A 12-V, 3-kWh module is shown in Fig. 5.

Comparison with Other Candidates for EV Batteries

Battery characteristics have a dominant influence on overall EV performance. For example, battery-specific energy (in watt-hours per kilogram) controls vehicle range. Similarly, battery power (in watts per kilogram) translates into vehicle acceleration. The Bertone Blitz, a high-performance prototype EV sports car (16), has achieved an impressive acceleration of 0 to 100 km per hour (0 to 62 miles per hour) in 6 s, in part through the use of Ni-Cd batteries with high peak power. Some candidate battery technologies for EV applications are listed in Fig. 6, which shows a comparison plot of peak power versus depth of discharge. These measurements were made independently at Argonne National Laboratories (17). High peak power (>150 W kg^{-1}), as required by the USABC goals shown in Table 1, must be maintained over the entire depth of discharge of the battery for satisfactory vehicle performance. The Ovonic NiMH battery provides the highest peak power and can maintain it over almost the full range of discharge.

Although Ni-Cd is a rechargeable battery technology with high peak power that is extensively used in consumer products such as electronic devices and power tools, its energy density does not meet USABC requirements, it uses toxic materials (Cd), and in the large sizes used for EVs, it is not a totally sealed system.

The Na-S battery has a high energy density, but its low peak power is a significant deficiency. In addition, the operating temperature of the battery is approximately 300°C, which must be maintained at all times because the battery can withstand only a few cycles of cooling and heating. The presence of molten sodium and sulfur is potentially hazardous, and corrosion has limited the reliability and life of prototype batteries.

Of the remaining batteries shown in Fig. 6, only the Pb-acid battery has been tested sufficiently to serve as a practical, immediate candidate for EV applications. However, its typical energy density of 30 Wh kg^{-1} is substantially below USABC requirements, and its limited cycle life would force it to be replaced every 32,000 km (20,000 miles).

Long cycle life is a feature of the Ovonic NiMH battery technology that will have economic consequences for EVs. Over 1000 charge-discharge cycles at 100% depth of discharge have been demonstrated (13) with Ovonic batteries. Under conditions of 30% depth of discharge, Ovonic NiMH cells designed for aerospace applications have demonstrated (18) a lifetime of more than 10,000 cycles. It is expected that in EV applications, batteries will experience a typical depth of discharge of about 80%. Under these conditions the cycle life of the Ovonic NiMH battery is projected to be 2000 to 3000 cycles, according to a numerical model (18).

Battery cycle life can be converted into EV battery-life driving range when the characteristics of the EV are specified. For example, in a GM Impact-type vehicle, replacement of the Pb-acid battery with an Ovonic NiMH system of the same volume increases its range to 480 km (300 miles). For 80% depth of discharge [385 km (240 miles)], even a conservative estimate of 500 cycles for the battery life will give a 200,000-km (120,000-mile) battery-life driving range. The electrical energy necessary to provide the 385-km range per charge costs only $2.32 at $0.08 per kilowatt-hour, compared with approximately $14 worth of gasoline needed to provide the same range for a typical IC-powered vehicle. Lifetime EV maintenance costs will also be smaller than for typical IC-powered vehicles. Therefore, EVs that are powered by batteries with long cycle lives and that meet the USABC initial cost goal of $150 per kilowatt-hour can be economically competitive on a lifetime basis.

Technology Improvements

The range of an EV will depend on many factors besides battery energy density, such as vehicle weight, tire rolling friction, and electric motor efficiency. Information published by GM on its pioneering Impact

vehicle can be used to establish a benchmark for conversion of battery energy density to vehicle range (19) for EVs of this type. The data from GM show that their vehicle will travel 180 km (113 miles) with a battery that stores 13.5 kWh. For a battery of the same weight, the current Ovonic NiMH technology will, therefore,

Fig. 5. A 3-kWh, 12-V series-connected Ovonic NiMH battery module and 250-Ah Ovonic NiMH single cell.

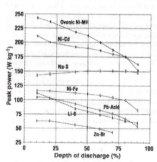

Fig. 6. Peak power versus depth of discharge, as measured (17) at Argonne National Laboratories, for a number of candidate EV battery technologies.

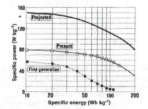

Fig. 7. Specific energy versus specific power for first-generation, present, and projected Ovonic NiMH batteries. Data shown for first-generation devices were obtained from 4-Ah "C" size cells; data for present devices were obtained from 50-Ah prismatic cells.

provide 31.6 kWh of energy storage, which will provide a vehicle range of 415 km (264 miles). For the same battery volume, the Ovonic NiMH battery will increase the range per charge to 480 km (300 miles). The environmental impact of eventual disposal of the Ovonic NiMH battery has also been studied (20). Knoll and colleagues concluded that, according to existing Environmental Protection Agency regulations, batteries that use this technology can be safely disposed of in landfills. It has also been shown (21) that with existing technology, Ovonic batteries can be recycled into metallurgical additives for cast iron, stainless steel, or new Ovonic NiMH battery electrodes. The commercial viability of each of these technologically feasible recycling programs will depend on process economics.

Future developments of Ovonic NiMH batteries will include improvements through the continued optimization of the MH materials and electrodes as well as improvements to the positive electrode and cell design (2). For example, some of the ongoing research at OBC focuses on application of the company's synthetic materials techniques to the development of an improved positive electrode with enhanced storage capacity through the use of engineered valence control. The chemical reaction that occurs during the charge of a conventional $Ni(OH)_2$ electrode involves transfer of one electron per Ni atom. We are developing materials that use the exchange of up to two electrons per atom. In addition, MH alloys with twice the storage capacity of first-generation materials have been measured in the laboratory, and cell designs in which lightweight substrates, current collection components, and containers are used are now being developed. Because the overall energy density of the battery is determined by the entire system, these combined approaches are targeted at the fabrication of batteries with both an energy storage density of 150 Wh kg^{-1} and the characteristics shown in Fig. 7.

Conclusion

In the development of the Ovonic NiMH battery, we have used aspects of physics, chemistry, metallurgy, and materials science. In particular, materials concepts (10–13) were focused on structural and compositional disorder to develop an NiMH battery with the characteristics necessary for practical EV use in the near, middle, and distant future.

REFERENCES AND NOTES

1. P. Jaret, *EPRI J.* 4, 4 (1992).
2. S. R. Ovshinsky and M. A. Fetcenko, U.S. Patent 5 135 589 (1992); 23 additional patents.

3. M. A. Gutjahr, H. Buchner, K. D. Beccu, H. Saufferer, in *Power Sources 4*, D. H. Collins, Ed. (Oriel, Newcastle upon Tyne, United Kingdom, 1973), p. 79.
4. A. Percheron-Guegen, U.S. Patent 4 107 405 (1978).
5. M. H. J. van Rijswick, in *Proceedings of the International Symposium on Hydrides for Energy Storage* (Pergamon, Oxford, 1978), p. 261.
6. G. Halpert, in *Proceedings of the Symposium on Nickel Hydroxide Electrodes*, Electrcchemical Society, Hollywood, FL, 16 to 18 October 1989 (Electrochemical Society, Pennington, NJ, 1990), pp. 3–17.
7. E. J. McHenry, *Electrochem. Technol.* 5, 275 (1967).
8. T. A. Edison, U.S. Patent 1 402 751 (1922).
9. S. U. Falk and A. J. Salkind, *Alkaline Storage Batteries* (Wiley, New York, 1969).
10. S. R. Ovshinsky, *J. Non-Cryst. Solids* 32, 17 (1979); for additional references, see S. R. Ovshinsky, *Disordered Materials: Science and Technology—Selected Papers*, D. Adler, B. B. Schwartz, M. Silver, Eds. (Institute for Amorphous Studies Series, Plenum, New York, ed. 2, 1991).
11. K. Sapru, B. Reichman, A. Reger, S. R. Ovshinsky, U.S. Patent 4 623 597 (1986).
12. M. A. Fetcenko, S. Venkatesan, K. C. Hong, B. Reichman, in *Proceedings of the 16th International Power Sources Symposium* (International Power Sources Committee, Surrey, United Kingdom, 1988), p. 411.
13. S. R. Ovshinsky, S. Venkatesan, M. Fetcenko, S. Dhar, in *Proceedings of the 24th International Symposium on Automotive Technology and Automation* (Automotive Automation, Croyden, United Kingdom, 1991), p. 29.
14. M. A. Fetcenko, S. Venkatesan, S. R. Ovshinsky, in *Proceedings of the Symposium on Hydrogen Storage Materials, Batteries, and Electrochemistry* (Electrochemical Society, Pennington, NJ, 1992), p. 141.
15. M. Tadokoro, K. Moriwaki, M. Nogami, T. Ise, N. Furakawa, in *ibid.*, p. 92.
16. L. Ciferri, *Autoweek* 1992, 14 (7 September 1992).
17. W. H. DeLuca, paper presented at the 1991 Annual Automotive Technology Development Contractors Coordination Meeting, Dearborn, MI, 24 October 1991.
18. B. Otzinger, in *Proceedings of the 6th Annual Battery Conference on Applications and Advances* (California State University, Long Beach, 1991).
19. *General Motors Electric Vehicles Progress Report* (summer 1992).
20. C. R. Knoll, S. M. Tuominen, J. R. Peterson, T. R. McQueary, in *Proceedings of Battery Waste Management Seminar*, S. Wolsky, Ed. (Ansum Enterprises, Deerfield Beach, FL, 1990).
21. C. R. Knoll, S. M. Tuominen, R. E. Walsh, J. R. Peterson, in *Proceedings of the 4th International Seminar on Battery Waste Management*, S. Wolsky, Ed. (Ansum Enterprises, Deerfield Beach, FL, 1991).
22. We thank the research staff at Energy Conversion Devices–OBC, particularly S. Venkatesan, for their contributions to the developments described in this article and S. J. Hudgens for his critical comments and helpful suggestions during preparation of the manuscript.

Appendix 6

04ANNUAL-606

A Hydrogen ICE Vehicle Powered by Ovonic Metal Hydride Storage

R. C. Young, B. Chao, Y. Li, V. Myasnikov, B. Huang and S. R. Ovshinsky

Texaco Ovonic Hydrogen Systems

ABSTRACT

Among the various alternative fuels, hydrogen is the only fuel, which is clean and sustainable. More importantly, if hydrogen is produced from renewable resources, virtually no CO_2 emissions are produced.

Texaco Ovonic Hydrogen Systems (TOHS) has converted a gasoline internal combustion engine (ICE) hybrid vehicle to a hydrogen vehicle using its advanced metal hydride storage. Compared to its gasoline counterpart, the converted vehicle demonstrated a reduction in CO_2 tailpipe emission of 220 grams per mile.

Ovonic metal hydride hydrogen storage systems consist of three critical elements: (1) an advanced metal hydride alloy, (2) an efficient heat exchanger and (3) a lightweight fiber wrapped pressure container. A 50 liter Ovonic metal hydride storage vessel installed in the vehicle provides a storage capacity of 3 kg hydrogen and a driving range of 130-150 miles.

BACKGROUND

Because of continuing growth in transportation energy demand, growing awareness of energy security, climate change, air pollution, and dwindling fossil fuel reserves, it is critical to identify a transitional path of adopting hydrogen as the transportation fuel of the future. Hydrogen can be generated from a variety of sources such as from coal, natural gas and from wind, solar, hydroelectric, etc. Although it would be most cost effective to generate hydrogen using fossil fuel sources in the short term, upstream greenhouse gas emissions can only be minimized if hydrogen is generated using renewable energy sources.

It is generally believed that it is no longer a question of *if* a hydrogen economy will come, but rather *when*. To pave the transition, a well-thought, well-planned hydrogen program targeted simultaneously to both hydrogen fueled vehicles and its supporting infrastructure will be crucial to a seamless transition. Attention should also be paid to minimizing well-to-wheels greenhouse gas emission. Ultimately, a cost effective renewable hydrogen generation and delivery system will have to be developed and implemented. In this paper, we will address the opportunity and challenge of adopting hydrogen as the transportation fuel and its impact on the tailpipe greenhouse gas emissions. The analysis of upstream greenhouse gas emissions is not included in the scope of this paper.

While hydrogen powered fuel cell vehicles would be the most desirable end goal, they are not quite ready to be a near term affordable solution. Hydrogen powered ICE vehicles could serve as a viable bridging technology option. These hydrogen vehicles, whether ICE or fuel cell, will share the same refueling infrastructure, adopt the same codes and standards, and provide the consumer with the same hydrogen safety awareness. A successful near term hydrogen ICE vehicle and supporting refueling demonstration can provide a positive impact in adopting hydrogen as a transportation fuel. It may even shorten the time frame for the commercialization of fuel cell vehicles, and the availability of a cost effective renewable hydrogen production.

In vehicle demonstrations, the safety aspect of fuel storage, the driving range and a user friendly refueling systems are of primary concerns. None of the hydrogen storage approaches employed in current OEM demonstration vehicles will meet these requirements. Each hydrogen storage approach has at least one major shortcoming: High-pressure (5000 psi) gaseous storage provides the limited driving range. Liquid hydrogen storage requires the handling of a cryogenic liquid. Use-once chemical storage (e.g. NaBH4) presents waste recycling challenges. Metal hydride onboard storage systems, even though it is heavier, are better able to satisfy these concerns than the aforementioned hydrogen storage methods.

Metal hydride onboard storage, due to its compactness, low pressure and safe operation, received much attention in the 70s and early 80s. (1). The first SAE paper with the concept of using metal hydrides as a fuel source for vehicle propulsion was presented by K.C. Hoffman et al as early as 1969. (2). However, many design challenges remain unresolved. For example the hydriding/dehydriding process is accompanied by the volume expansion and contraction, which not only decrepitates the coarse particles into fine powder, but also causes powder settling and vessel swelling. (3). Furthermore, because FeTi type of alloys were predominantly used in the early systems, material

issues, such as limited pressure tailorability, capacity degradation with cycles, were encountered. (4). To be practical, much more development was needed.

Unfortunately, the quest of using hydrogen as a transportation fuel and the research required to develop a better metal hydride onboard system declined and eventually reached a low in the early 80s. However, upon entering into the 21st century, the urgency of energy security and the awareness of climate change resulted in new national and worldwide hydrogen initiative once again. (5).

To pave the transition, ChevronTexaco and Energy Conversion Devices (ECD Ovonics) formed a joint venture in 2000 called Texaco Ovonic Hydrogen Systems, LLC (TOHS). Its mission is to develop and to advance solid hydrogen storage systems for portable power, stationary and onboard applications. In this paper, we report the advancement of the metal hydride onboard vessels made by TOHS. A vessel has been integrated into a converted hydrogen ICE hybrid vehicle. The heat integration and vehicle fuel economy and tailpipe emissions are measured. As anticipated, the greenhouse emission is virtually eliminated.

ONBOARD STORAGE CHALLENGES

Hydrogen has the highest heat of combustion among all fuels; 33.3 kWh per kg of H_2 vs 12.2 kWh per kg of gasoline. However, hydrogen, the lightest gaseous fuel, is very difficult to compactly contain. Under ambient temperature (20 ºC) and 1 atm pressure, one gallon (~ 3.8 liters) of hydrogen provides 0.011 kWh of energy; whereas 1 gallon of gasoline provides 33.6 kWh of energy. (Note: the energy content of 1 kg H_2 is equivalent to 1 gallon of gasoline).

To store sufficient amounts of hydrogen to provide a driving range of over 300 miles within the space and weight limitations of a passenger vehicle remains a major technological challenge. In the near term, it will be very difficult for hydrogen powered vehicles to compete with gasoline ICE vehicles in terms of convenience in refueling, driving range, and affordability. Adopting hydrogen as a transportation fuel will require a strong resolve and leadership not only from federal, state, and local governments, but also from automotive OEMs and energy companies.

SOLID HYDROGEN STORAGE

To date, compressed hydrogen has been used in most hydrogen demonstration vehicles, even though it is generally believed that solid hydrogen storage holds the key to the long-term solution. In this section, we will first give a brief review of solid hydrogen storage. We will then discuss various solid hydrogen onboard storage options. Finally, we will discuss the requirements of solid hydrogen storage systems.

SOLID HYDROGEN STORAGE. As the name implies, solid hydrogen storage is hydrogen stored in solid materials, in which hydrogen can be either physically adsorbed or chemisorbed to the solid.

Physical Adsorption. Hydrogen stored in activated carbon is a good example of physical adsorption. Here, molecular hydrogen is adsorbed to the high surface area of carbon by the weakly bonded Van der Waal force. Reducing temperature or increasing pressure dramatically increases the storage capacity of physical adsorption. It is also called cryoadsorption because H_2 is in a condensed form at cryogenic temperatures (77 °K). (6). Because of the high surface area required for storage, the volumetric energy density is not much better than compressed hydrogen storage. Activated carbon hydrogen storage has been known for many years. No practical onboard storage system has been demonstrated.

More recently, many investigators have focused on hydrogen in carbon nano-tubes or other nano forms of carbons. (7). However, complicated processing techniques and small quantities of inconsistent samples have resulted in a wide spectra of non-reproducible results. (8).

Chemical Absorption. Hydrides, in which atomic hydrogen is chemically bonded to the host elements, are typical examples of chemical absorption. Depending on the nature of chemical bonding and its bond strength, the hydride reaction can be either reversible or irreversible. Generally speaking, metallic and some of the ionic bonded hydrides are reversible, while covalently bonded substances are irreversible. For example, the ionic bonded MgH_2 and the metallic bonded $FeTiH_2$, $LaNi_5H_6$ are reversible; whereas the covalently bonded substances such as CH_4 (Methane), C_3H_8 (Gasoline), and most of the chemical hydrides such as $NaBH_4$, $LiAlH_4$ are irreversible.

Irreversible fossil fuels such as methane and gasoline leave no by-product in the fuel tank as they are depleted. Instead, the by-products (CO, CO_2, NO_x, etc.) are released to the air causing air pollution and climate change. Chemical hydrides, such as $NaBH_4$ require by-product removal ($NaBO_2$) at each refilling, as well as, replenishing the fuel tank with new chemicals. Not only are the waste recycling and/or disposal processes very costly, but perhaps more importantly, chemical hydrides are not considered to be a sustainable fuel. Unless, an abundant, low cost chemical hydride can be reprocessed cost effectively, it would be unlikely to be developed as a realistic onboard storage solution.

SOLID HYDROGEN ONBOARD STORAGE SYSTEM. Ultimately, a solid hydrogen onboard system should be reversible and have refilling characteristics similar to today's gasoline. Among the reversible solid hydrogen storage options, metal hydrides are the only solid

hydrogen storage medium, which can be realistically demonstrated in a vehicle today. In this sub-section, we will give a brief description of metal hydride onboard storage.

Metal hydrides are a broad class of materials that undergo a reversible reaction with hydrogen. The reaction is written as:

$$M_{solid} + x/2\ H_{2\ gas} \Leftrightarrow MH_{x\ solid} + heat$$

where M is the hydridable metal alloy, MH_x is the metal hydride and *heat* is the enthalpy of the reaction. The absorption reaction is exothermic - where heat is liberated; whereas the desorption reaction is endothermic - where heat is absorbed. A metal hydride system requires a delicate balance between heat transfer and hydrogen mass transfer. It is a self-regulated system. During absorption, if heat is not removed, absorption will automatically stop. During desorption, the hydrogen flow will stop if the heat supply is cut off. This self-regulating mechanism is another safety feature associated with metal hydrides.

Figure 1 shows a pressure, composition, temperature (PCT) diagram that represents a typical metal hydride system.

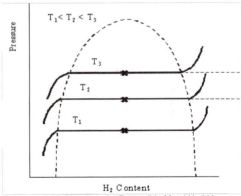

Figure 1. PCT Diagram of a Reversible Metal Hydride System.

Figure 1 depicts isotherms at three temperatures and shows the variation of the equilibrium pressure with the concentration of hydrogen in the metal alloy. The heat of formation and the entropy of a metal hydride can be derived from the PCT curves by means of the van't Hoff equation:

ln P = $\Delta H/RT$ - $\Delta S/R$; where ΔH is the enthalpy of the reaction or heat of formation, ΔS is the change of entropy and R is the gas constant.

At a given temperature, molecular hydrogen will first dissociate on the metal surface into atomic hydrogen, then dissolve in the metal alloy to form a solute solution. This is usually designated as the α phase. Hydride phase or the β phase, starts to grow, when the hydrogen reaches its solubility limit. The β phase formation is a nucleation and growth mechanism. During the β phase formation, the hydrogen pressure remains a flat plateau as more hydrogen is added. The α & β phases coexist in the plateau pressure region. The hydrogen pressure will rise sharply upon the completion of β phase formation. This phenomenon illustrated in Figure 2.

Pressure-Composition Isothermal Measurements: Determines Hydrogen Equilibrium Pressure at Various Temperatures

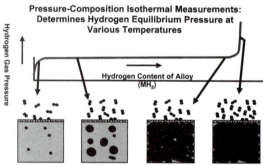

Figure 2.   The Nucleation and Growth Process of β Phase Formation.

Typically, at a given temperature and pressure, hydrogen content in the flat plateau region represents the usable hydrogen. In a metal hydride system, quite often, there is a slope in the plateau. Hydrogen stored in the low-pressure part of the plateau may not be able to release because of the insufficient amount of onboard waste heat. Therefore, a large difference between the total stored hydrogen and the usable hydrogen is observed, if the material is improperly designed.

Moreover, in the design of a metal hydride hydrogen storage system, special attention needs to be paid to issues such as, the volume expansion/contraction associated with the hydriding/dehydriding process, powder settling from powder decrepitation, insufficient heat transfer due to the poor thermal conductivity of hydride powders, etc.

In addition to the alloy and design challenges for onboard fuel storage, the system needs to satisfy the following criteria: lightweight, fast refueling, onboard waste heat for desorption, cycle stability, cold temperature start up, and durability.

TOHS METAL HYDRIDE ONBOARD SYSTEM

To satisfy these requirements, our efforts have focused on alloy design and selection, heat exchanger design, powder packaging, and lightweight pressure vessel selection.

ALLOY SELECTION. Over the years, Ovonic has developed a family of metal hydride alloys, from high temperature 7 wt% Mg alloys to low temperature multi-element intermetallic alloys.

In the selection of a particular alloy for onboard vehicle application, we first defined the type of waste heat available from the vehicle. For an ICE vehicle, there are two types of waste heat: the high temperature heat from the exhaust and the low temperature heat from engine-cooling loop. For a PEM fuel cell vehicle, there is no exhaust, the only available waste heat is from the fuel cell cooling loop. The heat of the cooling loop either from the engine or from the fuel cell stack is similar in temperatures, in the range of ~50-85 °C, only varies in its flow rate. To be versatile, our onboard vessel is designed to integrate with heat only from the cooling loop. In this case, low temperature metal hydrides (LTMH) were selected for onboard fuel storage.

Primary criteria in the selection of an appropriate LTMH are: (1) The alloy should be able to provide the highest usable hydrogen or to minimize the trapped hydrogen in the tank, and (2) The alloy would be able to release hydrogen to start the engine in cold weather without the engine heat supply.

Figure 3 shows the pressure-temperature tailorability of Ovonic LTMH. The appropriate alloy to be used in a particular vessel will depend on the required deliverable pressure to the fuel rail, the cold temperature start up requirement, and the maximum allowable filling pressure.

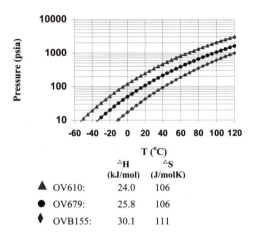

Figure 3. Pressure vs. Temperature of Ovonic alloys.

Figure 4 is the reversible capacity of the alloys as a function of the filling pressure. The measurement was done in a specially designed alloy-screening vessel with an active liquid heat exchanger. The sample size of the measurement was ~ 2 kg. The desorption was done with the water temperature of 85 °C.

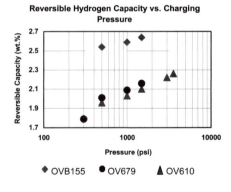

Figure 4. Reversible Hydrogen Capacity vs. Filling Pressure.

As can be seen from Figure 4, OVB155 has the highest reversible capacity of 2.6 wt% at 1500 psig . However, it will require 20 °C to provide the initial fuel to the engine at 30 psig. (See Figure 3). Due to its inability to provide cold temperature start up and other considerations,

OVB155 was not chosen for this prototype vehicle demonstration.

HEAT EXCHANGER. One of the most challenging issues associated with MH onboard storage is satisfying the fast refilling requirement. In order to accommodate fast refueling, a very efficient onboard heat exchanger as well as an off-board heat dissipation facility in the filling station are required. Figure 5 shows the average heat removal rate in kW as a function of refueling time for a 6 kg H_2 metal hydride vessel for an alloy with a heat of formation of 25 kJ/mol of H_2.

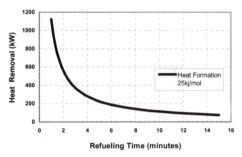

Figure 5. Filling Time vs. Heat Removal Rate (based on 90% of 6 kg hydrogen).

Because of the limited ΔT between the hydride bed and the cooling liquid, to facilitate the fast refueling, it is desirable to use a higher filling pressure. For example, with 20 °C cooling liquid, filling OV610 @ 500 psig, the hydride bed temperature will be about 40 °C (See Figure 3) which results a ΔT of 20 °C, whereas the ΔT will increase to 80 °C if 1500 psig is used for the refueling, which enhance the heat removal rate. For a given filling pressure, OV679, the lower plateau pressure alloy, will have a larger ΔT, than OV610, the higher plateau pressure alloy. However, other attributes of OV610 discussed below makes it a favorable alloy for vehicle applications.

To accommodate the fast refueling, we use a computer model to guide and to optimize the heat exchanger design. A mesh-less analytical model was developed to analyze the non-linear behavior of the metal hydride thermo-physical characteristics during hydrogen absorption. Based on the experimental PCT data and its heat of formation of a given alloy, this model calculates the heat generation and dissipation rate for a given heat exchanger geometry as a function of the filling pressure and coolant temperature. The initial conditions and boundary conditions were refined by comparison of the calculated and experimental kinetics data. Once these conditions were established, for a given heat exchanger geometry and coolant temperature, the simulation provided us with information of the filling time as a function of filling pressure.

Figure 6 is the hydrogen filling time (90% of the total capacity) as a function of the filling pressure of OV679 and OV610. The testing was done using a high-pressure stainless steel vessel with the same heat exchanger design as our current fiber wrapped onboard vessel. The cooling water was kept at 10 °C during the testing. Because of the higher bed temperature of OV679 compared to OV610 at a given filling pressure, OV679 provides a more efficient heat transfer and as a result, a faster refilling. Figure 6 shows the experimental data and the simulation. However, even though OV679 has a faster refilling time, OV610 has some desirable attributes from a vehicle integration and performance perspective. For example, the OV610 has a better cold temperature start up capability, can provide a sustainable hydrogen flow at a pressure higher than 150 psi, which is a condition required by some of the fuel cell vehicles. OV610 will also provide a better driving performance when the vessel is in the near empty condition. To further improve the refilling time of OV610, we need to either increase the filling pressure or improve the heat exchanger. An improved heat exchanger is currently under design, in which we will rearrange the geometry of the heat exchanger and double the surface area without compromising the system weight and volume. Based on the simulation, we predict that the refilling time of OV610 would be able to reduce from 14 minutes to about 6 minutes @1500psig filling pressure. We would like to point out that these experiments and simulations were conducted without the constraint of temperature rise during refilling.

THE LIGHTWEIGHT PRESSURE VESSEL. In order to reduce the weight of the vessel, we developed a proprietary technology to combine a lightweight fiber wrapped pressure vessel with our heat exchanger and liquid manifold. The fiber wrapped vessel was provided by Dynetek. The vessel with the heat exchanger and liquid manifold was hydrostatically pressure cycled between 290 psi and 4500 psi for 15,000 cycles without leakage. It was then hydrostatically burst. The burst pressure was 13,801 psi, which is above the minimum required burst pressure of 10,800 or 3 times the 3600 psi service pressure.

Figure 7 is an Ovonic prototype metal hydride onboard vessel. One end contains a hydrogen solenoid valve; the other end is the liquid inlet and outlet. The vessel has an internal volume of 50 liters with an external dimension of 32.8 cm OD and 84 cm in length.

Figure 7. Ovonic Prototype Metal Hydride Onboard Vessel.

Table 1 is a comparison chart of the metal hydride and compressed hydrogen using the same fiber wrapped vessel with an internal volume of 50 liters.

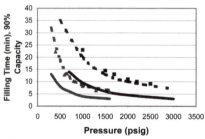

Experimental and Simulation, OV679
Experimental and Simulation, OV610
Adv. Heat Exchanger Simulation, OV679
Adv. Heat Exchanger Simulation, OV610

Figure 6. Refilling Time vs. Pressure. Coolant temperature 10 °C.

Table 1

	Metal Hydride@ 1500 psig	Compressed H_2 @ 3,600 psig
H_2 Capacity (kg)	3.0	0.88
Total weight (kg)	190	25.2
Weight %	1.58	3.49
Volume (g / liter)	60	17.6

THE PERFORMANCE OF AN OVONIC METAL HYDRIDE SYSTEM. The Testing Facility. A testing facility at ChevronTexaco's Richmond Technology Center (RTC) was designed and constructed to conduct performance and cycle life tests for Ovonic hydrogen storage vessels. Two test stands are in operation, each test stand is capable of controlling two vessels. Both systems are remotely controlled and operated.

Hydrogen flow rates of up to 15000 slpm and 1000 slpm can be monitored during absorption and desorption experiments, respectively. Other features include the recording of thermocouples and strain gauges attached to the vessels under investigation. Each of the test stands can provide up to 25 gal/min heating/cooling liquid (water-propylene glycol) between 8°C and 95°C. Figure 8 is a picture of the test stand.

Figure 8. The Test Stand.

A diaphragm compressor is available to supply hydrogen at pressures of up to 5500 psi, in addition to the RTC hydrogen supply at 3200 psi. The high-pressure storage capacity installed at the compressor is approximately 19 kg of hydrogen at 5500 psi. This storage unit is also used to recover and re-use hydrogen during long-term cycle life experiments.

The equipment was installed in accordance with RTC safety regulations and procedures. All pressurized parts are equipped with safety relief devices and pressure switches for emergency shut-down. Hydrogen and UV/IR detectors were installed in the test cells to trigger a safe shut off and to turn on the water sprinkler system in case of emergency.

The vessel was instrumented with ten strain gauges and eight thermocouples. The strain gauges were mounted on the aluminum liner underneath the carbon composite outer wrapping. Thermocouples were placed at coolant inlet and outlet locations, also at locations embedded in the metal hydride alloy and on the aluminum liner surface. The instrumented vessel was subjected to various absorption and desorption experiments. Because the glass transition temperature of the organic resin of the fiber wrapped vessel is about 110 °C, an e-stop was set at 85 °C on the liner during absorption testing.

Absorption Testing. Figure 9 shows an example of a hydrogen absorption experiment. The figure shows hydrogen delivery pressure, absorption capacity, metal hydride bed temperature (TC1) and aluminum liner surface temperature (TC6 ,) as functions of time. The flow rate of cooling liquid is about 20 gallons per minute (gpm) with the coolant temperature maintained at 8°C. The hydrogen delivery pressure was initially set at 1000 psig then ramped up to 1700 psig. The experiment ran for 20 minutes with a total storage capacity of 3 kg H_2, of which 2.7 kg or 90 % of the capacity was absorbed in 10 minutes.

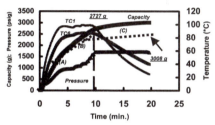

Figure 9. Absorption Experiment.

The capacity curve indicates that the filling process involves three stages, as marked (A), (B) and (C). The first stage (A) is characterized by a rapid hydrogen up-take, in which 1.5 kg of hydrogen is absorbed in the first 3 minutes. This rapid absorption is primarily due to the presence of a large heat sink from the heat capacity of the MH alloy. As can be seen from Figure 9, the rapid reaction during this stage is also accompanied by a rapid rise in both temperature and pressure.

During the second stage (B), an additional 1.2 kg of hydrogen is absorbed in about 7 minutes. The temperatures are kept fairly constant so that the heat generation and heat removal rate remain in balance. The duration of this stage is largely dictated by the effectiveness of the heat exchanger. In this particular experiment, a total of 2.7 kg H2 is absorbed by in the end of the second stage (approximately 10 minutes).

The third stage (C) is the end of the process, where the hydride vessel pressure approaches the delivery pressure. As a result, the hydrogen flow rate and the hydride growth rate are dramatically reduced. It takes an additional 10 minutes to absorb the remaining 300 g of hydrogen . During this stage, the vessel temperature starts to decline because the reaction slows.

Figure 10 illustrates the relationship between the strain and the absorption capacity. The data shows that at 90% of the total absorbed capacity or 2.7 kg H_2, the strain is ~ 1200 $\mu\varepsilon$, which is 33% of the allowable strain. The figure also shows that the strain rapidly increases as hydrogen is further absorbed into the vessel. The strain value is more than double for the last 0.3 kg H_2. Nevertheless, the 3000 $\mu\varepsilon$ measured at the completion of absorption remains below the maximum allowable working limit of 3600 $\mu\varepsilon$. The initial negative strain and the sharp rise of strain value observed in the last 10% of the absorption are currently under more detailed investigation.

One of the advantages of metal hydride hydrogen storage is the low pressure operation. Even though, the filling pressure is about 1500-1700 psi, the vessel operates at below 200 psi most of the time. Figure 12 shows the internal pressure of the metal hydride vessel at two different liquid inlet temperatures as a function of % of H_2 remaining in the vessel. For comparison, a 5000 psi compressed H_2 vessel is included in the graph. As can be seen from the graph, the pressure of the metal hydride vessel quickly decreases from the initial refilling pressure to below 200 psig, whereas, the pressure of the compressed H_2 vessel remains above 200 psi until almost empty.

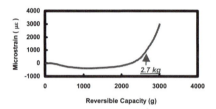

Figure 10. Microstrain During Absorption.

Desorption Testing. Figure 11 is an example of desorption experiment, which includes hydrogen flow rate, desorption capacity , internal vessel pressure, liquid inlet temperature (TC1) as functions of discharge time. The liquid temperature (TC1) was maintained at 75°C during the desorption experiment. The desorption flow rate is controlled @ 350 slpm (31.25 g/min) for approximately 90 minutes or 2.8 kg hydrogen. For a hydrogen ICE hybrid vehicle, a hydrogen flow in the range 17-300 slpm at 30 psi pressure is required. In this case, the vehicle can continue to run until the vessel is almost empty.

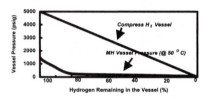

Figure 12. Vessel Pressures, MH vs. 5000 psi Compressed H_2 Vessel, as a Function of % of H_2 Remaining.

FROM LABORATORY TO REAL WORLD

Figure 13 shows a fully instrumented onboard vessel under laboratory testing, in which a chiller is used for cooling liquid for absorption and heat is provided from an electrical liquid heater for desorption.

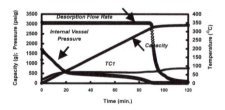

Figure 11. Desorption Data Recorded from an Ovonic MH On-board Hydrogen Storage Vessel.

Figure 13. Fully Instrumented Metal Hydride Onboard Hydrogen Storage Vessel.

Figure 14 shows the vessel installed into the trunk of an ICE hybrid vehicle (2002 Toyota Prius). The waste heat from the engine cooling loop through a liquid-liquid heat exchanger provides the heat for releasing hydrogen and feeding into the engine. Re-circulated water from an off-board water tank is used for heat removal during refilling. Details of vehicle integration and its performance data will be presented in a separate paper at this conference (9).

Figure 14. Metal Hydride Onboard Hydrogen Storage Vessel Installed in Converted H_2 ICE Hybrid Vehicle.

An onboard data logging system is installed in the vehicle, which automatically records data when the engine starts. In order to study transient response, data is recorded in one-second intervals. The data logging system records the vessel pressure, liquid inlet temperatures to the vessel from the engine cooling loop, the liquid outlet temperature from the vessel to the circulation pump and the hydride bed temperature.

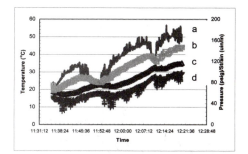

Figure 15. Sample Onboard Data Logged During a 45-Minute Drive.

Figure 15 shows a graph of the data during a 45 minute drive. When the engine starts, the hydride bed temperature is 18 °C, the inlet (a) and outlet (b) liquid temperatures are both about 20 °C, the pressure (d) is about 50 psi, and the vessel is about 1/3 full. At the end of the drive, the hydride bed temperature (c) has reached 34 °C, the liquid inlet/outlet temperatures are 52 °C and 44 °C respectively. The pressure rose to 110 psi and the liquid flow rate through the circulation pump is about 2.5 GPM.

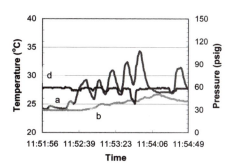

Figure 16. Onboard Data Logged During a 45-Minute Drive.

The spikes in the inlet temperature curve and the vessel pressure curve are an indication of the transient responses. An expanded section between the dotted lines of the figure is shown in Figure 16. The spikes of the inlet temperatures (a) are in good correlation with the pressure drop (d) with an approximate 10-second delay. The pressure drop in the vessel is caused by the acceleration of the engine. Since there is no temperature spike in the outlet (b), the extra engine heat is consumed by the metal hydride to provide a higher hydrogen flow into the engine. It is a self-regulating mechanism.

Figure 17 shows that the vehicle is driven with the vessel near empty. The hydride bed temperature (c) is maintained about 55 °C while the pressure steadily decreases (d). This indicates that the hydrogen in the metal hydride has reached the tail part of the PCT curve. Yet, the vehicle still functions well with good response.

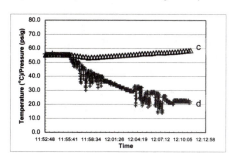

Figure 17. Onboard Vessel Data Logged with a Near Empty Vessel.

A driving range of 137 miles was demonstrated at 55 MPH constant speed with the vessel filled @1200 psi to about 2.7 kg H_2, which has the fuel economy similar to that of a fuel cell vehicle (9).

Table II shows the emission data of the hydrogen Prius vs. gasoline Prius. As can be seen from the table there is about 220 gram/mi CO_2 reduction and 0.385 gram/mi CO reduction in the hydrogen vehicle. The NO_x emission also meets the SULEV standard.

Tailpine Emissions, g/mi				
	NMOG	CO	NOx	CO₂
Hydrogen Prius With Prius Catalyst	0.001	0.001	0.018	3.2
Gasoline Prius	0.010	0.386	0.004	222.8
SULEV / PZEV standard	0.010	1.0	0.020	na

Table II. Emissions data.

Figure 18 shows the fueling port. The top connector is the hydrogen filling nozzle. The two bottom connectors are the cooling inlet and outlet. The small connector on the top left corner is a six pin electrical connector which is connected to the refilling dispenser. The electrical connector provides data such as bed temperature, tank pressure, strain, and hydrogen sensor readings during refilling for this prototype demonstration vehicle.

Figure 18. The Fueling Port.

Figure 19 is a portable refilling dispenser, which is designed to be connected to existing 5000 psi compressed hydrogen refilling stations. The dispenser, designed and constructed by TOHS to be user-friendly, will regulate the pressure down to the specified pressure for metal hydride refilling with a pre-programmed refilling algorithm.

Figure 19. Portable Low-Pressure Refilling Dispenser.

Because 5000 psi compressed H_2 vessels will not be able to provide vehicles with sufficient driving range, the DOE and some automotive OEMs are pushing toward the use of 10,000 psi vessels. To provide a vehicle with a driving range of 300 miles (assuming 50 miles per kg H_2), 6 kg H_2 will be needed. Table III is a comparison of a Ovonic metal hydride onboard vessel and a 10,000 psi vessel.

6 Kg H₂ Vessel		
	MH	10,000 psi compressed
Internal Vol (l)	100	153
Weight (kg)	375	171
Filling pressure (psi)	1500	12,500

Table III. Comparison of a Ovonic Metal Hydride Onboard Vessel and a 10,000 psi Vessel.

While a 6 kg H_2 storage system using an Ovonic metal hydride vessel will be 200 kg heavier in weight, it is 50 % less in volume. More importantly, its refilling pressure is 8 times less and its operational pressure is about 50-100 times less. Further, because low-pressure gaseous hydrogen is used, instead of liquid H_2 or 10,000 psi compressed H_2, a metal hydride system will also benefit from substantially simpler and lower fuel cost.

CONCLUSION

In this paper, we demonstrated that hydrogen hybrid ICE vehicle powered by metal hydride fuel storage system can virtually eliminate the CO_2 tailpipe emission. The NO_x level can also meet the SULUV standard. It would be an ideal bridging technology in the adapting of hydrogen as the transportation fuel.

Hydrogen onboard storage, however, presents the major technological challenge. The storage system needs to be light in weight, compact in volume, safe in operation, low in fuel cost, fast and user friendly in its refilling operations.

While none of the current storage systems can meet all these requirements, with today's technology, an Ovonic metal hydride system's benefits such as long range, low fuel cost, safe low pressure operation etc. surpass the weight disadvantage. Our strategy is to work on and perfect today's technology while brainstorming and continuing the research on a much improved solid hydrogen storage system which will lead to a long-term hydrogen economy solution.

ACKNOWLEDGMENTS

We acknowledge Franz Gingl and Ming Wang for performing the vessel testing; Isaak Fidel, Nestor Kropelnyckyj, and Alexander Gerasimov for vessel design and assembly; Dick Geiss, Bruce Falls, and Alwin Lutz for vehicle conversion; Bob Stempel, Gene Nemanich and Greg Vesey for encouraging and supporting the project; and Angela Goddard for editing the manuscript.

REFERENCES

1. See for example, HYDROGEN POWER, by L.O. Williams, Pergamom Press Inc. New York, 1980. Turillon, P.P. " Design of Hydride Containers for Hydrogen Storages" in Proceedings of the 4th World Hydrogen Energy Conference, CA, USA. 13-17 June 1982, p. 1289.

2. Hoffman, K. C., Wische, W.E., Wiswall, R.H. , Reilly, J.J., Sheehan, T.V. and Waide, C.H. " Metal Hydrides as a Source of Fuel for Vehicular Propusion". SAE paper 690232 presented at the International Automotive Engineering Conference, Jan, 13-17, 1969, Detroit, USA.

3. Lynch, F.E. and Snape, E., "The Role of Metal Hydrides in Hydrogen Storage and Utilization" in Alternative Energy Sources, Vol. 3, p 1479. Veziorglu, T.N. Ed., Hemisphere Publishing, Washington D.C. 1978.

4. Strickland, G., "State-of-the-Art Summary of the Technical Problems Involved in the Storage of Hydrogen via Metal Hydrides" in Alternative Energy Sources, Vol. 8, p 3699. Veziorglu, T.N. Ed., Hemisphere Publishing, Washington D.C. 1978.

5. See for example; the DOE web site: www.eere.energy.gov/hydrogenandfuelcells/.

6. Noh, J. S. Agarwal, R. K. and Schwarz, J. A. " Hydrogen Storage System Using Activated Carbon" Int. J. Hydrogen Energy. Vol 12, p 693, 1987.

7. Dillon, A.C. etal. Hydrogen Storage in single-wall Carbon Nanotubes, 14th World Hydrogen Energy Conference, Montreal, Canada (June of 2002).

8. Schlapbach, L., Züttel, A. Hydrogen Storage Materials for Mobile Applications, Nature, Vol 414, 353 (2001).

9. Geiss, R., Webster, B., Ovshinsky, S.R., Stempel, R. Young, Li, Y., Myasnikov, V., Falls, B., Lutz, A., "Hydrogen-Fueled Hybrid: Pathway to a Hydrogen Economy". This conference.

CONTACT

Rosa C Young received her PhD in physics from Rensselaer Polytechnic Institute, Troy, New York. Prior to joining Energy Conversion Devices (ECD Ovonics) in 1984, she was a research staff member in the Solid State Division of Oak Ridge National Laboratory. Currently, she is the Vice President of Technology of Texaco Ovonic Hydrogen Systems; a joint venture between ChevronTexaco and ECD Ovonics. The venture's web address is: www.txohydrogen.com, her e-mail address is: ryoung@ovonic.com.

Appendix 7

Presented at the Hydrogen and Fuel Cells 2004 Conference and Trade Show
Toronto, Canada, September 2004

The Ovonic® Regenerative Fuel Cell, A Fundamentally New Approach

S. R. Ovshinsky, S. Venkatesan, D. A. Corrigan

Ovonic Fuel Cell Company
Rochester Hills, Michigan, USA

The Ovonic® Regenerative Fuel Cell utilizes Ovonic metal hydride materials in place of traditional noble metal catalysts in the hydrogen fuel electrode. This provides unique features including the ability to capture and utilize regenerative braking energy at high efficiency and the ability to operate for a significant period upon interruption of the hydrogen fuel supply. Additionally, this novel fuel cell does not use high price components, such as platinum catalysts, microporous membranes, and graphite bipolar plates, used in PEM fuel cells. Proof of concept has been demonstrated in full-size multicell prototypes delivering about 100 W power. The Ovonic® Regenerative Fuel Cell is yet another component of ECD Ovonic technology contributing to the emerging hydrogen economy which already includes Uni-Solar PV solar cells, Ovonic solid-state hydrogen storage devices, and Ovonic nickel-metal hydride batteries from Cobasys, a joint venture between ECD Ovonics and ChevronTexaco.

Introduction

The development of fuel cells has had a long history dating back to the basic discovery of Grove in 1839. The alkaline fuel cell (AFC) developed by F. T. Bacon in 1930 was the first practical device. Alkaline fuel cells with platinum electrodes were predominantly the system of choice for manned space applications by NASA since the time of Apollo [1]. They were also utilized in early demonstration programs for transportation applications such as the GM Electrovan [2].

Subsequent to the development of the AFC, other fuel cell types have been developed that utilize other electrolyte media [1,2] including the proton exchange membrane fuel cell (PEMFC), the phosphoric acid fuel cell (PAFC), the molten carbonate fuel cell (MCFC), and the solid oxide fuel cell (SOFC). Since 1990, the development of PEM fuel cells has received focused attention from the U.S. Department of Energy and the industries associated with fuel cell development [3]. Significant and substantial progress has been achieved, particularly in terms of power performance, where there are now claims of power performance around 1000 W/kg [3]. PEMFC systems have been developed and demonstrated in a variety of applications including automotive propulsion. Hurdles remain in meeting application life targets and particularly cost targets. High cost due to inherently high cost PEMFC materials are the main obstacle to commercialization. Life and cost issues have also retarded the commercial introduction of high temperature MCFC and SOFC technologies aimed at large stationary applications [4].

The Ovonic® Regenerative Fuel Cell is a fundamentally new approach to fuel cells that utilizes hydrogen storage technology such as Ovonic metal hydrides in the hydrogen electrode active material. This provides intrinsic energy storage functionality in the fuel cell stack, and unique performance attributes utilizing non-noble metal catalysts as a low cost approach. Attributes include instant start and the unique capability to store regenerative braking energy in the fuel cell stack also with excellent low temperature operation. Additionally, this new approach provides alternative reaction pathways to enable higher voltage operation with the potential for dramatic improvements in efficiency.

Ovonic Metal Hydride Technology

Our parent company, Energy Conversion Devices, Inc. (ECD Ovonics, see www.ovonic.com) has pioneered the development of metal hydride materials [5] and their subsequent commercialization into Nickel Metal-Hydride (NiMH) batteries [6] and solid state hydrogen storage devices [7]. NiMH consumer batteries are now a billion dollar a year business with billions of cells manufactured and sold annually under ECD Ovonics licenses. NiMH batteries have also become the battery of choice for the emerging electric and hybrid vehicle industries. Cobasys (see www.cobasys.com), a joint venture between ECD Ovonics and ChevronTexaco, is gearing up to be a volume manufacturer of large NiMH batteries for transportation and stationary applications. Rare Earth Ovonic Battery Company, a joint venture between ECD Ovonics and Inner Mongolia Baotou Steel Rare Earth High-Tech Holding Co., Ltd. in China, manufactures metal hydride materials for the global NiMH battery business.

Additionally, ECD Ovonics has developed novel solid state hydrogen storage technology applicable to several aspects of the emerging hydrogen economy [8]. ECD Ovonics has recently demonstrated the utilization of metal hydride storage systems to enable a hydrogen-powered Toyota Prius to achieve a range of 150 miles [9,10].

Most recently ECD Ovonics has developed a new fuel cell technology, the Ovonic$^{®}$ Regenerative Fuel Cell, which utilizes Ovonic metal hydride materials in the fuel cell anode. Ovonic Fuel Cell Company has been formed to commercialize this new technology.

The Ovonic$^{®}$ Regenerative Fuel Cell

The Ovonic$^{®}$ Regenerative Fuel Cell utilizes an anode active material having hydrogen storage capacity [11] and can also utilize a cathode active material having oxygen storage capacity [12-14]. This provides for a fuel cell with intrinsic energy storage functionality resulting in several unique and exceptional performance attributes. The Ovonic$^{®}$ Regenerative Fuel Cell concept can be utilized in conjunction with any ionic electrolyte type and thus the full variety of fuel cell technologies including AFC, PEMFC, PAFC, SOFC, and MCFC technologies. This is a fundamentally new concept that for the first time provides fuel cell stacks with intrinsic energy storage.

Our initial product direction utilizes alkaline electrolyte as shown in Fig. 1. This allows for the facile introduction of metal hydride materials developed for NiMH battery applications. These materials have already fully demonstrated their capability for high energy and high power with excellent durability in the alkaline environment. The choice of alkaline electrolyte also provides for better kinetics at the air cathode and enables the utilization of non-noble metal catalysts at this electrode as well. Finally, the utilization of alkaline electrolyte avoids the necessity of expensive membrane materials utilized in PEMFC technology. We are initially utilizing a circulating potassium hydroxide (KOH) electrolyte which minimizes the impact of carbon dioxide absorption and provides for an electrolyte replacement option to maximize life.

Additionally, the circulating electrolyte provides an excellent and very effective method for heat rejection needed in high power applications.

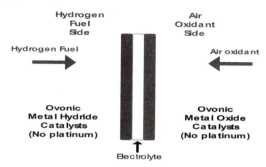

Fig.1   Schematic diagram of Ovonic® Regenerative Fuel Cell.

The energy storage functionality is provided by the metal hydride material in the anode which can be charged chemically from gas phase hydrogen or electrochemically from the oxidation of water. Additional energy storage functionality can be provided by proprietary metal oxide materials that can be oxidized chemically by oxygen or electrochemically. The energy storage functionality provides several key features including regenerative operation, instant start, and excellent low temperature performance.

Regenerative Operation

The most exceptional feature of the Ovonic® Regenerative Fuel Cell is the ability to store energy in the fuel cell stack in regenerative mode operation. This fuel cell can be run backwards and store energy within the fuel cell stack without resorting to the electrolysis of water to hydrogen and oxygen gases. Regenerative mode operation is illustrated in Fig. 2 showing charge-discharge operation.

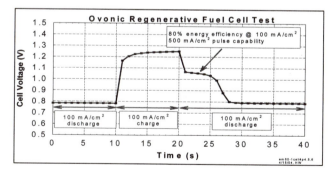

Fig. 2 Regenerative operation.

In Fig. 2, a fuel cell stack operated at 100 mA/cm^2 is interrupted by a 100 mA/cm^2 charge pulse. During the 10-second pulse, the cell voltage increased to about 1.25 V, indicating the storage of energy without the electrolysis of water. Upon return to discharge operation, the operational voltage was elevated from 0.8 V to over 1 V as a result of energy stored in the charge pulse. The charge-discharge energy efficiency is estimated to be about 80% under these operating conditions.

The elevated cell voltage during discharge subsequent to the charge pulse also indicates a high pulse capability. In a series of experiments, we found the pulse discharge capability was increased to over 500 mA/cm^2 when preceded by a 100 mA/cm^2 charge pulse. This is a very promising characteristic for applications requiring high pulse power capability, such as vehicle propulsion which requires pulse charge and discharge capability for braking and acceleration which normally alternate over time in automotive applications.

Our term "regenerative" in regenerative fuel cell refers in part to its ability to accept regenerative braking energy. The Ovonic® Regenerative Fuel Cell is not to be confused with the more "conventional" regenerative fuel cells that combine fuel cell and electrolyzer functions to store energy albeit with low efficiency in hydrogen and oxygen gases stored externally to the fuel cell stack. Our regenerative fuel cell provides for the high efficiency solid state storage of hydrogen in metal hydride materials internally in the fuel cell stack.

Instant Start Operation

Also as a consequence of the energy storage functionality, the Ovonic® Regenerative Fuel Cell provides for instant start operation on the order of microseconds as shown in Fig. 3. Cold start has been a development issue, not only for high temperature fuel cells such as PAFC, MCFC, and SOFC where hours can be required to reach operating temperatures, but even for lower temperature PEMFC systems which do not operate below freezing and require warming from room temperature to achieve rated power performance. In contrast, the Ovonic® Regenerative Fuel Cell provides excellent power instantly even at temperatures well below freezing.

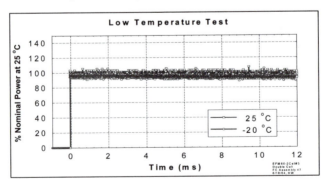

Fig. 3   Instant start operation at ambient and low temperatures.

Furthermore, other fuel cell types require the fuel cell anode to be in direct contact with hydrogen gas to generate power. With the Ovonic® Regenerative Fuel Cell, power is available even in the absence of hydrogen gas flow to the anode. Operation without hydrogen is illustrated in Fig. 4 where power was sustained for several minutes at near peak levels. Instant start without hydrogen again is a result of the intrinsic hydrogen storage in the metal hydride anode. An energy storage capacity of about 5 Wh/kg was demonstrated.

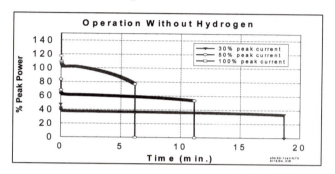

Fig. 4   Instant start operation without hydrogen gas fuel supply.

Low Temperature Performance

Another attribute of the charge storage capability of our fuel cell is its exceptional low temperature performance. Metal hydride batteries operate well at low temperatures and this battery functionality in the Ovonic® Regenerative Fuel Cell also provides for excellent low temperature performance as shown in Fig. 5. PEMFC stacks operate best at 60°C or higher. Although systems solutions have provided for operation at lower ambient temperatures, PEMFC devices typically do not operate below the freezing point of water and PEMFC manuals caution against operation below 5°C. Our fuel cell stack generates 75% of peak power performance at 25°C, 50% of peak power at 0°C, and operation down to below -20°C.

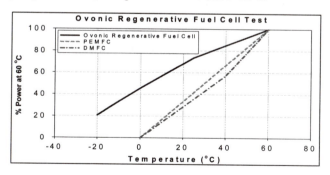

Fig. 5   Low temperature performance.

Power Performance

We have built full size multi-cell stack prototypes up to over 100 W in size. An example of the electrical performance data is shown in Fig. 6. The voltage and power as a function of current are shown. Early prototypes have shown peak power operation at about 150 mA/cm^2, a cell voltage of 0.6 V, and a temperature of 60°C. In more recent results, higher power operation has been demonstrated with current densities up to 250 mA/cm^2 in continuous mode operation and current densities exceeding 500 mA/cm^2 in power pulse mode operation.

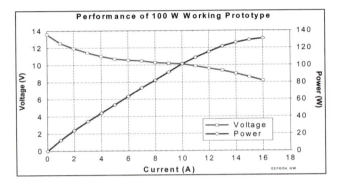

Fig. 6 Voltage and power vs. current for early 100 W prototype stack.

Life Performance

Life tests of Ovonic® Regenerative Fuel Cell prototypes are underway and initial results are promising. Individual electrode half cell tests have exceeded 5000 hours of continuous operation at rated currents. Full cells and full cell stacks are also under test. An example is shown in Fig.7 with over 1000 hours of continuous operation. Utilizing alkaline electrolyte, we can avoid membrane degradation modes. When early AFC devices developed for space applications were adapted for terrestrial applications, absorption of atmospheric carbon dioxide was an acute issue because of the limited electrolyte available in these static (starved) electrolyte systems [2]. Our system which utilizes a more ample electrolyte volume in a circulating liquid electrolyte system is much slower to carbonate and carbonation can be easily handled by electrolyte change out [2]. Additionally, disposable and regenerative scrubber technologies are now available [1].

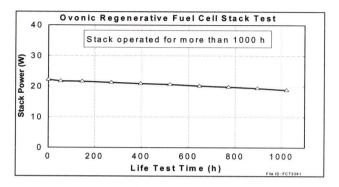

Fig. 7   Early life test of prototype fuel cell stack.

Low Cost Opportunities

One of the biggest obstacles to the commercialization of PEM fuel cells and fuel cells in general is cost. Despite diligent effort for many years, the costs of PEM fuel cells remain high and efforts to achieve cost targets have been discouraging. This is largely due to high materials costs in the fundamental components of the PEM fuel cell including the platinum catalysts, the Nafion membrane, and the graphite bipolar plates. While impressive cost reduction of other components has been achieved, the costs of these components remain over 80% of the total materials costs in high volume production.

Initial cost projections for the Ovonic® Regenerative Fuel Cell indicate materials costs lower by more than a factor of two, principally due to the costs of active materials for the electrochemical catalyst layer (ECL) and electrolyte being an order of magnitude less expensive than the noble metal catalysts and membrane used in the PEMFC membrane electrode assemblies. Our preliminary materials costs are principally in auxiliary hardware components such as the nickel screens and tabs used as current collectors in our existing monopolar design. Volume costs for these commodity materials can be expected to decline dramatically in mass production. These components are currently priced typically at more than an order of magnitude over the raw materials cost.

Finally, our fuel cell technology also has the capability to otherwise lower system cost and complexity by obviating the need for a startup or buffer battery or a battery to handle regenerative braking energy storage.

Prototype Products

After several years of intensive R&D yielding 8 issued U.S. Patents and over 25 published U.S. Patent Applications, we are now involved in prototype product development. A wide variety of cells and stacks sized from a few watts to about 100 W have been built and tested. We are now pursuing a low cost modular approach with molded electrode frames that provides a rugged product. For demonstration purposes, we have selected an electrode surface area of 60 cm^2 for our early prototypes. A 40 cell module provides over 250 W with a conservative monopolar design. Our baseline prototype product is specified in Table I. With our modular approach, shorter or longer stacks can be produced. Additionally, a variety of systems are available by connecting stacks in series and parallel.

Table I   Specifications for OV-60 Prototype Product

OVONIC 40-OV-60 FUEL CELL STACK

Configuration:	40 cells in series	
Electrode Surface Area:	60 cm^2	
Module Dimensions:		
Width	11.8 cm	
Length	26.2 cm	
Height	13.5 cm	
Volume	4.2 L	
Module Weight:	3.9 kg	
Nominal Performance:		
Power	260 W	
Voltage	26 V	
Current	10 A	
Specific Power	67 W/kg	
Power Density	62 W/L	
Temperature	60 °C	

Several-fold improvements in specific power and power density are under development utilizing improved electrodes and current collection. Enhanced pulse power is also available utilizing regenerative mode operation. Improved specific power is also available in larger sizes through the improved design to reduce the contributions of hardware.

Our technology is easily scalable to applications requiring 50 W to 100 kW.

Market Opportunities

The Ovonic® Regenerative Fuel Cell has strong favorable attributes for fuel cell electric vehicle applications, including the capability to store regenerative brake energy. This capability is critical to achieve sufficient overall system efficiency to provide a net improvement in greenhouse gas avoidance. Additional useful features include the instant start capability and excellent low temperature performance, both also derived from the energy storage functionality. However, the strongest advantage over PEM fuel cells now under development for automotive applications is probably in the area of cost. After many years of intensive development there are increasing doubts about whether PEM fuel cells will ever be able to meet the automotive cost requirements of less than $100/kW. We believe the Ovonic® Regenerative Fuel Cell offers the best approach to meet the challenging cost goals of the automotive application.

Particularly because of concerns about fuel cell costs, it is now acknowledged that fuel cell electric vehicle introduction may be delayed by at least one decade and the initial focus of fuel cell commercialization is being diverted to alternative applications including UPS (uninterruptible power supply), emergency power, portable electronics, telecommunications, electric scooters, forklifts, and various military applications. For these applications, the regenerative operation, the instant start operation, and the excellent low temperature performance of the Ovonic® Regenerative Fuel Cell are invaluable attributes. Additionally, the low cost opportunity with our new technology applies across the board, as the cost issue has been the single largest issue holding back the commercialization of the fuel cell industry.

Acknowledgements

We gratefully acknowledge the many contributions of our former and current Ovonic Fuel Cell Company and ECD Ovonics colleagues including Mr. Subhash Dhar, Dr. Boyko Aladjov, Mr. Zdravko Menjak, Dr. Hong Wang, Dr. Konstantin Petrov, Mr. Tom Hopper, Mr. Rajeev Puttaiah, Ms. Latchezara Gradinarova, and Mr. Kevin Fok.

References

1. J. Appleby and F.R. Foulkes, "Fuel Cell Handbook", Van Nostrand Reinhold, New York (1989).
2. K. Kordesch and G.Simader, "Fuel Cells and Their Applications," V.C.H.Verlagsgesellschaft mbH, New York (1996).
3. 2004 Annual DOE Hydrogen Program Review, US Department of Energy, Philadelphia, PA, May 2004.
4. J. Larminie and A. Dicks, "Fuel Cell Systems Explained," Fuel Cell Systems Explained", John Wiley and Sons Ltd., West Sussex, England (2003).
5. S. R. Ovshinsky, M. A. Fetcenko, and J. Ross, Science, 260, 176 (1993).
6. R. C. Stempel, S. R. Ovshinsky, P. R. Gifford, and D. A. Corrigan, IEEE Spectrum, 35, 29 (November 1998).
7. S. R. Ovshinsky, Mat. Res. Soc. Symp. Proc. Vol. 801, G. Nazri, M. Nazri, R. Young, and P. Chen, Eds., p. 3 (2004).
8. B. Chao, R. Young, V. Myasnikov, Y. Li, B. Huang, F. Gingl, P. Ferro, V. Sobolev, and S. R. Ovshinsky, Mat. Res. Soc. Symp. Proc. Vol. 801, G. Nazri, M. Nazri, R. Young, and P. Chen, Eds., p. 27 (2004).
9. R. Young, B. Chao, Y. Li, V. Myasnikov, B. Huang, and S. R. Ovshinsky, SAE Paper No. 04ANNUAL-606, Society of Automotive Engineers, Warrendale, PA (2004).
10. R. Geiss, B. Webster, S.R. Ovshinsky, R. Stempel, R. Young, Y. Li, V. Myasnikov, D. Falls, A. Lutz, SAE Paper No. 04ANNUAL-583, Society of Automotive Engineers, Warrendale, PA (2004).
11. S. R. Ovshinsky, S. Venkatesan, B. Aladjov, R. Young, T. Hopper, U.S. Pat. 6,447,942, Sep 10, 2002.
12. S. R. Ovshinsky, S. Venkatesan, B. Aladjov, S. Dhar, K. Fok, T. Hopper, U.S. Pat. 6,783,891, Aug 31, 2004.
13. S. R. Ovshinsky, B. Aladjov, S. Venkatesan, S. Dhar, U.S. Pat. 6,620,359, Sep 16, 2003.
14. S. R. Ovshinsky, S. Venkatesan, B. Aladjov, S. Dhar, K. Fok, T. Hopper, U.S. Pat. 6,703,156, Mar 9, 2004.

Appendix 8

Characteristics of OUM Phase Change Materials and Devices for High Density
Nonvolatile Commodity and Embedded Memory Applications

Tyler A. Lowrey, Stephen J. Hudgens, Wally Czubatyj, Charles H. Dennison, Sergey A.
Kostylev, and Guy C. Wicker
Ovonyx, Inc 1030 E. El Camino Real #276, Santa Clara, CA 94087
Tel: 408-653-9742 Fax: 408-653-5244 Email: tlowrey@ovonyx.com

ABSTRACT

Phase change memory devices were originally reported by Stan Ovshinsky [1] in
1968. A 256-bit phase-change memory array based on chalcogenide materials was
reported by R.G. Neale, D.L. Nelson, and Gordon E. Moore [2] of Energy Conversion
Devices and Intel in 1970. Recent advances in phase change materials, memory device
designs, and process technology have resulted in significant advances in phase change
device performance, and a new memory device, called Ovonic Unified Memory (OUM)
has been developed. This paper will discuss various device and materials characteristics
of OUM phase change memory materials of interest in applications for non-volatile high-
density memories. These materials are generally Te chalcogenide based, exploiting the
congruent crystallization of the FCC phase and the associated reduction in resistivity that
results from crystallization from the quenched amorphous state. Data storage is a
thermally initiated , rapid, reversible structural phase change in the film. While
rewriteable DVD disks employ laser heat to induce the phase change and modulate
reflectivity, OUM technology uses a short electrical current pulse to modulate resistivity.
The device geometry and thermal environment dictate the power and energy required for
memory state programming.

We will review the device structure, characterization data, device performance, and
reliability as well as device modeling results. Characteristics of key material and device
performance metrics such as crystallization and amorphization programming speed will
be presented. Programming algorithms will be discussed for optimizing operating margin
for high-density applications. Data retention characteristics will be reviewed along with
means for accelerated statistical evaluation. Potential high-density memory array data
disturb issues will be identified and their impact on scalability will be assessed. Scaling
attributes and issues will be reviewed.

INTRODUCTION

OUM is a random access memory with read/write for user addressed bit, byte, or word without the requirement for Flash-like block erase. Low voltage and energy read/write requirements are compatible with CMOS feature and power supply scaling and attractive for mobile and wireless applications. The ultra-small volume of phase change material programmed minimizes the power and energy needed for heating to produce the phase transition.

The chalcogenide phase change alloys in OUM contain at least one element Group VI in the periodic table: Te, Se, or S. Early phase change devices were based on materials containing substantial amounts of Te, which phase segregated into a "filament like" electrically conductive region between two contacts. These devices were inherently slow and power hungry, taking milliseconds and many milliamperes to write, but could be read relatively fast. Most importantly, however, they could be integrated with baseline silicon processing and were used to fabricate a read mostly memory (RMM) in 1970 [2].

Further work at Energy Conversion Devices [4] and elsewhere [5,6] led to improved chalcogenide materials for optical and electrical memories. Alloys along the GeTe – Sb_2Te_3 tie line in the Ge Sb Te ternary phase diagram were developed which could exist in both the amorphous and crystalline states with simple bond re-arrangement, as opposed to diffusion and phase segregation of an element. This, of course, made phase change extremely fast, in the nanosecond range, with programming energy to a first order, proportional to volume and scaling with area. Phase change is an extremely efficient way of changing material resistivity, which for some alloys is over six orders of magnitude (Fig. 1). Electrical conductivity exhibits an activated behavior with activation energydependent on the structural phase as shown,

Semiconductor memory devices, based on these new alloys, in particular Ge2 Sb2 Te5 or GST225, have come to be known as Ovonic Unified Memory – OUM devices.

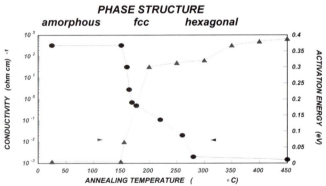

Figure 1. Effect of 10 min isochronal anneal on bulk electrical properties of as-deposited GST225 phase change alloy

Fig. 2 shows a typical IV curve for an OUM device. It contains two traces, one for a set devicein the low resistance state, and one for a reset devicein the high resistance state. The reset device exhibits a phenomenon characteristic of amorphous semiconductors with S type negative differential conductivity, that is a switching or snap-back to a conducting "on" state. It is this phenomenon that allows both reading the OUM bit without disturb (for applied voltages less than the threshold voltage) and programming with current after the switching event at a nominal voltage. Once in the dynamic on state, programming occurs by heat generated in the active region and causing the material to either crystallize (requiring both time and temperature) or amorphise (requiring temperatures above the melting point and rapid quenching to freeze in the disordered amorphous state). Thus, lower temperatures resulting from smaller amplitude pulses with wider pulse widths will cause the device to nucleate and grow crystals and "set" the device to a low resistance state. Shorter but higher amplitude pulses with rapid falling edges perform the "reset" function, putting the device into the high resistance state. Extrapolating the I-V characteristic of the dynamic state backward onto the X-axis gives the holding voltage, V_h. V_h is the voltage which is dropped across the bulk of the active region during programming. This voltage times the current passing thru the device, IV_h, generates the power needed to program the device. Joule heating is also provided from I^2R power dissipation from a resistive heater electrode.

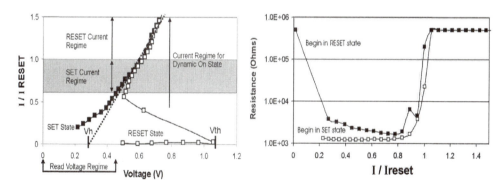

Figure 2. OUM I-V [3]   **Figure 3. OUM R-I [3]**

Fig. 3 shows a plot of resistance vs. current pulse amplitude (R-I curve) which characterizes the programming operation of the OUM device. It shows that starting in the set state, by applying higher and higher amplitude pulses, the device at first stays set, since no part of the device has reached the melting point. Then, at about I/Irest ~ 0.8, a small part of the crystallized region melts and quenches after the pulse ends and the bit becomes partially reset causing the device resistance to start to rise. The resistance continues to increase with increasing pulse amplitude until the whole crystallized region has been amorphized and the device exhibits a saturated reset level. It is interesting to note that the rising portion of the R-I curve can be generated by pulses of appropriate magnitude and width regardless of the previous state of the bit. In other words, this part of the R-I demonstrates "direct overwrite" when using sufficient pulse width. Direct overwrite is useful if one wants to utilize multi-level cell (MLC) memory capability. To perform stable MLC operation, the OUM device structure design should be optimized to provide a gradual transition from the set to the reset state

PHASE CHANGE KINETICS

Programming a phase change device into the low resistance polycrystalline set state involves both nucleation and crystal growth.   It is highly desired to optimize both processes for speed and reliability. Here we propose three approaches that greatly reduce set programming time.

Nucleation time can be reduced or eliminated by a pre-nucleation technique and the first approach provides for pre-nucleation by device structure design. Polycrystalline phase change material itself is used as a virtual electrode for the media programming volume providing an envelope of nucleation sites promoting rapid media crystallization (Fig. 6). The resistivity of polycrystalline phase change alloysis in the range of 25 mΩ-cm, sufficient low to provide good electrical continuity to the programming region with minimal parasitic R during the read operation.

Crystal growth rate is strongly a function of temperature so   programming at an optimum temperature can greatly decrease set time.   This optimum temperature, historically termed the "nose temperature"determined from Isothermal Transformation Diagrams is a result of competition between an increase in crystallization rate and the melting process as temperature is increased. A tailored high performance crystallization temperature can be accomplished by providing on die or block trimming for an optimized set current programming pulse within a memory device.

A third approach to optimize the set programming operation is shown in Fig. 4 where a repetitive write 1/read/write 0/read waveform is show. The waveform uses a sloped falling edge to crystallize (set) a bit, which we term "set sweep". The set sweep insures each bit sees the optimum nose temp for high-speed crystallization in every region of the programming volume. With set sweep, the media programmable volume is provided with an epitaxial "phase front" that insures all local regions see strong nucleation and the optimum   crystallizing   temperature   for   high-speed   robust   homogeneous   phase transformation to the polycrystalline state. This results in a lower and more consistent set resistance for memory read margin.   The set pulse amplitude can start with a peak amplitude current level near that used for resetting and sweep down in a controlled sloped fashion to crystallize the media from the top down. An amorphising reset programming pulse can be used with a similar amplitude current pulse, but with a fast falling edge. Thus the programmed state is determined by the falling edge rate instead of the pulse amplitude. A fall time less than several ns is used to reset a bit and a fall time greater than 50-200ns is used to fully set a bit with present devices. The set sweep approach provides margin over a wide distribution of required bit programming currents.

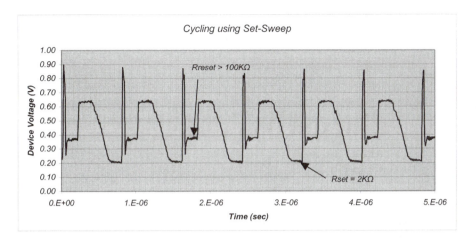

Figure 4. Memory cycling utilizing set sweep

Crystallization occurs at approximatly 60% of the reset pulse amplitude, so it is possible to terminate the sloped falling edge of the set sweep pulse (bring it to zero) at approximately ½ amplitude to further improve performance (25-100ns). Intentional variation in programmed resistance for MLC applications can be obtained by choosing the falling edge slope between these extremes. Using set sweep for MLC has advantages due to the increased resistance dynamic range and the reduced sensitivity to device manufacturing variation providing for faster algorithmic placement.

Turning now to resetting, rapid amorphization is an important characteristic of phase change devices. Sub 10 ns pulses can readily provide fully saturated Rreset > 100Kohms. The phase transformation to the amorphous phase requires sufficient power to heat the phase change material in the programmable volume to the melting temperature. A subsequent rapid quench (rapid pulse falling edge) will freeze in the high R amorphous state. However, as device design continues to reduce the required programming current by improving the thermal environment through better thermal isolation of the programmable element, the thermal time constant of the device will increase. For thermally optimized device designs, this thermal time constant can increase to the order of ns become a factor in the heating rate of the element. Thus for very short reset pulses a higher current amplitude may be needed due to the finite thermal response time. By approximating the geometry of an OUM cell as a sphere and assuming uniform heating within the programmed volume of GST, one can solve the equation analytically and this provides a good approximation of both the time dependence and the contact area dependence of current required to program the cell. We can calculate the temperature distribution $T(r,t)$ at time t and radius r during application of constant source power, P, by integrating the heat flow equation for the spherical source solution over time from zero to t:

$$T(r,t) = P \, erfc(r/\delta)/4\pi\alpha C_v r \qquad (1)$$

$$\delta^2 = 4\pi\alpha t \qquad (2)$$

$$\alpha = \kappa/C_v \qquad (3)$$

Where P – applied power, r distance from source power, α – insulator thermal diffusivity, C_v – insulator specific heat, κ – insulator thermal conductivity, and T_m – melting Temp. Thus for $P = V_h$ Ireset:

$$Ireset = 4\pi \, r \, \kappa T_m V_h/erfc(r/\,\delta) \qquad (4)$$

This effect is shown in Fig. 5. where the reset current amplitude required to fully reset a bit is plotted as a function of pulse width. As seen, for very short pulses, a higher amplitude is needed and experimental results closely matche calculated values..

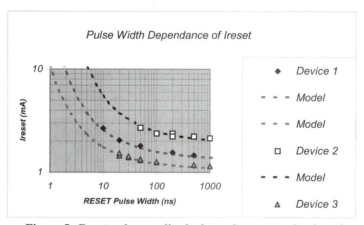

Figure 5. Reset pulse amplitude dependence on pulse duration

OUM MATERIAL REQUIREMENTS

Materials requirements for the various parts of an OUM cell can be understood with reference to the generic device cross section structure shown in Fig. 6. Here, the device is shown as a cylindrical resistive electrode embedded in a dielectric film upon which is deposited a planar film of the GST225 memory material. The hemispherical region that is switched between the amorphous and polycrystalline structural state when the bit is programmed is indicated in the diagram. Because of the relatively low crystallization temperature of the GST225 alloy (~ 200C), it is fully crystallized by the normal processing steps used in device fabrication. The high electrical conductivity of the polycrystalline GST225 (~25 mohm-cm) makes it possible to provide the top electrical contact to the GST material anywhere outside of the hemispherical programmed volume.

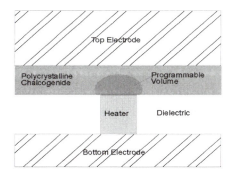

Material	k (W/cm K)
SiOx	1.4E-02
SiNx	2.0E-02
GST225 (xtal)	5.3E-03
ZnS – SiO2	5.8E-03

Figure 6. OUM cell basic structure [3]   **Table I Thermal conductivity**

Requirements for the dielectric layer in which the resistive electrode is embedded can be satisfied by SiOx or many other commonly available dielectrics. These requirements include low thermal and electrical conductivity, good adhesion to the GST film, and no chemical interaction with the GST film at temperatures near the melting temperature of the GST (~ 610C).

Although SiOx and SiNx are normally considered good thermal insulators, it is apparent in Table I that they are considerably more thermally conductive than the GST phase change material itself and SiNx is ~60% more conductive than SiOx. Heterogeneous ZnS-SiO2 films in which ZnS microcrystals are dispersed in an SiO2 matrix have been routinely employed in phase change optical disk fabrication as a thermal isolation layer and these materials, although not commonly available in a semiconductor manufacturing environment, offer thermal conductivity values comparable to the GST alloy and can improve the thermal efficiency of programming.

Material requirements for the resistive electrode are more demanding. This material must be adherent to and chemically compatible with the GST material and, in addition, it must have an electrical resistivity in the range of a few mohm-cm to tens of mohm-cm -- ideally with little or no temperature coefficient. The low temperature coefficient is necessary, since, during programming, the top of the heater will be at T > 600C, but during a read operation, it will be near room temperature. The heat used to melt or crystallize the phase change material during application of a programming current pulse is generated in part from self-heating in the GST, but also from joule heating in the resistive electrode. Finally, the resistive heater should have as low a thermal conductivity as possible consistent with the Wiedeman-Franz relation. This is important because heat lost down the resistive heater from the programming volume represents a source of programming inefficiency leading to higher programming current.

Cermets and nonstochiometric refractory metal nitrides have been used in the past for resistive electrodes in OUM cells and the temperature dependence of the resistivity of a typical electrode material is shown in Fig. 7. In this case, the resistivity drops by about a factor of two between room temperature and the device programming temperature, ~ 600C.

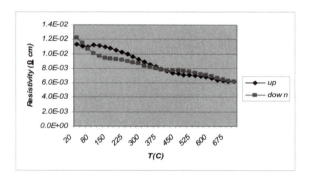

Figure 7. Temperature dependence of refractory nitride resistive electrode material

The resistivity of refractory metal nitrides can be adjusted over a considerable range by changing the nitrogen content, however, as the materials become more resistive, the resistivity also becomes less metallic and shows and increasing negative temperature coefficient.

The requirements for the phase change material itself are the most complex. In addition to showing a large change in resistivity as a function of its polycrystalline or amorphous structural state, the material must have very low thermal conductivity, low melting temperature, good glass forming characteristics, rapid crystallization without phase segregation at elevated temperature but slow crystallization at normal storage and working temperatures, and it must exhibit field dependent threshold switching. This last requirement is necessary for a memory device using a programmable resistive element if low voltage operation and a high dynamic range of resistance change are to be accomplished. The GST225 alloy used in OUM meets all of these requirements.

The large change in resistivity in GST225 results from a change in the density of charged traps in the material as it transforms from the amorphous to the polycrystalline phase as described in the paper by Pirovano et al. [7]. In the amorphous state, naturally occurring disorder-produced valence alternation pair defects [8] pin the fermi level at mid gap resulting in few carriers in high mobility "band-like" states which spatially extend throughout the material. When the material crystallizes, the density of valence alternation pair states is drastically reduced, unpinning the fermi level and new crystalline defects which act as acceptors are created. This results in the nearly degenerate p-type conductivity exhibited by the crystalline material.

THERMAL AND ELECTRICAL DEVICE SIMULATION

A number of thermal or combined electrical and thermal simulations of OUM device operation have been reported [3,7,9,10]. Simulation of the dynamic or steady state temperature rise in a cell during programming is straightforward in that it only requires solution of the heat flow equation as discussed above.

More sophisticated numerical simulations take into account the temperature and structural state dependence of the thermal and electrical conductivity in the GST and surrounding materials and these approaches can be used on actual device geometries to provide more accurate results. In Wicker's simulation results [9], the percolative nature of the heterogeneous, partially crystallized state of the GST is explicitly taken into account to calculate both the thermal and electrical conductivity of the material. Finally, melting and crystallization processes can be included in a self-consistent manner in numerical simulations and these results can be used to model both the set and reset (crystallization and amorphization) processes.

OUM SCALING

In evaluating any new memory technology, a critical factor is how well the performance and cell size scale with decreasing technology lithography nodes. Performance is measured primarily by overall speed of the memory (both read and write), endurance, and the programming energy per bit, which is of increasing importance for mobile portable applications. As an OUM cell is scaled down the programming electrode area is scaled and the volume of the Chalcogenide programmed material is reduced. The decrease in programming material volume provides the performance improvements with scaling to smaller technology nodes as illustrated in Table II.

Scaling of OUM Cell vs. Select Device for Embedded Applications											
						Max Current of Select Device vs. Tech. Node					
		Cell size		MOS T	Tech node	180	130	100	65	45	32
		SAC	non-SAC	width	IDS/um	900	900	900	900	1200	1500
Select Device	MOS select	$6F^2$	$9F^2$	F		162	117	90	58.5	54	48
		$8F^2$	$12F^2$	2F		324	234	180	117	108	96
		$12F^2$	$16F^2$	4F		648	468	360	234	216	192
		$16F^2$	$20F^2$	6F		972	702	540	351	324	288
	BJT select	$5F^2$	$5F^2$						???	Yes	Yes
		$6F^2$	$6F^2$			???	Yes	Yes	Yes		
		$8F^2$	$8F^2$			Yes					
Write Energy R / S (pJ / bit)						20 / 60	8 / 25	4 / 15	2 / 6	1.5 / 4	1 / 3
Write Speed Reset (nS)						8	6	4	3	3	3
Write Speed Set (nS)						50	38	25	20	20	20
Read Speed (nS)						<20	<20	<20	<20	<20	<20

Table II. Roadmap of scaling OUM memory

MEMORY CELL SIZE SCALING

In evaluating a future memory technology one of the most critical factors that impacts cost is the cell size for a given technology node and the ability to reduce the cell size with each subsequent lithography reduction. To compare memory cell size across lithography nodes it is useful to normalize the cell size as a function of a minimum square feature, F^2 (where F is minimum 1/2 pitch feature size). In an ideal memory technology the cell size would be able to take full advantage of the lithography scaling and remain at the same or lower factor of F^2 at subsequent technology nodes. Up to now this has clearly been the case for the dominant memory technologies of DRAM and Flash for many generations and has been the driving factor for the continued 27-30% cost reduction per year for these mainstream memory technologies. However for Flash, the leading non-volatile memory, and also for some potential new technologies there are emerging physical limitations that may lead to roadblocks for continued cell size reduction.

A key differentiating factor for scaling an OUM cell compared to main competing non-volatile memory technologies is that as the cell is scaled down the volume of the chalcogenide programmed material is directly reduced which results in a significant reduction in the write programming current leading to the OUM cell size decreasing as a function of F^2 as illustrated in Table II. An OUM memory cell can be divided into two components, the select device and the chalcogenide resistor element. Either a MOS transistor or a bipolar transistor/diode element can be utilized as a select device [3,11]. For embedded applications it would be more desirable to utilize a MOS select device, but at the 180 nm technology node the width of the MOS device width needs to be increased to over 6F resulting in a cell size of 16-20 F^2 to provide sufficient current with margin to reset the chalcogenide element (Table II). However, as the technology is scaled down from 180 nm to 45 - 32nm the MOS select device OUM cell is reduced to 6 - 12 F^2. This cell size reduction is a consequence of the chalcogenide element requiring lower reset current to program a smaller volume while the CMOS transistor drive currents per unit width remaining constant from 180 thru 65 nm and then increasing at the 45 and 32 nm technology nodes [12].

A potential limiting factor for memory technology cell size scaling is thermal proximity disturb on adjacent bits while programming a target bit Heat emanating from a cycled cell could raise the temperature of adjacent cells, converting an adjacent bit from reset to set over time.

We know that the steady state temperature profile around a point source goes as $1/r$ (the complete expression for T[r,t] is discussed previously and at steady state, infinite time, T goes like $1/r$), a 3-D "thermal resistive divider" is created. Since T goes like $1/r$ and with current scaled down with each generation to cause $T > T_m$ at the edge of the bottom electrode, then if the separation between the bits is scaled proportionally to the lower electrode width, the temperature profile looks the same for each generation. The key aspect of scaling an OUM cell is to scale contact area of heater (bottom electrode) to the phase change material thereby reducing the volume of programmable material with each technology node. As shown in Fig. 8 there is no disturb issue at the 180 nm technology node, consistent with simulations. The margin for thermal proximity disturb (increase of adjacent cell temperature) is expected to remain constant through scaling as shown in Fig. 9. Thus thermal disturb is not anticipated to be a key issue with future scaling

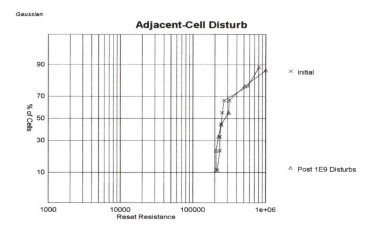

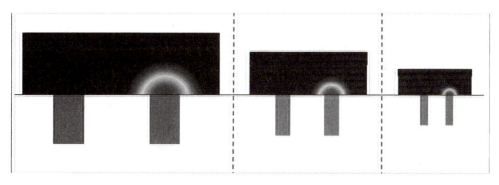

Figure 9. Scaling of Temperature Plume in OUM

PHASE CHANGE MEMORY RELIABILITY

Data retention of phase change devices follows a thermally activated behavior with an activation of 3.5-4.0 eV [3]. Data retention testing can be readily performed with a data retention bake at 2 or more temperatures to accelerate failures, extrapolate retention life or 10 year retention temperature, and to identify weak bits with outlying activation energies or pre-factors. Intrinsic data retention for 10 years is projected with the devices stored at 120C [3]. Further, the consistency of activation energy and pre-factor over a broad range of temperatures provides a useful cost-effective tool for the test engineer to identify outlying bits.

Economical testing of high cyclelife memory devices is a difficult challenge for giga scale capacity memory products. Despite high-speed programming and reading, parallelism, and on chip test modes; the expense of test time to cycle past 1E7 cycles for each bit becomes significant. A means of estimating operating cyclelife using pulse energy acceleration has been developed. Applying overstress pulse energy at various levels can accelerate cyclelife failures and be extrapolated back to normal use conditions. Weak bits can be identified and failure modes can be investigated and engineered for improved statistical cyclelife performance without cumbersome and expensive use of extended high-speed tester time.

CONCLUSIONS

OUM Phase Change memory devices offer performance advantages including high-speed programming and reading, non-volatility, random access, direct over-write, high endurance, and low voltage/energy requirements. They also offer cost advantages including cell size, high density, strong scalability, relative device structure process simplicity, and compatibility of CMOS process integration. A number of material, device structure, and programming algorithm approaches are suggested to further enhance phase change crystallization performance. Material property requirements for optimized phase change memory devices are discussed and can be determined through simulation. No major OUM scaling barriers are anticipated for the foreseeable 3-4 generations. Reliability testing techniques for high endurance OUM devices have been identified. These attributes make OUM an attractive alternative to Flash and other proposed non-volatile memory technologies.

ACKNOWLEDGEMENTS

The authors wish to acknowledge the support and many contributions from Intel Corporation, ST Microelectronics, and Energy Conversion Devices personnel in many areas including wafer processing, clean room support, product engineering, device engineering, test, CAD, and analytical support. We also wish to acknowledge Stan Ovshinsky for his pioneering efforts discovering and engineering the phase change memory device, materials, and related amorphous thin film science for multiple practical applications.

REFERENCES

[1] S. R. Ovshinsky, Phys. Rev. Lett. 21, 1450 (1968)

[2] R.G. Neale, D.L. Nelson and Gordon E. Moore, "Nonvolatile and reprogrammable, the read-mostly memory is here," Electronics, pp56-60, Sept. 28, 1970.

[3] Stefan Lai and Tyler Lowrey, "OUM - A 180 nm Nonvolatile Memory Cell Element Technology For Stand Alone and Embedded Applications," IEDM 2001.

[4] J. Hernandez, B. Chao, D. Strand, S. Ovshinsky, D. Pawlik, P Gasiorowski, Appl. Phys. Comm 11(4), 557 (1992)

[5] M. Terao, T. Nishida, Y. Miauchi, S. Horiguchi, T. Kaku, and N. Ohta, Proc. Soc. Photo-Opt Instrum. Eng. 695, 105 (1986)

[6] T. Ohta, K. Inoue, M. Uchida, K. Yoshida, T. Akiyama, S. Furakawa, K. Nagata, and S. Nakamura, Proc. Int. Symp. on Optical Memory (Kobe 1998), Jpn. J. Appl. Phys. 28, Suppl. 28-3, 123 (1989)

[7] A. Pirovano, A. L. Lacaita, D. Merlani, A. Benvenuti, F. Pellizzer, and R. Bez, "Electronic Switching Effect in Phase-Change Memory Cells", IEDM 2002.

[8] M. Kastner, D. Adler, and H. Fritzsche, Phys. Rev. Lett. 37, 1504 (1976)

[9] G. Wicker, "A comprehensive model of submicron chalcogenide switching devices," Ph.D. Dissertation, Wayne State University, Detroit, MI 1996.

[10] Y. H. Ha, J. H. Yi, H. Hori, J. H. Park, S. H. Joo, S. O. Park, U-In Chung, J. T. Moon, IEEE 2003 Symposium on VLSI Technology, Kyoto, Japan, June 12-14, 2003.

[11] J. Maimon, J. Rodgers, L. Burcin, NVMTS (Nonvolatile Memory Technology Symposium, Goddard Space Flight Center), Nov. 6, 2002.

[12] International Technology Roadmap for Semiconductors: 2002 update

Appendix 9

**"A New Information Paradigm -
The Cognitive Computer"**

**Innovation Providing New Multiple Functions in
Phase-Change Materials To Achieve Cognitive Computing**

Stanford R. Ovshinsky and Boil Pashmakov
Energy Conversion Devices, 2956 Waterview Drive, Rochester Hills, MI 48309

ABSTRACT

This paper describes a basic new scientific and technological approach for information and computing use. It is based on Ovonic cognitive devices that utilize an atomically engineered Ovonic chalcogenide material as the active medium. We demonstrate how such a device possesses many unique functions including an intrinsic neurosynaptic functionality that permits the processing of information in a manner analogous to that of biological neurons and synapses. Our Ovonic cognitive devices can not only accomplish conventional binary computing, but are capable of non-binary generation of information, storage, encryption, higher mathematics, modular arithmetic and factoring. Uniquely, almost all of these functions can be accomplished in a single nanosized device. These devices and systems are robust at room temperature (and above). They are non-volatile and also can include other volatile devices such as the Ovonic Threshold Switch and Ovonic multi-terminal threshold and memory devices that can replace transistors.

INTRODUCTION

The global computer industry is based upon silicon in a binary mode where information is processed sequentially. The transistor is fabricated from crystalline silicon where periodicity is fundamental and where doping in the ppm and above range of donor and acceptor atoms such as P and B is required.

Computers are characterized by two fundamental attributes. First, operation is based on binary logic. The storage and manipulation of data occurs through conversions to binary strings and transformations of binary strings. Second, today's computers operate sequentially in a manner first described by John Von Neumann. Completion of a computational function is inherently a step by step process. Computer programs are simply line by line instructions that outline a sequence of steps to be implemented. They are executed in a one by one fashion in which the results of preceding steps are typically forwarded to later steps.

Despite their tremendous successes, certain computations, functions and tasks remain largely unamenable to solution or implementation by conventional silicon computers. Such computers become increasingly inefficient as the complexity of computation increases. Computational problems whose time of computation scales exponentially with the input size (number of bits) become intractable with conventional computers. Examples of such problems include the factoring of large numbers and searching or sorting large databases.

Quantum computing has recently been proposed as a solution for overcoming these limitations of conventional computers. Proposed quantum computers seek to exploit the quantum mechanical principle of wavefunction superposition to achieve more than binary state computing through the massive parallelism inherent in entangled, yet coherent states. These states are not accessible for detection and utilization except upon wavefunction collapse. Quantum algorithms such as Shor's factoring algorithm [1] and Grover's searching algorithm [2] demonstrate the benefits potentially available from such computation. However, the systems involved are operable mostly at very low temperatures with states stable only for very brief periods of time.

The statistical nature of the quantum activity requires very complex error correction. Decoherence is a fundamental problem, and device states are volatile with short lifetimes. Therefore quantum computing is a topic of scientific interest, but it will be far in the future before it can become a viable industry [3]. Laboratory quantum computer experiments at exceedingly low temperatures received worldwide attention by showing that it is possible to factor the number 15. With our approach, we can factor 15 trivially and stably at room temperature with none of the above problems. Our approach is demonstrable now, not only for factoring, but also for the many functions described below.

We have taken the position since the 1950's that information is physical; it is encoded energy. Our computer principles are therefore based upon generating and storing units of energy so that they can be added, subtracted, multiplied and divided to provide simple arithmetic and to be utilizable for higher mathematics, while having the inherent plasticity needed for neurosynaptic operation, all in a stable, non-volatile manner.

Our devices are able to emulate the biological functions of memory, switching, learning, adaptability, higher mathematics etc. occurring in the brain, see e.g. refs. 4, 5. The materials of choice through which we achieve our unique mechanisms replicating these functions, are inorganic and polymeric. The devices can operate as neurons, synapses and dendrites, all in a single nanostructure. The devices are able to generate, store, and transform information within a single multifunctional entity in the nanostructure range, assuring high density and high speed. These devices and their systems, while not being quantum computers in any sense, are still able to emulate in a much improved and practical manner some of the quantum computing operations that have been proposed.

The devices must be cost effective, manufacturable and near term. To accomplish this, we utilize thin film structures in the nanoscale at room temperature and above, with both non-volatile as well as volatile operation. We construct multi-terminal devices which achieve the equivalent function of the transistor with far faster speed, increased current capacity and smaller size. One example is a device of nanometer size made of Ovonic threshold material [6] showing a normal threshold voltage of less than 2V with a third electrode that modulates the threshold voltage, while at the same time reducing the holding current to essentially zero, keeping the conducting state intact. When the third electrode is turned off, the original threshold voltage appears [7]. This behavior clearly demonstrates the electronic nature of Ovonic switching by establishing that the conducting filament is a plasma as orginally proposed [8]. The lifetimes of the threshold and memory devices have been proven to be the same as that of other semiconductor devices.

The basis of our work in chalcogenide based materials (e.g. $Ge_{22}Sb_{22}Te_{56}$) is well known [8-11]. Ge, Sb and Te have been the archetypical elements for the Ovonic memory material from its beginnings [8,12-15] to which other elements can be added. Ovonic optical phase-change materials are utilized throughout the world in devices such as rewritable DVD's. Our Ovonic electrical phase-change memories are the basis of our joint venture Ovonyx with Tyler Lowrey, Intel and others [16]. Ovonyx has several licensees, including STMicroelectronics, and the work is progressing very well [17]. Both the Ovonic optical and electrical memory are currently binary in nature, and the latter are intended as replacements for flash, DRAM and SRAM.

Current implementations of artificial intelligence utilize conventional transistor technology. We have many more degrees of freedom in material and device design that, while non-biological, permit achievement of higher level functionality of intelligence. We describe here the principles permitting this higher level functionality. We show that we are able to use our proven materials, production techniques and devices to achieve functions that cannot be achieved in any other known manner.

From a socioeconomic viewpoint, our economics are far more favorable than those of conventional computing. The capital costs of equipment can be lowered by adapting our eighth generation, continuous-web, multijunction nanostructure layer machines. These fabrication facilities can produce complex multilayer materials such as our Ovonic triple junctions by miles and tons with very high yield. The materials can have as many as eleven layers in an overall thickness of less than 0.5 □m with individual layer thicknesses of 80 - 100Å [18,19]. The cost of our machines is in the millions instead of the billions of dollars required for silicon wafers, including the cost of complex photolithography for the latter, however.

The first step along the path to full realization of the potential of cognitive computing may well be the implementation of a hybrid technology. Arrays of our devices can be compatibly fabricated upon a silicon chip engineered to contain all necessary drivers and other auxiliary circuits if desired.

A NEW COMPUTING PARADIGM

The familiar consumer computer and semiconductor industries are now cyclical, approaching important fundamental limits of the science, technology and costs. A new tranformative approach is needed. We offer one that operates in the nano-range with new physical mechanisms on various thin film substrates, assuring mechanical flexibility. We have already described the transformative potential of our technology for a new information age [20].

Figure 1 presents a comparative summary of the features of the current silicon paradigm and those of our approach. We emphasize that the functions described in Figure 1 have been and are being demonstrated on the benchtop. Since the field of application is so large, building integrated systems is required now as the first task on our critical path to commercialization. It is important to recognize that the device can be used to perform in the binary or in higher modes as required for particular tasks, emulating various functions within the brain. More explicitly, our proprietary devices can also perform as non-binary processors capable of manipulating and storing data in high level arithmetic bases (e.g. decimal, hexadecimal, base 8) which provide for additional operational capabilities via multi-valued logic. The Ovonic Cognitive Computer also has remarkable encryption possibilities and has the plasticity to show adaptive learning and cognitive functions, hence the name.

We can make full use of the unique functionality of individual devices to increase dramatically the functionality at the array level. The device principles make possible the variable interconnection strengths among cognitive devices needed to emulate the biological plasticity and complexity needed for adaptive and learning capabilities. Each cognitive device can further be connected to a very large number of devices in an array, with three-dimensional interconnectivity made possible with large fan in and fan out of the connections. **As a result, a highly dense, interactive, and massively parallel architecture is achievable. This makes possible the use of dynamical states of activity for computation, as in human brains, instead of the sequential switching from static state to state in conventional computers.**

Conventional Silicon Computers	Ovonic Cognitive Computer Multifunctionality in a Single Element
Each Element: • Computes based on single bit (binary) manipulation • Manipulates data sequentially, bit by bit	Each Element: • Manipulates, processes and stores information in a non-volatile fashion • Hardware and software are unified • Low voltage and low current operation • Performs arithmetic operations (+,-,x,÷) on multi-bit numbers $(0,1,2,3\ldots n)$ • Performs modular arithmetic • Executes multi-valued logic • Stores the result in a non-volatile manner • Simple, powerful encryption • Acts as a neurosynaptic cell; i.e. possesses intelligence capability • Scales down to nanoscale dimensions; huge density • Device speed is in the picosecond range • Capable of massive parallelism • Combines logic and memory in a single device • Has attributes of proposed quantum computers without their limitations, such as analogs of quantum entanglement and coherence at practical conditions and environments
Arrays of computation and storage elements are combined in a conventional computer which: • Requires separate storage and processor units or regions • Has limited parallel processing capability • Is limited to Von Neumann operations	**An Array of Ovonic Cognitive Elements working as a System:** • Easily factors large numbers • Performs high level mathematical functions (e.g. vector and array processing) • Has high 3-dimensional interconnectivity, huge density, giving rise to high speed, hyper-parallel processing (i.e. millions of interconnected processors) • Has adaptive learning capability • Interconnectivity is simply and inherently reconfigurable • Can generate dynamic activity **The Ovonic Cognitive Devices are:** • Mass produced in exceptionally dense, all thin film, uniquely interconnected arrays • Mass manufactured as a thin film, flexible device using proven technologies • Ovonic "transistor" unique high speed low cost 3-terminal device. Nanostructure capable of carrying large amounts of current both in nonvolatile and volatile modes

Figure 1. A comparison of the features and operational characteristic of conventional silicon elements and arrays with those of the Ovonic Cognitive Element and Computer.

HOW DOES THE OVONIC COGNITIVE DEVICE WORK?

There are two kinds of Ovonic materials, the Ovonic threshold switch material (OTS) and the Ovonic memory switch (OMS) or phase-change material. The OTS material has a strongly crosslinked polymeric structure and strong interbond interactions which ensure its structural stability during the electronic transitions associated with switching. The OMS, on the other hand, has a different polymeric structure which is designed to have fewer, weaker crosslinks and strong interactions between lone pairs, all of which facilitates reversible structural transitions between the amorphous and crystalline states.

The active material in our cognitive device is our Ovonic, solid-state, chalcogenide phase-change material, the same material that is used in commercial applications. Those applications, however, are binary in nature. In them, the devices utilize only the reversible phase-change from amorphous (high resistance, low reflectivity state) to crystalline (low resistance, high reflectivity state) in current commercial applications. In contrast, we show here the deep and rich new physics that be utilized in single or multiple elements, especially in the amorphous state.

The basic operation of the active material is illustrated by the data presented in Figure 2, showing the resistance characteristics of a representative Ovonic chalcogenide material, $Ge_{22}Sb_{22}Te_{56}$. This is the material used in the binary mode by our optical phase-change licensees and in the electrical Ovonic memory device now called the Ovonic Unified Memory (OUM) currently so successfully pursued by Tyler Lowrey, a towering figure in the memory field, and his talented group at Ovonyx.

We show in Figure 2 the response of our Ovonic Cognitive device as a function of electrical energy (lower axis) applied to the cognitive device in the form of current pulses. The amorphous regime, which in the past has been considered silent regarding information, is where the pre-threshold pulses act. The pre-threshold states are the equivalent of the coherent and entangled states of the quantum computer. In contrast to quantum computers, they are non-volatile; new pulses needed to complete a computation or encryption can be added much later (e.g. over forty years later). The devices are also radiation hard.

The response of the material to the current pulses can be described via the two general response regimes depicted in the folded presentation format shown in Figure 2. The fold coincides with a minimum in the resistance and demarcates a low constant amplitude pulse regime to the left from a higher current variable amplitude pulse regime to the right. The higher current range shows the multistate activity of our Ovonic electrical memory [10,11]. Operation in the variable amplitude regime (VAR) requires a minimum current pulse amplitude and this minimum amplitude pulse produces the lowest resistance (highest crystallinity) state in the VAR regime. The amorphous-crystalline transition utilizes a reversible phase-change mechanism.

Our new Ovonic cognitive devices make use of new mechanisms in the deceptively simple single, amorphous, nano-dimensional spot in the low current operational regime shown to the left of the fold in Figure 2. As current pulses are applied in the cognitive regime, minute nanocrystalline regions form, the volume fraction of such crystalline phases increasing with each current pulse. Crystallization can occur through nucleation/growth upon the application of a current pulse. The microcrystallites generated by a sequence of pulses form a temporally sequence of statcoherentes.

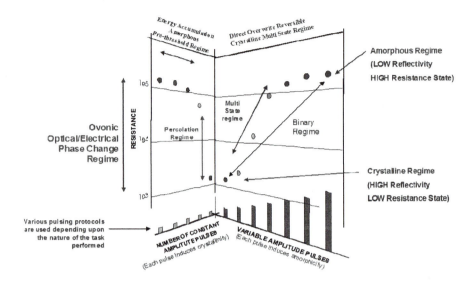

Figure 2. Resistance characteristics of an Ovonic Cognitive Device. The cognitive amorphous pre-threshold synaptic regime (left side) culminates in a percolative transition to crystalline material, the equivalent of neurosynaptic switching. The resistance change accompanying the transition to the crystalline regime can provide readout and transferring of a completed signal to other devices. The leftmost and rightmost data points of Figure 2 (the high resistance endpoints) both correspond to material that is substantially amorphous and the material becomes increasingly crystalline toward the center of the figure, with the lowest resistance states having the greatest crystallinity. The right side is the multistate crystalline cognitive regime (CCR). One should look upon the left side as being either standalone when the crystalline sums up the synaptic information or united with the activities of the right side.

The nanocrystallites are distributed randomly throughout the chalcogenide material. As they grow, a percolation path results, a continuous, high-conductivity pathway across the material between the contacts. Once percolation has occurred, the material exits the amorphous cognitive regime and enters the right side, the CCR regime, if desired. Otherwise, the material can be reset to an amorphous state [12].

Accumulated energy, rather than current pulse amplitude, is a more fundamental representation of the modification of the Ovonic chalcogenide material in the cognitive regime. The increment of crystallization that occurs upon application of a current pulse is dictated by the energy deposited by the pulse into the material. This is an essential feature of the cognitive functionality of our new device because the structural state (defined by its crystalline volume fraction) of the material at any point in the cognitive regime is a manifestation of the total accumulated energy applied to the material. The crystallites represent stored energy that has encoded meaning. This stored energy represents what we mean when we say information is encoded energy.

The accumulative nature of the cognitive regime also provides a close analogy to the neurosynaptic functionality essential to cognitive behavior in biological organisms [21-23]. In the cognitive regime, each application of energy to our adaptable polymeric material induces a partial crystallization of the material to an extent characteristic of the applied energy. Upon removal of the energy source, the material remains in the partially crystallized state until exposed to energy once again. Since the pulse energies in the cognitive regime are sufficiently low to prevent reversion of crystallized regions back to the amorphous phase, the crystallization process is stable until one desires to erase it or make it reversible as in the Ovonic memory.

The structural state is thus a record of the energy accumulated by the material. Continued application of energy to the structural state induces additional crystallization and further accumulation of energy until sufficient energy has been applied to reach the percolation transition. The energy required to induce percolation is a threshold for a transition from a high resistance state to a low resistance state. In optical applications, we replace resistance with reflectivity. We have proposed that an Ovonic hybrid optical-electrical memory will precede the emergence of the all-optical memory [20].

The ability of our cognitive device to undergo an abrupt change in a readily detectable manner after accumulating its threshold energy provides for neurosynaptic functionality [21-23]. A biological neuron receives energetic inputs at its dendritic synaptic terminals and accumulates them until it reaches a threshold and fires. Before firing, a neuron "acts" as if uncognizant of the signals it has accumulated, and yet it fires when the net signal reaches the threshold value. Our cognitive device exhibits analogous accumulation and threshold activated firing capabilities. The accumulation response is a series of pre-percolation structural states with altered local order having similar resistances and crystalline volume fractions, increasing in proportion to the accumulated energy. Since the resistances of the pre-percolation states are similar, these states are functionally equivalent and analogous to the pre-threshold states of a biological neuron. The abrupt reduction in resistance that occurs at the percolation transition is analogous to the firing event of a biological neuron. This apparently silent zone is the basis of our encryption and other functions.

The firing pulse, which represents crystallization (or in quantum analogy terms, collapse of the wavefunction) gives meaning to the pre-threshold events which could not be interrogated individually. These events are correlated in such a way as to provide functionality analogous to that derivable from quantum entanglement, while representing a significant number, symbol, or information value, etc. The firing pulse in effect reveals the meaning of information stored in forensically inaccessible pre-percolation states. Upon firing, that which was inaccessible becomes tangible and can be read out and interacted with other devices and functions. What was once inaccessible in the "silent" processes of information gathering and storage in a pre-percolation state becomes detectable and manipulable by other devices.

Keep in mind that we are thus far speaking of a *single* cognitive device in the *nanosize range* that can perform a wide variety of mathematical operations, neurosynaptic functions etc. Such activity is unique and exemplifies the deep and rich physics of our nanostructured amorphous material.

APPLICATIONS OF THE OVONIC COGNITIVE DEVICE

We offer a fundamental new approach to computing that enables Ovonic cognitive devices and networks to provide new strategies for doing not only conventional computing but, even more importantly, a whole new approach to informational and computational applications. It also opens up a new phase in the use of non-silicon material for semiconductors. Several illustrative examples of the dramatic increase in multifunctionality are discussed below.

Non-Binary Storage

Non-binary data storage is a unique aspect of the Ovonic cognitive device. In non-binary data storage, a single Ovonic cognitive device can be programmed to store any one of three or more numerical values. Each distinct numerical value corresponds to a distinct structural state in the cognitive regime. Programming or storage of a particular numerical value occurs by providing energy to the Ovonic cognitive device in an amount sufficient to transform the device to the structural state corresponding to the information or value (e.g. letter, number, symbol). In a typical application, the programming energy is provided to the Ovonic cognitive device in its reset state (the initial state (amorphous endpoint) in the cognitive regime) and becomes characteristic of the numerical value being stored. Distinct numerical values are assigned to each of a series of selected structural states in the cognitive regime. Since each structural state has a unique programming energy, a numerical value is encoded through the programming energy and retained by the material through its structural state in a non-volatile manner.

The assignment of numerical values to specific selected structural states can occur in many ways. From an operational point of view, it is most convenient to assign increasing (or decreasing) consecutive integer values to the structural states in order of increasing accumulated energy relative to the initial, reset state of the cognitive regime. In its simplest operation, it is desirable to separate consecutive integer values by equal intervals of accumulated energy so that repeated application of a particular pre-threshold energy pulse increases the stored value by one. This pulsing is done in the amorphous state. The energy relative to the reset state required to store an integer is proportional to the integer. This is advantageous because it renders the cognitive device inherently additive. The reproducibility of the values is assured because the materials always respond in the same way, making for a very stable computer.

Transformations of the Ovonic cognitive device from a structural state assigned to one integer to a structural state assigned to a different integer is a basic operation of the Ovonic cognitive device in mathematical computations. These transformations correspond to incrementing the device from one state to another through the application of energy, typically in the form of one or more electrical current (or optical) pulses of the same energy. Pulse energy can be varied through the pulse amplitude, pulse duration and even the shape of the pulse. In practical operation, non-binary storage and incrementing are most conveniently accomplished with pulses having a common amplitude and variable duration so that energy is proportional to pulse duration and different structural states separated equally in energy are separated by equal pulse durations. New degrees of freedom of electronic and material design can also be utilized.

An inherent feature of our cognitive device is the ability to operate it according to many different non-binary storage protocols. Figure 2 presents an example of a five state protocol in which the threshold energy separating the reset and set states is divided into five intervals so that five incrementing pulses are required to transform the material from its reset state to its set state. The energy threshold can be divided into a desired number of intervals to provide arbitrary multistate storage in which an arbitrary number of pulses is used to transform the material from its reset state to its set state. Storage protocols based on three states, four states, etc. can be realized by dividing the threshold energy into three intervals, four intervals etc. Devices that operate using a large number of states are readily realized and operate reproducibly over a large number of reset-set-reset cycles. Our cognitive device can easily be reconfigured from one non-binary storage protocol to another. A device utilizing a three state protocol in one computation, for example, can be reconfigured to operate in a seven state protocol in another computation.

Encryption

The reconfigurable storage capability of our cognitive device provides a unique and remarkably effective mechanism for encrypting information. The encryption capabilities of our cognitive device originate from the non-uniqueness of the relation between the structural state of the active material and the information stored in the device. Reconfigurability precludes a unique one-to-one correspondence between the structural state and the stored information. The information content of a particular structural state in the cognitive regime depends on the number of states included in the non-binary storage protocol of the device. Different information can be encoded in the same structural state. In the absence of knowledge about the number of storage states and the energy increments separating energy states, knowledge of the structural state of the cognitive device provides no insight about the information value (alphanumeric, symbolic or otherwise) assigned to the structural state.

Another level of security provided by our cognitive device involves the difficulties in inferring the structural state of the device. Except for the set state, the structural states in the cognitive regime of our device are pre-percolation states that consist of a random, non-contiguous distribution of nanocrystallites within an amorphous matrix. The pre-percolation crystallites can be nanoscale particles that are below the size resolution of common analytical techniques. Furthermore, efforts to identify the structural state necessarily require exposing the device to energy in the form of electron beams, photons etc. Any manipulations or probes of the device that alter its structural state have the effect of deleting the stored information because a change in structural state corresponds to changing the information content of the device. Even if one were able to deduce the structural state, one would still be faced with the impossible task of decoding the information content of the state since a particular structural state is determined by the accumulated energy and this accumulated energy can be provided in a variety of different ways through variations in the pulse amplitude, pulse duration, and number and shape of pulses. Each of the different ways of transforming the material to a particular structural state corresponds to a different way of encoding information. The information content of our cognitive device cannot be determined merely through knowledge of the structural state.

Non-Binary Arithmetic

The multistate, non-binary storage capability of our cognitive device provides a natural basis for calculations in non-binary arithmetic systems. Whereas conventional computers are limited to binary computations, our cognitive devices can operate in a non-binary fashion and permit computations in base 3, base 4, etc., where the arithmetic base of operation corresponds to the number of states included in the multistate, non-binary protocol. Decimal (base 10) operation, for example, is a particularly intuitive mode of operation and may be accomplished using a ten state protocol in which ten current pulses are used to traverse the energy threshold of a cognitive device. The important factor is that we can go to any base up to the resolution of our ability to distinguish distinct states in the cognitive regime. We can even use base 60, the sexagesimal base of the ancient Sumerians, which persists to this day in angular and temporal measurements.

Addition

Because of its intrinsic accumulative functionality, our device is naturally suited to addition. Since each pulse applied to the device signifies the operation of incrementing by one, the structural state of our device provides a record of the cumulative number of increments applied to the device since its last reset. Addition of two numbers is accomplished by storing one of the addends in the device and subsequently applying pulses to the device in a number equal to the other addend.

Division

Division exploits the accumulative nature and reconfigurability of our cognitive device. In division, the divisor is used to define the arithmetic base of computation for a cognitive device and a number of pulses equal to the dividend is applied to the device with a requirement that the device be reset each time it sets until all of the pulses have been applied. The quotient of the division is equal to the number of times the device sets while applying the pulses corresponding to the dividend and the remainder corresponds to the final state of the device.

Modular Arithmetic

Implementation of modular arithmetic with our cognitive device is similar to the method of division described above. Determination of the modulo X equivalent of the number Z is accomplished by applying Z pulses to a cognitive device whose cognitive operational range is partitioned into X intervals, resetting the device each time it sets and reading the final state of the device to obtain the result. The modulo 7 equivalent of 17, for example, can be obtained by applying 17 incrementing pulses to a cognitive device requiring 7 incrementing pulses to progress from its reset state to its set state. Application of the 17 incrementing pulses causes the device to set twice and leaves the device in a state removed from the reset state by 3 incrementing pulses. Hence, 17(mod 7) = 3.

Factoring in Parallel

Our cognitive device offers a new approach to factoring that is efficient and amenable to parallel operation. During factoring, a number of pulses equal to the input number is applied to each of several devices configured to divide by a different prime number and each device is reset every time it sets. After all pulses have been applied, each device is in a state that corresponds to the modular equivalent of the input number in the modulus of a different prime number. Since any factor of the input number necessarily has a modular equivalent of zero, the prime numbers that are factors of the input number are those associated with cognitive devices that are in their set state after applying pulses in a number equal to the input number. This method can also factor information that is not numerical; for example, intelligent database searching and associative memory.

SUMMARY

We have described and demonstrated a unique new computational/information device that possesses the neurosynaptic functionality necessary to achieve cognitive computing. The cognitive device shows threshold activated firing, possesses a threshold energy that is variable, records experiential history, combines memory and processing in a single device, and responds to stimuli of many types. The cognitive devices can be connected into densely interconnected, highly parallel networks that exhibit plasticity and learning capabilities. The neurosynaptic properties of individual devices and the connection strengths between devices in a network are adjustable and permit reconfiguration and adaptation of a network as it confronts new situations. A single device can do both logic and memory.

In addition to providing a new concept in computing, our cognitive devices make possible the redefining of the manufacturing of computers. The atomically engineered chalcogenide materials used in our cognitive devices and networks can be deposited uniformly as thin films on a variety of substrate materials, including silicon, using methods such as sputtering, physical vapor deposition, and chemical vapor deposition. These processes are inexpensive and adaptable to large scale manufacturing. Post-deposition processing and patterning can be achieved using existing techniques that are well-known in silicon technology and can be incorporated into our continuous-web technology.

The era of truly cognitive computing in which machines utilize higher order reasoning capabilities to process, interpret and respond to information is now upon us. Our continuing efforts will focus on interconnecting devices, scale up of cognitive networks from the few to the many, optimizing learning protocols and answering emerging needs by developing task-specific devices that display adaptability within a bounded range of input conditions with first implementation via a hybrid technology. Space prohibits the description of our multiterminal junction devices that have the potential to replace the transistor, providing great performance advantages [6,7].

ACKNOWLEDGEMENTS

We thank the information team of Wally Czubatyj, my longtime collaborator in information; David Strand, for his leadership of our optical phase-change memory activities; Genie Mytilineou, for her contributions and continuous help; Kevin Bray, for his invaluable work on the preparation of the paper; and the technical staff of our Information Group. We are grateful to Morrel Cohen, a long-time collaborator, for his helpful comments. As always, SRO pays homage to his inspiration and loving collaborator, Iris.

REFERENCES

1. P.W. Shor, Proceedings of the 35th Annual Symposium on the Foundations of Computer Science (IEEE Computer Society Press, Los Alamitos, CA, 1994), p. 124.
2. L.K. Grover; Phys. Rev. Lett. **79**, 325 (1997).
3. M.A. Nielsen and I.L. Chang; Quantum Computation and Quantum Information; Cambridge University Press, Cambridge, 2000.
4. A. Nieder, D.J. Freedman, E.K. Miller; Science **297**, 1708 (2002).
5. S. Dehaene; Science **297**, 1652 (2002).
6. S.R. Ovshinsky, B. Pashmakov, E. Mytilineou; to be published.
7. A new volume updating our work since 1991 is in preparation.
8. S.R. Ovshinsky; Phys. Rev. Lett. **21**, 1450 (1968).
9. Disordered Materials: Science and Technology, Selected Papers by Stanford R. Ovshinsky; D. Adler, B.B. Schwartz, M. Silver, eds.; Plenum Press, New York, 1991.
10. Disordered Materials: Science and Technology: Selected Papers by S.R. Ovshinsky; D. Adler, ed.; Amorphous Institute Press, Bloomfield Hills, Michigan, 1982.
11. S.R. Ovshinsky; MRS Symp. Proc. **554**, 399 (1999).
12. S.R. Ovshinsky; Revue Roumaine de Physique, **26**, 893 (1981).
13. S.R. Ovshinsky; "The Quantum Nature of Amorphous Solids"; in Disordered Semiconductors; M.A. Kastner, G.A. Thomas, S.R. Ovshinsky, eds.; Plenum Press, New York (1987); p. 195.
14. S.R. Ovshinsky, H. Fritzsche; IEEE Trans. Elect. Dev. **ED-20**, 91 (1973).
15. S.R. Ovshinsky; Memoires, Optiques et Systemes, No. 127, Sept. 1994, p. 65.
16. Ovonyx is a joint venture between ECD, Tyler Lowrey and Intel Capital, among others.
17. T. Lowrey, C. Dennison, S. Hudgens, W. Czubatyj; "Characteristics of OUM Phase Change Materials and Devices for High Density Nonvolatile Commodity and Embedded Memory Applications"; 2003 MRS Fall Meeting, Dec. 1-5, 2003, Boston, MA; Symp. HH, paper 2.1.
18. S.R. Ovshinsky; Proc. of the Intl. Ion Engr. Cong., ISIAT '83 & Ipat '83, Kyoto 12-16 September 1983, p. 817.
19. D. Adler, S.R. Ovshinsky; Chemtech **15**, 538 (1985).
20. For a more recent discussion of our work in phase change optical memory, see: S.R. Ovshinsky, "Optical Cognitive Information Processing – A New Field"; presented at the International Symposium on Optical Memory '03; Nara, Japan; Nov. 3 – 7, 2003 (to be published in the Japanese Journal of Applied Physics).
21. F. Morin, G. LaMarche, and S.R. Ovshinsky; Anat. Rec. **127**, 436 (1957).
22. F. Morin, G. LaMarche, and S.R. Ovshinsky; Laval Medical **26**, 633 (1958).
23. S.R. Ovshinsky, I.M. Ovshinsky; Mat. Res. Bull. **5**, 681 (1970).

Appendix 10

To appear in Physics and Chemistry of Glasses, 2005

Why chalcogenides are ideal materials for Ovshinsky's Ovonic threshold and memory devices.

H. Fritzsche, Louis Block Professor Emeritus, University of Chicago
3140 E. CMO Juan Paisano, Tucson AZ 85718

ABSTRACT

A theory of electronic switching of Ovonic threshold switches and memory devices is presented, and the highly conducting ON state is explained, which allows many billion reproducible switching cycles. These features are related to the defect chemistry and the unique properties of chalcogenide glasses. Some of Ovshinsky's new Ovonic Universal Memory devices are described which are capable of non-binary information storage and encryption, and of neurosynaptic functions.

INTRODUCTION

Today we are honoring an extraordinary human being, a superb scientist and prolific inventor: Stan Ovshinsky. Nearly half a century ago, he started the field of amorphous semiconductors, at that time, an unexplored field of material science.

It happens very rarely that the materials used for an original invention turn out to be the best materials for the invention in later years. For instance Bardeen and Brattain made their first transistor out of germanium in 1947; and selenium was used in the original Xerox machines, materials no longer in use for these purposes. In general, new materials are developed and replace the original ones to improve the performance of the inventions. This has not happened with Ovshinsky's Ovonic threshold switches and memory devices: chalcogenide glasses remain the ideal materials for them, and today I will explain why that is so.

First, I will briefly describe the performance of the Ovonic devices, and second the physics of their operation. Understanding the physics of these devices allows us to answer the question why no other material has been able to perform their unique functions, i.e., why chalcogenides are the best.

PERFORMANCE OF OVONIC THRESHOLD SWITCHES

Figure 1 shows the current –voltage characteristic of the threshold switch which consists of a thin (less than 1 micron thick) chalcogenide glass film between two electrodes [1]. The first remarkable feature is its symmetry for positive and negative voltages. John Bardeen was astonished when he saw this because there is no other solid state device that behaves the same for positive and negative voltages. The device whose characteristic is shown in Fig.1 has been switching 120 billion times since 1968; it has outlived two oscilloscopes that needed replacement. This long life is another remarkable feature that I will try to explain.

In its OFF-state, the resistance of the device is many megohms, as expected for a chalcogenide glass having a bandgap of 0.7 to 1.0 eV. As the voltage exceeds the threshold value, however, the device switches in less than a fraction of a nanosecond to the conducting ON-state where the current increases nearly vertically at a holding voltage of between 0.5 and 1.2V. When the current falls below a critical holding current, the device switches back to its original OFF-state. In order to understand the physics of the device, you should know (1) that the current of the OFF-state increases with the area of the device, the current therefore flows uniformly through the chalcogenide before switching and (2) that the threshold voltage is proportional to the thickness of the chalcogenide film, which means that switching occurs at a critical electric field strength. Its value is typically between 500,000 and 700,000V/cm.

Figure 1

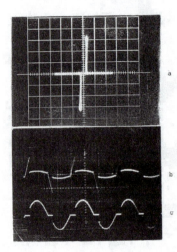

Fig.1. Response of Ovonic threshold switch to 60Hz voltage; after ref.[1].
    a. Vertical: 2mA/div., horizontal: 5V/div.
    b. Vertical: 10V/div., horizontal: 5msec/div.
    c. Vertical: 20mA/div., horizontal: 5msec/div

  Now some more information about the ON-state: (1) The holding voltage is nearly independent of the chalcogenide thickness. From that we conclude that most of the holding voltage drop occurs at the contacts. (2) The ON current and the holding current are independent of the area of the device down to area diameters of 100nm. That tells us that the ON current does not flow uniformly through the chalcogenide film, but is restricted to a current filament of 100nm diameter or less. In order to support typical ON-state currents of 0.5-5mA the current densities in the current filament must be 5-50 million A/cm^2. Any theory needs to explain these essential observations. But before we proceed with the theory for threshold switching, let us look in more detail at the pre-threshold current.

Before switching, the OFF current rises rapidly with increasing voltage. The first super-ohmic increase is due to space charge limited currents. This is followed by an exponential current increase with voltage or electric field due to the Poole-Frenkel effect [2]. This effect essentially delocalizes an increasingly larger section of localized states with increasing field, thus reducing the effective mobility gap and increasing the mobile carrier concentration. Just before and at threshold voltage the current rises rapidly as excess carriers are produced somewhere in the bulk of the material by what I believe is field-induced interband tunneling breakdown.

THEORY OF SWITCHING
First I remind you that chalcogenide glasses differ greatly from tetrahedral semiconductors such as Si, Ge, or the III-V compounds. In tetrahedral semiconductors, the uppermost filled band, called the valence band, is formed by the bonding orbitals of covalent bonds. Not so in chalcogenide glasses. Chalcogenides have 4 p-electrons, of these only 2 are used to covalently bond to two neighboring atoms, leaving a pair of 2 p-electrons untouched. These are called lone-pair electrons and they form the highest filled band [3]. Valence alternation pair defects are a unique feature of the defect chemistry of chalcogenide (group-VI) and pnictide (group-V element) glasses [4,5]. They are positive and negatively charged defect pairs that form easily and are at equilibrium with the glass above the glass transition temperature. They have a negative correlation energy and are associated with under- coordinated (negative) and over- coordinated (positive) chalcogenide or pnictide elements in the glass. Their concentration is

$$N(defect) = N(chalc) \exp(-Evap/2kTg) \tag{1}$$

Where Evap is the defect pair creation energy and Tg is the glass transition temperature, the temperature at which the equilibrium concentration of valence alternation pairs freezes in [4,5]. For typical threshold switching alloys this concentration is about $5 \times 10^{18} < N(defects) < 10^{20} cm^{-3}$.

The electronic states associated with the negatively and positively charged valence alternation centers are imbedded in the distributions of localized states which originate from the structural and compositional disorder of the chalcogenide glass. These distributions form exponentially decreasing tails of localized states extending from the electron and hole mobility edges into the gap. The mobility edge energies mark the transition from localized states in which carriers are immobile to extended states were electrons and holes are free to move with their respective mobility in response to an electric field. The separation of the electron and hole mobility edge energies is called the mobility gap.

As mentioned above, the Poole-Frenkel effect delocalizes an increasingly larger fraction of tail states, thereby decreasing the mobility gap and producing the exponential rise of the pre-threshold current. A further increase in field initiates somewhere in the bulk a Zener breakdown, that is a rapid rise in carrier concentration due to field-induced interband tunneling [6]. Interband tunneling is rare in crystalline semiconductors: one observes it only in Esaki tunneling diodes [7]. Zener proposed interband tunneling as the explanation for the sudden rapid rise of the reverse current in Zener diodes. However, the correct explanation turned out to be impact ionization breakdown in these reversed biased crystalline diodes [8]. Why do we believe that in chalcogenide glasses switching is initiated by Zener interband tunneling rather than by impact ionization? The answer is that the carrier mobilities in chalcogenide glasses are very small, less than 1 cm^2/Vs. This corresponds to mean free paths of about 2 A, which makes the concept of a mean free path and of occasional scattering meaningless. Whatever it's meaning, the mean free path is too short for carriers to gain the 0.6eV or 0.7eV energy necessary to ionize charges from the valence alternation defects to the conduction band. Interband tunneling, on the other hand, is greatly favored in chalcogenides. The localized wave functions of the tail states and of the numerous valence alternation defects form extensions and bridges for the tunneling wave functions crossing the gap.

After the onset of Zener tunneling breakdown, the excess carriers swamp the traps and recombination centers and are produced faster than the recombination rate. This allows the current to move at a much reduced internal field. The rapid increase of the drift mobility of excess carriers, as the traps get filled, contributes to the positive feedback that leads to a negative differential i-V characteristic which is usually hidden by the load line. The current-controlled S-type negative resistance leads then naturally to filament formation.

Switching has occurred and the ON-state needs a different sustaining mechanism, which we will discuss now.

THE ON-STATE

The ON-state deserves even greater attention than the breakdown phenomenon. All insulators and high- resistivity semiconductors experience breakdown around fields of about 1MV/cm and in essentially all cases such breakdown is destructive. In contrast, chalcogenide switching devices exhibit after breakdown a highly conducting ON-state that protects the device from permanent damage so that with falling current the original high resistance OFF-state is restored. Repeatable switching, billion and trillion times without damage, is possible thanks to the conducting ON-state.

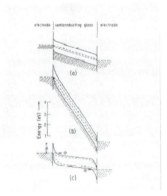

Fig.2. Potential profiles of device. (a) at low voltages and (b) at high voltage before switching. (c) In the ON-state after switching.

In the ON-state, current densities of order 1 MA/cm^2 flow in a 100nm diameter filament [9]. The voltage drop is confined to the vicinity of the contacts. Moreover, there is no polarity dependence. When the voltage drop is confined to the contacts, the current is contact limited. Indeed it is difficult to visualize how contacts to a semiconductor can supply a current density of order MA/cm^2. This problem is illustrated in Fig.2. The first panel shows an ohmic contact. Since the Fermi level of a chalcogenide glass is located near midgap, there is a barrier B of magnitude half the gap to overcome before electrons or holes can enter the semiconductor. The maximum current density which a metal contact can supply over the barrier is the thermionic emission current density given by the Richardson- Dushman equation [10]:

$$J= 120 \ T^2 \exp(-B/kT) \ (A/cm^2) \tag{2}$$

This thermionic current density is much smaller than the current densities flowing in the ON-state filament.

In the third panel of Fig.2, I have confined the voltage drop to the contact regions. Again there are the barriers B. The image potentials will round the barrier tops and decrease their heights, but still thermionic emission cannot supply the observed current densities. The only process that can yield the high current densities is Fowler-Nordheim field emission [11], that is tunneling of charge carriers through the potential barriers. This Fowler- Nordheim field emission is well known from metal contacts into vacuum. Current densities as large as 10^{10}A/cm^2 have been observed [12]. At even higher current densities the metal contact disintegrates because of excessive heating. In the ON-state, the barriers at the contacts to the chalcogenide are at most 0.4eV high compared to the work functions of 4-5 eV of metals. This allows for tunnel current densities of the magnitude we observe in chalcogenides with contact fields of order $2x10^5$V/cm, provided that the tunnel barrier width is narrow. The width or the screening length is small in chalcogenides in part because the negative correlation energy gives the valence alternation defects some unusual screening properties; despite the fact that they are located closer to the mobility edges than to the Fermi level at the gap center, they change their charge state as soon as the band bending exceeds a few kT [13]. Furthermore, their number counts double in screening because they change by two charges. As the Fermi level moves into the exponential tail of localized states, the shape of the screening potential changes from parabolic to exponential. These two factors, the negative correlation energy defects and the exponential tail states produce strong screening and the narrow potential barriers needed for Fowler-Nordheim tunneling.

As one decreases the chalcogenide thickness, that is, the electrode separation, there comes a point where the two space charge regions touch and the threshold voltage becomes equal to the holding voltage. No voltage breakback is observed between the OFF and ON states for such thin devices. The physics of these very interesting devices requires a separate discussion.

WHY CHALCOGENIDES ARE IDEAL MATERIALS FOR OVONIC SWITCHING
Very importantly the negative correlation energy of the valence alternation defect centers pins the Fermi level near the gap center [13]. As a consequence, and in contrast to most other materials, chalcogenide glasses are highly resistive despite the presence of defects and impurities. This special circumstance provides the high resistance OFF-state of the Ovonic devices. That situation is almost never found in other semiconductors having comparable band gaps [13].

The large densities of localized gap states bridge the tunneling wave functions for interband Zener tunneling which initiates switching from the OFF-state.

The localized gap states play an additional role. After the onset of breakdown one needs a positive feedback that provides excess carriers in the bulk at fields lower than the threshold field, in order to initiate the current controlled negative differential resistance that leads to filament formation. The filling of these states rapidly increases the drift mobility and life time of excess carriers.

The large density of negative correlation energy defect centers as well as the localized tail states provide strong screening and hence provide the narrow potential barriers at the contacts that are necessary for allowing, by Fowler- Nordheim field emission, the high current densities of the ON-state.

There is no substitute for chalcogenides when it comes to selecting the composition of a material that can easily and quickly undergo reversible structural transitions between the amorphous and crystalline states observed in Ovonic phase change memory devices. The logic of their synthesis and even most of the compositions used in modern optical and electrical phase-change devices date back to the pioneering work of Stan Ovshinsky [14-16].

MEMORY DEVICES

The Ovonic memory devices store the programmed information in a non-volatile manner using the high contrast between the high resistance, low optical reflectivity amorphous state and the low resistivity, high reflectivity crystalline state [1,15,17]. The phase change is initiated by short light or electrical pulses of different intensity and time shape.

High speed and low energy programming requires a material that undergoes the phase changes with minimum motion of the constituent atoms. There is no time for diffusion and phase separation. The flexibility of 2-fold coordinated chalcogen atoms and 3-fold coordinated pnictide atoms provide the ideal building blocks for designing materials with the desired energy balance between the amorphous and crystalline phases. The special character of their lone-pair orbitals, the non-bonding p-electron pair in group-VI elements and the non-bonding s-electron pair of group-V elements gives rise to a rich spectrum of phenomena that are unique to chalcogenide glasses [18]:

1. Non-thermal Photo-induced morphological change such as
   a. photo-induced fluidity
   b. photo-induced crystallization and amorphization
   c. photo-polymerization and giant densification
2. Reversible Isotropic Changes
   a. photo-darkening (photo-induced decrease of the optical band gap)
   b. structural changes
3. Photo-induced Anisotropies
   a. photo-induced dichroism and birefringence
   b. anisotropic optomechanical effect
   c. light scattering
   d. anisotropic photocrystallization
4. Photo-induced Chemical Modification
   a. photodissolution of Ag
   b. reversible chemical modification of Ag-chalcogenides

Many of these fascinating phenomena can be traced back to local bonding changes associated with excited exitons that momentarily change the charge state and hence the effective valency of adjacent chalcogen or pnictide atoms [18,19]. The structural flexibility of chalcogen and pnictide atoms provides these glasses with unique properties. However, some changes must be avoided in order to assure a trillion time repeatability of switching or of the programmed phase changes: the basic and desirable composition of the chalcogenide in the device must not change. This is no trivial task and has led to predictable failures in some laboratories. The problem is the prevention of electro-migration that is aggravated by the high contact fields of order 200,000V/cm and the high current densities in the filament of order 10^7A/cm^2. Some contact materials are truly terrible, such as Cu, Ag, Au, Al, and NiCr, others appear to serve for some time; but the very best results are obtained with carbon contacts.

BEYOND BINARIES

Conventional computers work in a binary mode and operate sequentially. The first Ovonic memory devices, as well as the Ovonic optical phase change memory discs, store information in the binary mode: the high resistance, low optical reflectivity amorphous state and the low resistivity, high reflectivity crystalline state. I now wish to describe Stan Ovshinsky's exciting new Ovonic Universal Memory (OUM) that transcends the binary mode of computing [20-22].

Figure 3 shows that an OUM device is capable of storing multiple memory states, in this case sixteen [20,22]. The same device can be programmed to fewer or more memory states as desired and depending on the resolution of reading the different resistance states. What are plotted along each step are the resistance values obtained with the programming current pulse indicated before the step. For example, a resistance of 1E+5 Ohm is programmed with a pulse of 2.35 mA regardless of the prior resistance state. Each state is non-volatile until it is overwritten by a different programming current pulse. The multi-state storage capability of the OUM obviously increases its memory storage density manifold.

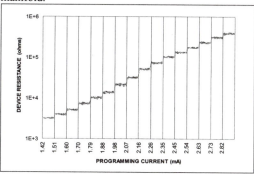

Fig.3.   Multi-state programming of OUM device. Each resistance state can be reached from any other state with the programming pulse current shown before each step. After ref.[20].

Figure 4 shows an overview of programming the resistance of OUM devices with current pulses [20,22]. In each case the resistance is read at a low voltage which does not change the state of the device in any way. Let us start with a device in its low resistance crystalline state. The state is not changed until the programming pulse amplitude is large enough to initiate amorphization. This first occurs at the smaller of the two contacts. As the programming pulse is increased an increasingly larger fraction of the chalcogenide gets amorphized thereby increasing the devise resistance in steps. This is the origin of the multi-state storage capability discussed in the previous Fig.3. This process saturates when essentially most of the chalcogenide between the electrodes is amorphous. Any of these states is non-volatile with time or the application of a read pulse.

I now describe another novel and exciting programming mode [20,22]. Look at the left hand side of the programming curve of Fig.4. We just ended up with the device in the amorphous, high resistance state. As one increases the current pulse amplitude, the

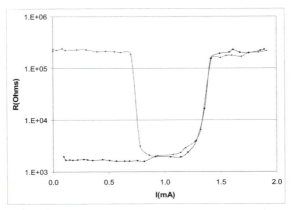

Fig.4. Programmed resistance as a function of pulse amplitude for OUM device either starting from the low resistance crystalline state or the high resistance amorphous state. After ref.[20].

resistance drops suddenly at a certain current amplitude when the conditions for crystallization are reached. It takes a certain amount of energy for crystallization. Let us now divide this energy into say five pulses as shown in Fig.5. The first 4 pulses do not change the resistance even though their energy is accumulated such that the fifth pulse achieves the change of state. Similarly one can divide the crystallization energy into say 10 parts such that the effect of nine pulses is accumulated and the tenth pulse produces the resistance change. What is happening? Each of the sub-pulses produces some crystallization and each sub-pulse increases the crystalline volume fraction until the percolation threshold is reached at which the resistance drops by one or two orders of magnitude. What you see in Fig.5 are resistance readings of 1000 repeat cycles of amorphization and crystallization in this pulse accumulation mode. Plotted are the minimum and maximum resistances recorded of these 1000 cycles. The reproducibility is very satisfactory. The behavior of the device reminds you of a biological neuron that receives energy inputs at its dendritic synaptic terminals and accumulates them until it reaches a threshold and fires.

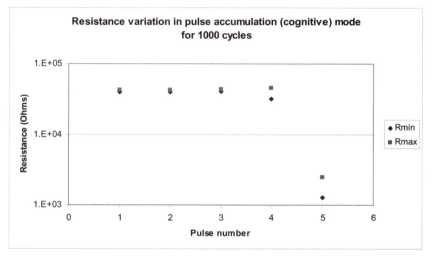

Fig.5. Pulse accumulation mode of the OUM device. The device has been cycled and programmed 1000 times. The minimum and maximum resistance value of these 1000 cycles are shown. After ref.[20].

The Ovonic Universal Memory is therefore a cognitive device; it exhibits analogous accumulation and activated firing capabilities with a choice of the number of pulses in the silent zone, the zone before the percolation threshold and the rapid resistance change. The scope of possible applications is immense. The fact that the silent zone hides the stored information which can only be obtained when one knows the exact parameters needed to encode it, the pulse widths and amplitudes, gives it unique encryption capabilities. Moreover, the non-binary storage and pulse accumulation capabilities provide the conditions for calculations in non-binary arithmetic systems [20-22].

CONCLUSIONS

Ovshinsky's invention of a variety of devices initiated a thorough study of the unique chemistry and the interesting electro-optical properties of chalcogenide glasses. His discovery of certain chalcogenide compositions that transform easily and reversibly between amorphous and crystalline states in response to optical or electrical pulses enabled the large industry of high information density optical and electrical phase change memories. His new multilevel memory and cognitive devices indicate that the applications of chalcogenide glasses are far from exhausted.

ACKNOWLEDGEMENTS

I am deeply indebted to Stan Ovshinsky for opening a new and promising field of material science that offered many interesting problems, which challenged me for many years.

REFERENCES

1. S.R. Ovshinsky, Phys. Rev. Lett. 21 (1968) 1450.
2. H. Fritzsche, Ch.5 in "Amorphous and Liquid Semiconductors" ed. J. Tauc, Plenum Press (1974) pp.221-312.
3. M. Kastner, Phys. Rev. Lett. 28 (1972) 355.
4. M. Kastner, D. Adler and H. Fritzsche, Phys. Rev. Lett. 37 (1976) 1504.
5. M. Kastner and H. Fritzsche, Philos. Mag. B37 (1978) 199.
6. C. Zener, Proc. Roy. Soc. (London) 145 (1934) 523.
7. L. Esaki, Phys. Rev. 109 (1958) 603.
8. K. G. McKay and K. B. McAffee, Phys. Rev. 91 (1953) 1079.
9. S. A. Kostylev, Ovonyx, Inc., private communication.
10. S. Dushman, Rev. Mod. Phys. 2 (1930) 381.
11. R. H. Fowler and L. Nordheim, Proc. Roy. Soc. A119 (1928) 173.
12. See, for example, Electron Emission in Encycl. Appl. Phys. Ed. G. L. Trigg (VCH Publ. 1994).
13. D. Adler and E. J. Yoffa, Phys. Rev. Lett. 41 (1978) 1755.
14. Disordered Materials-Science and Technology: Selected papers by Stanford R. Ovshinsky, eds. D. Adler, B.B. Schwartz, M. Silver (Plenum Press, New York,1991).
15. S.R. Ovshinsky and H. Fritzsche, IEEE Transactions on Electronic Devices, ED-20, (1973) 91.
16. S.R. Ovshinsky, Mater. Res. Soc. Symp. Proc. 554 (1999) 399.
17. Disordered Materials-Science and Technology-Selected Papers by S.R. Ovshinsky, ed. D. Adler, (Amorphous Institute Press, Bloomfield Hills MI,1982).
18. H. Fritzsche, in Insulating and Semiconducting Glasses", ed. P. Boolchand (World Scientific Press, 2000), p.653.
19. R.A. Street, Solid State Commun. 24 (1977) 363.
20. B. Pashmakov, S.R. Ovshinsky, D. Strand and T. Ohta, Asia Pacific Data Storage Conf. 27-30 Sept. 2004, Taiwan, ROC.
21. S.R. Ovshinsky and B. Pashmakov, Mater. Res. Soc. Symp. Proc. 803 (2004) 49.
22. S.R. Ovshinsky, in "Non-Crystalline Materials for Optolectronics" p.1, eds. G. Lucovsky and M. Popescu, Vol.1 Series: Optoelectronic Materials and Devices, (INOE, Bucharest, 2004).

FIGURE CAPTIONS

Fig.1. Response of Ovonic threshold switch to 60Hz voltage; after ref.[1].
   a. Vertical: 2mA/div., horizontal: 5V/div.
   b. Vertical: 10V/div., horizontal: 5msec/div.
   c. Vertical: 20mA/div., horizontal: 5msec/div.

Fig.2. Potential profiles of device. (a) at low voltages and (b) at high voltage before switching. (c) In the ON-state after switching.

Fig.3. Multi-state programming of OUM device. Each resistance state can be reached from any other state with the programming pulse current shown before each step. After ref.[20].

Fig.4. Programmed resistance as a function of pulse amplitude for OUM device either starting from the low resistance crystalline state or the high resistance amorphous state. After ref.[20].

Fig.5. Pulse accumulation mode of the OUM device. The device has been cycled and programmed 1000 times. The minimum and maximum resistance value of these 1000 cycles are shown. After ref.[20].

Appendix 11

Stan's and Iris' Acknowledgements

Many people have joined us in building ECD. We would like to mention all of them, but it is impossible.

We have already spoken of the importance of Bob Stempel – his vital contributions cannot be overstated.

Hellmut Fritzsche, whose great achievements have also been discussed earlier, has been a consistently wonderful collaborator.

Tyler Lowrey is an extraordinary talent and a great leader of our Ovonyx joint venture whose importance in the information area will in many ways be parallel to that of our energy activities. Remember, energy and information are the twin pillars of our global economy.

The Office of the Chairman is composed of Bob Stempel, Jim Metzger and Stan. Jim had a very senior position with Texaco, who were not only investors but had various joint ventures in energy with us. As everyone knows, Texaco was taken over by Chevron and we were so impressed with Jim that we asked him to join us as chief operating officer of ECD. His contributions to the expansion of the company's operations are very much appreciated.

Nancy Bacon, Senior Vice President of ECD, is in charge of much of our activity in finance and with the U.S. government. She is exceptionally talented, hardworking and committed and has through the years been a major contributor to building the company. She is a whirlwind of activity and has achieved recognition as a leader in international business.

We are very proud to have Marv Siskind as our chief patent counsel. He is an incredible talent who has a unique ability to get to the heart of an invention, obtain basic patents and at the same time be a wonderful negotiator with a great sense of strategy. There is no one like him.

Obviously, intellectual property is the bedrock of the company. Larry Norris, a talented and close colleague who has made critical contributions to the company, was one of our first patent attorneys.

Kevin Bray and Dave Schumaker are outstanding members of our patent department.

Subhendu Guha is president and chief operating officer of United Solar Ovonic. He came from the famous Tata Institute in India and joined our Ovonic photovoltaic research and development team. When Masat Izu, the first president of our Ovonic solar activities, transferred to building the new generations of Ovonic multi-junction continuous web machines, Subhendu became president. He has an admirable international scientific reputation.

It is unfortunate that we still use our joint venture name of United Solar Ovonic not only because it is now again 100% owned by ECD, but it always was and is now an integral unified, very talented group of colleagues and collaborators, some who came from the machine shop, but all as one unity. That unity is what is meant by our slogan and our trademark, Ovonics@work.

Masat Izu and Herb Ovshinsky pioneered with Stan the Ovonic photovoltaic activities. Masat was the first president of our Ovonic Solar manufacturing and sales and did a marvelous job of keeping costs down and production up on the machines that are now in the 9th and 10th generations. Herb's exceptional machine design talents and machine building experience were crucial to achieving the present generations of the Ovonic photovoltaic processor as well as the efficient and effective layout of the plants. ECD's Machine Division is the basis of the success and growth of our photovoltaic manufacturing. Its integral relationship with the United Solar Ovonic operating group is a wonder in itself. Not only for photovoltaics, but the wonderful work of Bud Dotter through the years on microwave and Vin Cannella's many important contributions that are lately being seen in our continuous web GE machines.

The profitability of Ovonic photovoltaics had its basis in our decision to build a 25MW machine which was strongly supported by Bob Stempel. His involvement was crucial. We felt that the only way that we could succeed in having our unique and superior technology take over the field was to expand from a 5MW to a 25/30MW machine which would give us the critical mass and platform for future machines where we could be directly competitive to fossil fuels, a world changing need and over a trillion dollar a year industry.

There are individual talents that are hard to characterize because they have so many facets and yet their work is part and parcel of the fabric of ECD. Alastair Livesey came to us from Shell where he had won our admiration working with him and observing how he could organize a team of strangers into a very productive creative group. He was an early recognizer of our work which he followed for many years. He has been a contributor to such disparate activities as algorithms for the Ovonic cognitive computer and being an aid to Jim Metzger's organizational activities. His potential is great.

Gary DiDio and Kevin Hoffman, with their accomplished and talented operating team, have had an extraordinary impact on the operation of the United Solar Ovonic production machines. Each has his own great strengths, together they are terrific. They continue working in complete harmony with ECD's Machine Division, using the latest lean manufacturing methods which contribute greatly to the groundbreaking work of this important division.

Prem Nath was an early pioneer with Stan who did superb work in Mexico and on the "back-end" activity of the operating group. Of course, many, many others contributed, of whom we must mention the outstanding work of John Call. Mark and Jackie Dahlin, Greg DeMaggio, Irv Rosenstein and Kais Younan deserve special mention for their significant contributions, both past and present. This tradition of service and talent began with Pat Dahlin who for many years represented the human side of our organization through her empathic abilities as head of ECD's human resources.

The 25/30MW machine is the engine of the great growth and commercial acceptance of the Ovonic solar company that is now taking place.

Our very close collaborators, the exceptionally creative Joe Doehler and Scott Jones, are the very best. The rest of the Machine Division's engineers, machine builders, engineering specialists, and everyone in the Machine Shop…what a dream team! They work so closely with the splendid operating group that runs the photovoltaics plant. Members of the Machine Division include our electrical genius, Arun Kumar and Tim Ellison, whose uniquely creative contributions are prize-winning. Many others, naming only a few such as Hank Bianchi, Gennady Bondarenko, Ervin Brooks, Barry Clark, Ray Crucet, Larry Fralalski, Eugene Ginzburg, Tim Laarman, Mark Lycette, Wayne Messing, Art Myatt since the early '60s, George Uzoni, Ken Whelan, and Roger Woz have earned our respect and admiration.

Jeff Yang joined us many years ago. While he worked on other projects, his contributions to the advancement of our Ovonic photovoltaics has been key to its many successes—increased efficiency is just one of the important areas of his work. He is a great group leader and developer of talent. He deserves much honor for his dedication, commitment, his great talents and for continuously moving the ball ahead both scientifically and technologically.

Dick Blieden, a great pioneer in photovoltaics, described earlier, continues to make important contributions in the marketing of our Ovonic solar products.

Qudrat Delawari, who pioneered Ovonic photovoltaics commercial marketing development, particularly in California, is a person of great talent, integrity and insight. His contributions to our photovoltaic success should be more widely known.

Homero delBosque is a very important figure in alternative energy. He is an industry builder, not only for Mexico and Latin America, but internationally. Homero's work is key to our efforts in bringing energy to developing countries around the world.

Steve Heckeroth is an extraordinary talent whose creativity, dedication and commitment to alternative energy, particularly photovoltaics, is of a legendary nature. His knowledge of roofs and building integration has no peer. It is a pleasure to see that our long struggle for building integrated photovoltaics, which has been the company's focus since before 1980, is now the order of the day.

Ben Ovshinsky has been a great help to ECD. In the early days, we set him up alone in England to build ECD in Europe and he succeeded. Varta, the famous battery company, became our first licensee. Ben has made ECD-Ovonics highly visible and respected on the West coast. He is a great asset of the California alternative energy community which is the most important of its kind in the United States.

Ovonic photovoltaics are part of our hydrogen energy loop. Obviously the sun fuses hydrogen to obtain its energy and our triple junction photovoltaic cells break apart water to provide hydrogen, the ultimate fuel.

Now to the people who are building the hydrogen economy with us.

Rosa Young is a unique, extraordinarily innovative talent whose important contributions have spanned almost all of our areas in a remarkable manner. She is in charge of our Ovonic hydrogen systems and is truly a force of nature. Rosa heads a wonderful group including Franz Gingl, Bao Huang (a great materials person), our veteran Ted Jurczak, Patrick Morris, Greg Schmidt, Jeff Schmidt (a vital part of our vehicular activity), Vicki Wong and Mike Zelinsky.

Ben Chao is not only head of our analytical laboratories but an incredibly important leader of many of ECD's material activities of which hydrogen is now of prime importance. Dave Pawlik is an important asset of ECD. His talent and leadership in the analytical lab are of major importance to the entire company. Alan Chan has made continuous contributions to the success of the analytical lab. Kim Huffman had been a vital part of this team. Having played an important role in our hydrogen activities, Yang Li is now utilizing his special talents in the Machine Division.

Vitaliy Myasnikov, a great metallurgist, is head of the inspired team, mostly Russian, who have done such outstanding work on the hydrogen storage vessel systems: Isaak Fidel, Alexandr Gerasimov, Jerzy Giedzinski, Vadim Itskov, and Nestor Kropelnyckyj.

Frank Ingriselli, formerly president of one of Texaco's operations is now working with us to build the hydrogen economy. He combines a great many talents in one person.

Subhash Dhar, a very close collaborator with Stan, formerly president of our Ovonic Battery Company, is a wonderfully multifaceted talented individual, uniquely good in business as well as in advanced technology operation. His leadership role in making a success of our vehicular batteries must always be recognized. The hybrid cars enabled by our Ovonic nickel-metal hydride batteries are a symbol of what a great team can accomplish.

Mike Fetcenko, Senior Vice President of Ovonic Battery, has exceptional multiple talents and has been a long time collaborator at ECD. His contributions have been critical to the success of the Ovonic nickel-metal hydride battery. Mike's ability to represent our company with Marv Siskind, head of our intellectual property, has been outstanding. Kwo Young has been a very important assistant to Mike's team. Benny Reichman's vital contributions date back to the earliest days of the Ovonic battery. Rose Bertolini, Cristian Fierro, William Mays, Avi Zallen and the rest of the team have much to be proud of.

Krishna Sapru is a wonderful colleague and one of our earliest collaborators in the atomic modeling of our materials. She helped Stan set up our first Ovonic nickel-metal hydride team which she led. Krishna continues her hydrogen activities, especially in developing countries.

Dennis Corrigan is a great contributor and team builder of the Ovonic Battery Company who is now head of the very important Ovonic Regenerative Fuel Cell activity. He is an industry builder whose personal contributions to our electric and hybrid vehicles are greatly appreciated. He represents our culture and is successful in passing it along to new employees who now join us.

Donn Fillmore has the potential to become one of our finest engineers. It is good to see him tapping into this potential, making him a sought-after addition to the various technology teams of ECD.

Srini Venkatesan—quiet, committed, and talented—is a superb electrochemist who has a long history of important contributions to our Ovonic batteries and fuel cells. He has been a collaborator in many of our fundamental activities that have been important to the commercial success of our batteries.

Kevin Fok is a young, talented contributor, particularly to our fuel cell unit. He has a great future with us and we look forward to his being an important builder of our Ovonic Regenerative Fuel Cell.

Meera Vijan can be placed in any position of management and be successful. She played an important role in our pioneering liquid crystal work as did Vin Cannella. Meera ran our production hydride foundry and is now acting head of the Ovonic Battery Company. She plays a critical role in our international battery work with China and India.

Our Ovonic Battery Company enabled the hybrid vehicles which are the future of the automotive industry. We are fortunate indeed to have John Smaga, a great talent who continues to advance our battery work; Lin Higley, all around creative genius; Marshall Muller, now on a special project continuing to make his mark on new hydride materials; Boyko Aladjov, whose next generation work with Stan is showing great progress.

We honor all of our "young tigers" who literally are the ones who changed the automotive industry by their talent, incredibly hard work and leadership ability that has made COBASYS, our joint venture with Chevron, the leading company that it is, manufacturing our Ovonic nickel-metal hydride batteries. There are many names, exemplified by Erik Hansen, Nick Karditsas, Ivan Menjak and Tony Osgood, who have much to contribute to ECD's future.

Arthur Holland is a fine engineer and machine builder whose work has always been key to our success. He can be depended on to build industries whether they are in the U.S, India or China. Art has been a dependable resource for many years as well as continuing to provide significant contributions.

David Tsu is one of our house theoretical physicists. He thinks carefully and deeply, always making himself available to help. He aids us in a wide range of projects.

Now to our work in information.

Wally Czubatyj who heads the Ovonic Universal Memory team, has been an incredibly valuable colleague and collaborator as well as an inspired leader of our semiconducting activity. He is a wonderful and great human being.

The team both old and new deserves acclaim for building the information side of ECD and Ovonyx. Starting with Pat Klersy who has played such an important role in developing our manufacturing technology, Steve Hudgens for his early contributions and leadership, now in Ovonyx, Sergey Kostylev for his creative advice, Guy Wicker, our computer whiz, Jeff Fournier who for many years has made sure that the technology and the clean room activities are of the highest caliber, and the new "young tigers" who are now making their contributions to our Ovonyx joint venture.

Contributors from an earlier day must certainly be mentioned —John deNeufville, Charlie Sie, Ed Fagen, Simon Moss, Raphael Tsu and others are seamlessly connected with our present group of important contributors such as David Strand. Dave is head of our optical phase change memory work and leader of our Ovonic cognitive computer activities. He has always been on a fast track for his recognized technical and management talents. Dave's stellar group includes his remarkable assistant Mike Hennessey, Dave Beglau, Kelly Daly Flynn, Dave Jablonski and Brenda Walton. Together with the rest of their team, they are very productive and their advanced work represents an integral part of our company's future. Ted Ohta has done so much to make our Ovonic optical phase change memory a commercial success by his important work at Matsushita and his continuing relationship with us. Boil Pashmakov is our collaborator on the Ovonic cognitive computer and the Ovonic 3-terminal device. This work has the potential to transform the computer industry as we know it.

The above-mentioned people are just a portion of the exceptional community of colleagues that has made ECD the unique company it is today.

We would like to acknowledge colleagues who have had unusual positive effects on not only our company's history but its integrity. They represent the best of us. Chester Kamin, an incredible intellect, strategic genius and our shield and sword has been our corporate attorney for many years, representing his law firm, Jenner and Block. Words actually fail us in describing his many, many contributions.

Ghazaleh Koefod has been an indispensable part of ECD. From her early beginnings with us as Stan's secretary in 1970 to her current position of great importance as board secretary, but more than that, there is no other person who works as hard as she, representing our company to the outside world with great intelligence, integrity and talent.

Ghazaleh's sisters, Laleh and Shahnaz, carry on her work ethic and high standards. We are so appreciative of their many, many contributions to making ECD the admired company that it is.

Lee Bailey was our internal corporate attorney whose sterling performance during periods of great challenges and change was equaled only by his superior intellect, his humor and his strength of character. He went on to become an important figure in government and then in investment banking.

Henry Lee has worked with us since we set up a small factory for the gases needed for photovoltaics that was headed by John deNeufville. He is a plasma chemistry expert, a very capable safety officer and a talent always ready to be of help. Every company should be as lucky to have such a talented and good person.

Loretta Yang, a stalwart of our company, is now head of Human Resources. Intelligent, efficient, effective and professional are words that jump to mind in describing her. Loretta's long, successful history with ECD has earned the respect of all of us.

We have been indeed blessed to have Freya Saito come back to us after her children grew up. She is bright, extremely competent with just the right values. Freya is an exceptional human being whose intelligence, scientific taste and ability have led us to consider her not only our administrative assistant but also our aide in science. Who needs Google?

Georgina Fontana, head of our administrative group and assistant to Bob Stempel, is outstanding. In all our years in industry, we have never seen anyone who is as good as she is under sometimes trying circumstances. She is talented, committed, effective, efficient, hard working and a good "boss".

After many years of working with Barb Wolff whom we miss greatly, Iris is lucky to have as her assistant Jeannie Sharon whose work provides the productive climate for Iris and Stan to work together and accomplish the things we do. JoAnn Osman, Stan's secretary for several years is now a great help in the Machine Division. Her warmth and friendly help, always at the ready, has earned our respect and appreciation and friendship.

Janis Delaney and Angelo Jacovetti, who are in charge of Plant Engineering, have shown themselves to be dedicated, hard-working people whose efforts allow the company to run smoothly. Like the proverbial postmen, they and their valued team work successfully in all conditions, climatic and otherwise.

We feel deep pride that we have built a culture for such talented people to reach their potential. Even if this culture is eroded or destroyed, ECD will be remembered as a place where human beings, regardless of race, religion or opinion, were able to live and work in a manner that brought out the very best in them, where merit, equity and the desire to make the world a better place were the guiding principles. May that torch of what society could become shine as an example to the world and its heart and soul continue.

Writing acknowledgements is an impossible task. We have gone this far and have only just begun. As we look through the names of all the people who have contributed mightily to our success, We feel we have to stop and give incredible thanks to ECD as a whole – it has been one great team working together with exceptional individuals throughout the organization. If we stop now, we will be inadvertently leaving out many people who have been extremely important to us. We find it very difficult to accept that we have not included all who should be mentioned here. We extend our deep apologies to those colleagues and collaborators who have not been singled out.

In closing, we must mention an ECD icon, Max Powell, Vice President of African Affairs. Now ninety-five years old, he has worked with us since the beginning in 1960. Admired by Nobelists, appreciated by everyone, Max has served as our ambassador to our incredible group of visitors from all over the globe. Always working hard for the company's success, Max is an inspiration.

Finally, we wish to acknowledge George Howard and Nancy Gulanick for their patience, humanity, insight and skill. We were not easy subjects either to understand or to put up with because of our incredible work load. For example, as we write this, we still haven't had dinner and it's after 8pm. We're still at the office. And our work continues, both when we get home and on weekends. O, woe... but what happiness!

We owe George and Nancy another great thanks. We have vicariously become a part of the Notre Dame culture. The students we met over the years from Notre Dame gave us great pleasure. Most of all, we were so moved by Father Hesburgh's forward for this book. As everyone knows, Father Ted is a living spirit and an illuminating human who shows that humanity has great potential for having better and more peaceful days. We thank him from our hearts.

Stan & Iris Ovshinsky
March 2006

Appendix 12

A Partial Listing of Stanford Ovshinsky's Publications and Papers

Physics and Chemistry

1. The Ovonic Switch as an Amorphous Switching Device, Presented at IV Symposium on Vitreous Chalcogenide Semiconductors, Academy of Sciences of the USSR, Leningrad (May 23-27, 1967).
2. Ovonic Switching Devices, Presented at the International Colloquium on Amorphous and Liquid Semiconductors, Academy of the Socialist Republic of Romania, Bucharest (September 28-October 3, 1967).
3. Ovonic Switching Devices, Presented at the 2nd Conference on the Characterization of Materials, Rochester, NY (November 8-10, 1967).
4. Reversible Electrical Switching Phenomena in Disordered Structures, *Phys. Rev. Lett.* **21**, 1450 (1968).
5. Ovonic Switching Devices, Presented at the American Ceramic Society Meeting, Chicago, IL (April 20-25, 1968).
6. Ovonic Switching Devices, Presented at the 1968 Electronic Components Conference, Washington, D.C. (May 9, 1968) p. 313.
7. Radiation Hardness of Ovonic Devices (with E. Evans, D. Nelson and H. Fritzsche), *IEEE Trans. Nuclear Sci.* **NS-15**, 311 (1968).
8. Ovonic Switches and Their Applications (with D. Nelson), Proceedings of IEEE International Convention, New York (March 1969).
9. Switching Devices, Presented at the Dalhousie Seminars on Solid State Physics, Dalhousie University, Halifax, Nova Scotia (June 30-July 2, 1969) p. 76.
10. Amorphous Semiconductors, *Science Journal* **5A**, 73 (August 1969).
11. The Ovshinsky Switch, Proceedings of the 5th Annual National Conference on Industrial Research, Chicago, IL (September 1969) p. 86.
12. Amorphous Semiconductors, *Electronic Material* (Japan) **8**, 30 (1969).
13. Simple Band Model for Amorphous Semiconducting Alloys (with M.H. Cohen and H. Fritzsche), *Phys. Rev. Lett.* **22**, 1065 (1969).
14. Hopping Conduction in an Amorphous Chalcogenide Alloy Film (with E.A. Fagen and H. Fritzsche), *Bull. Am. Phys. Soc. II* **14**, 311 (1969).
15. Photostimulated Conductivity in an Amorphous Chalcogenide Alloy Film (with H. Fritzsche and E.A. Fagen), ibid.
16. Electronic Conduction in Amorphous Semiconductors and the Physics of the Switching and Memory Phenomena (with H. Fritzsche), Presented at SEAS Symposium, NYC (May 14-17, 1969); *J. Non-Cryst. Solids* **2**, 393 (1970).
17. An Introduction to Ovonic Research, ibid., p. 99.
18. Reversible Conductivity Transformations in Chalcogenide Alloy Films (with E.J. Evans and J.H. Helbers), ibid., p. 334.
19. Structural Studies of Amorphous Semiconductors (with A. Bienenstock and F. Betts), ibid., p. 347.
20. Conduction and Switching Phenomena in Covalent Alloy Semiconductors (with H. Fritzsche), Proceedings of the International Conference on Amorphous and Liquid Semiconductors, Cavendish Laboratory, Cambridge, England (September 24-27, 1969); *J. Non-Cryst. Solids* **4**, 464 (1970).
21. A Qualitative Theory of Electrical Switching Processes in Monostable Amorphous Structures (with H.K. Henisch and E.A. Fagen), ibid., p. 538.
22. Radial Distribution Studies of Amorphous $Ge_x Te_{1-x}$ Alloys (with F. Betts and A. Bienenstock), ibid., p. 554.
23. Reflectivity Studies of the Te (Ge, As)-Based Amorphous Semiconductor in the Conducting and Insulating States (with J. Feinleib), ibid., p. 564.
24. Time Delay for Reversible Electric Switching in Semiconducting Glasses (with K.W. Boer and G. Doehler), ibid., p. 573.
25. Physics and Device Applications of Switching and Memory Effects in Vitreous Semiconductors (with H. Fritzsche), Presented at V Symposium on Vitreous Chalcogenide Semiconductors, Leningrad, USSR (May 25-29, 1970).
26. Switching Effects in Amorphous Semiconductor Thin Films (with H.K. Henisch and R.W. Pryor), Presented at the International Congress on Thin Films, Cannes, France (October 5-10, 1970).
27. Development and Application of Amorphous Semiconductors (with R.G. Neale), Presented at 4th International Congress Microelectronics, Munich, Germany (November 9-11, 1970).
28. Ovonics and Its Applications, Presented at 1970 International Hybrid Microelectronics Symposium, Beverly Hills, CA (November 16-18, 1970).
29. Amorphous Semiconductors, *Detroit Engineers* **34**, #5, 13 (1970).
30. Analog Models for Information Storage and Transmission in Physiological Systems (with Iris M. Ovshinsky), *Mat. Res. Bull.* **5**, 681 (1970). (Mott Festschrift)
31. Calorimetric and Dilatometric Studies on Chalcogenide Alloy Glasses (with H. Fritzsche), *J. Non-Cryst. Solids* **2**, 148 (1970).
32. Electrical Conductivity of Amorphous Chalcogenide Alloy Films (with E.A. Fagen and H. Fritzsche), ibid., p. 170.
33. Electrothermal Initiation of an Electronic Switching Mechanism in Semiconducting Glasses (with K.W. Boer), *Appl. Phys.* **41**, 2675 (1970).

34. Reversible High-Speed High-Resolution Imaging in Amorphous Semiconductors (with P.H. Klose), Presented at 1971 Society for Information Display International Symposium, Philadelphia, PA (May 4-6, 1971); Digest of Technical Papers (May 1971) p. 58.
35. Glass Switch, McGraw-Hill Encyclopedia of Science and Technology **13**, 360 (1971).
36. New Materials for Electronics (with H. Henisch), Encyclopedia of Science and Technology, Italy (1971) p. 400 [I semiconduttori amorfi, Stanford R. Ovshinsky e Heinz K. Henisch, in Encyclopedia della Scienza e della Tecnica 71, A. Mondadori, Editore, 1971, p. 402].
37. Rapid Reversible Light-Induced Crystallization of Amorphous Semiconductors (with J. Feinleib, J. deNeufville and S.C. Moss), *Appl. Phys. Lett.* **18**, 254 (1971).
38. Reversible Structural Transformations in Amorphous Semiconductors for Memory and Logic (with H. Fritzsche), *Metallurgical Transactions* **2**, 641 (1971).
39. Imaging in Amorphous Materials by Structural Alteration (with P.H. Klose), Presented at 4th International Conference on Amorphous and Liquid Semiconductors, Ann Arbor, MI (August 9-13, 1971); *J. Non-Cryst. Solids* **8-10**, 892 (1972).
40. Reversible Optical Effects in Amorphous Semiconductors (with J. Feinleib, S. Iwasa, S.C. Moss and J.P. deNeufville), ibid., p. 909.
41. The Transmission, Storage and Control of Information in Amorphous Materials, Presented at 4th Annual Spring Meeting of the Metallurgical Society of AIME, Boston, MA (May 8-11, 1972).
42. New Thin-Film Tunnel Triode Using Amorphous Semiconductors (with R.F. Shaw, H. Fritzsche, M. Silver, P. Smejtek and S. Holmberg), *Appl. Phys. Lett* **20**, 241 (1972).
43. Ovonics Revisited, *Industrial Research* **14**, 48 (1972).
44. Optical Information Encoding in Amorphous Semiconductors, Presented at the Topical Meeting on Optical Storage of Digital Data, Aspen, CO (March 19-21, 1973).
45. Amorphous Materials and the Computer, Presented at Engineering Society of Detroit (October 11, 1973).
46. Amorphous Semiconductors for Switching, Memory, and Imaging Applications (with H. Fritzsche), *IEEE Trans. on Electron Devices*, **ED-20**, 91 (1973).
47. Mechanism of Reversible Optical Storage in Evaporated Amorphous AsSe and $Ge_{10}As_{40}Se_{50}$ (with J.P. deNeufville, R. Seguin and S.C. Moss), Proceedings of the 5th International Amorphous and Liquid Semiconductors Conference, Garmisch-Partenkirchen, Germany (September 1973), edited by J. Stuke & W. Brenig (Taylor and Francis, London, 1974) p.737.
48. Three Dimensional Model of Structure and Electronic Properties of Chalcogenide Glasses (with K. Sapru), ibid., p. 447.
49. Photostructural Transformations in Amorphous As_2Se_3 and As_2S_3 Films (with J.P. deNeufville and S.C. Moss), *J. Non-Cryst. Solids* **13**, 191 (1973/1974).
50. Amorphous Materials as Information Storage Media, Presented at Iowa State University, Joint Electrical Engineering and Physics Colloquium (January 28, 1974).
51. Applications of New Memory Material to Electronic Imaging, Presented at University of Pittsburgh, Medical School, Pittsburgh, PA (February 13, 1974).
52. Amorphous Read Mostly Memory, Presented at University of Illinois, Urbana, IL (March 12, 1974).
53. Optical Information Encoding in Amorphous Semiconductors (with Iris M. Ovshinsky), Presented at the 14th Annual Fall Symposium of Society of Photographic Scientists and Engineers, Washington, D.C. (October 23-26, 1974).
54. Imaging by Photostructural Changes (with P.H. Klose), Proceedings of the Symposium on Nonsilver Photographic Processes, held at New College, Oxford (September 1973); *Non-Silver Photographic Processes*, edited by R.J. Cox (Academic Press, London, 1975) p. 61.
55. Electronic and Structural Changes in Amorphous Materials as a Means of Information Storage and Imaging, Proceedings of the 4th International Congress for Reprography and Information, Hanover, Germany (April 13-17, 1975) p.109.
56. A New Means of Information Storage, Presented at the 1975 Summer Symposium of the Society of Photographic Scientists and Engineers, Bloomington, MN (June 24-27, 1975).
57. Amorphous Materials as Optical Information Media, Presented at the International Laser Exposition and Electro-Optical Systems Design Conference, Anaheim, CA (November 11-13, 1975); *J. Appl. Photographic Eng.* **3**, 35 (1977).
58. Amorphous Materials as Interactive Systems, Proceedings of the 6th International Conference on Amorphous and Liquid Semiconductors, Leningrad (November 18-24, 1975) p. 426.
59. An Experimental Study of Threshold Switching in Some Binary Chalcogenide-Based Glass Films (with R.A. Flasck, M.P. Shaw and K. Dec), ibid., p. 490.
60. The Basic Concepts of Amorphous Semiconductors, Presented at Stanford University, Stanford, CA (January 21, 1976).
61. Lone-Pair Relationships and the Origin of Excited States in Amorphous Chalcogenides, Proceedings of the International Topical Conference on Structure and Excitation of Amorphous Solids, Williamsburg, VA (March 24-27, 1976) p. 31.
62. Localized States in the Gap of Amorphous Semiconductors, *Phys. Rev. Lett.* **36**, 1471 (1976).
63. Amorphous Materials as Optical Information Media, Presented at SPIE/SPSE Technical Symposium, East Reston, VA (March 22-25, 1976); *J. Appl. Photographic Engineering* **3**, 35 (1977).

64. Chemical Modification of Amorphous Chalcogenides, Proceedings of the 7th International Conference on Amorphous and Liquid Semiconductors, Edinburgh, Scotland (June 27-July 1, 1977) p. 519.

65. Optical and Electronic Properties of Modified Amorphous Materials (with R.A. Flasck, M. Izu, K. Sapru, T. Anderson and H. Fritzsche), ibid., p. 524.

66. Modification of SiO_x (with K. Sapru and K. Dec), Proceedings of the International Topical Conference on the Physics of SiO2 and its Interfaces, Yorktown Heights, NY (March 22-24, 1978) p. 304.

67. Local Structure, Bonding and Electronic Properties of Covalent Amorphous Semiconductors (with D. Adler), Presented at the APS March Meeting, Washington, D.C. (March 27-30, 1978); *Contemp. Phys.* **19**, 109 (1978).

68. Amorphous Photovoltaic Cells (with A. Madan), Proceedings of the Solar Energy Symposia of the 1978 Annual Meeting of the American Section of the International Solar Energy Society, Inc., Denver, CO (August 28-31, 1978).

69. Photovoltaic Solar Energy Conference, book review, edited by A.S. Strub, *American Scientist* **66**, 616 (September-October 1978).

70. Solar Electricity Speeds Down to Earth, *New Scientist* **80** (November 30, 1978), p. 674.

71. A New Amorphous Silicon-Based Alloy for Electronic Applications (with A. Madan), *Nature* **276**, 482 (November 30, 1978).

72. Low-Cost Photovoltaic Devices Using Amorphous Materials (with A. Madan), Presented at the Symposium on Applied Technology to Solar Energy Systems, Jurica, Queretaro, Mexico (January 29 - February 3, 1979).

73. New Amorphous Materials for Computer Use, Presented at the 18th IEEE Computer Society International Conference, San Francisco, CA (February 26-March 1, 1979) p. 158.

74. The Inventor as a Catalyst, Proceedings of the 33rd National Conference on the Advancement of Research, Pennsylvania State University State College, Pennsylvania (October 7-10, 1979).

75. An Innovative Approach to New Sources of Energy Through Amorphous Materials, Presented at the UNITAR Conference on Long Term Energy Resources, Montreal, Canada (November 26-December 7, 1979) p. 783.

76. Electrical and Optical Properties of Amorphous Si:F:H Alloys (with A. Madan and E. Benn), *Phil. Mag.* **B.40**, 259 (1979).

77. The Shape of Disorder, *J. Non-Cryst. Solids* **32**, 17 (1979). (Mott Festschrift)

78. Some Electrical and Optical Properties of A-Si:F:H Alloys (with A. Madan, W. Czubatyj and M. Shur), Presented at the 21st Electronic Materials Conference, University of Colorado, Boulder, CO (June 27-29, 1979); *J. Elect. Mat.* **9**, 385 (1980).

79. Properties of Amorphous Si:F:H Alloys (with A. Madan), Presented at the 8th International Conference on Amorphous and Liquid Semiconductors, Cambridge, MA (August 27-31, 1979); *J. Non-Cryst. Solids* **35/36**, 171 (1980).

80. Book Review on The Physics of Selenium and Tellurium, edited by E. Gerlach and P. Grosse, *American Scientist* **68** (May-June 1980) p.316.

81. The Chemistry of Glassy Materials and Their Relevance to Energy Conversion, Proceedings of the International Conference: Frontiers of Glass Science, Los Angeles, CA (July 16-18, 1980); *J. Non-Cryst. Solids* **42**, 335 (1980).

82. Effect of an Interfacial Oxide in Amorphous Si:F:H Alloy Based MIS Devices (with A. Madan, J. McGill, W. Czubatyj, J. Yang and M. Shur), Presented at the SPIE – The International Society for Optical Engineering Conference on Role of Electro-Optics in Photovoltaic Energy Conversion, San Diego, CA (July 31-August 1, 1980); SPIE Proc. Vol. 248, p. 26.

83. Electronic and Vibrational Properties of Glow-Discharge Amorphous Si:F:H (with R. Tsu, M. Izu and V. Cannella), Proceedings of the 15th International Conference on Physics of Semiconductors, Kyoto, Japan (September 1-5, 1980); *J. Phys. Soc. Japan* **49** (1980) Suppl. A, p.1249.

84. The Important Roles Played by Selenium and Tellurium in Amorphous Materials, Presented at the International Symposium on Industrial Uses of Selenium and Tellurium, Toronto, Canada (October 21-23, 1980).

85. Electroreflectance and Raman Scattering Investigation of Glow-Discharge Amorphous Si:F:H (with R. Tsu, M. Izu and F.H. Pollak), *Solid State Comm.* **36**, 817 (1980).

86. Metal-Insulator-Semiconductor Solar Cells Using Amorphous Si:F:H Alloys (with A. Madan, J. McGill, W. Czubatyj and J. Yang), *Appl. Phys. Lett.* **37**, 826 (1980).

87. New Experiments on Threshold Switching in Chalcogenide and Non-Chalcogenide Alloys (with K. Homma and H.K. Henisch), *J. Non-Cryst. Solids* **35/36**, 1105 (1980).

88. Threshold Switching in Chalcogenide Glass Thin Films (with D. Adler, M. Shur and M. Silver), *J. Appl. Phys.* **51**, 3289 (1980).

89. The Immediacy of Alternative Energy, presentation sponsored by Nihon Keizai Shimbun, the Japanese Economic Journal and Science, *Japanese Scientific American* (February 26, 1981) and several presentations in the 1970s.

90. High Efficiency, Large-Area Photovoltaic Devices Using Amorphous Si:F:H Alloy (with A. Madan, W. Czubatyj, J. Yang and J. McGill), Presented at the 9th International Conference on Amorphous and Liquid Semiconductors, Grenoble, France (July 2-8, 1981); *J. de Physique* **42**, Suppl. 10 (1981) p. C4-463.

91. The Nature of Intermediate Range Order in Si:F:H:(P) Alloy Systems (with R. Tsu, S.S. Chao, M. Izu, G.J. Jan and F.H. Pollak), ibid., p. C4-269.

92. Principles and Applications of Amorphicity, Structural Change, and Optical Information Encoding, ibid., p. C4-1095.

93. The Chemical Basis of Amorphicity: Structure and Function, *Revue Roumaine de Physique* **26**, 893 (1981). (Grigorovici Festschrift)

94. This Week's Citation Classic [S.R. Ovshinsky, Reversible Electrical Switching Phenomena in Disordered Structures, *Phys. Rev. Lett.* **21**, 1450 (1968)], *Current Contents* **22**, 18 (March 8, 1982).

95. Progress in Large Area Photovoltaic Devices Based on Amorphous Silicon Alloys (with J.P. deNeufville and M. Izu), Proceedings of the 16th Intersociety Energy Conversion Engineering Conference, Atlanta, GA (August 9-14, 1981); *Photovoltaics, The Solar Electric Magazine* **3**, 2217 (August/September 1982).

96. Correlation Between the Superconducting and Normal State Properties of Amorphous Molybdenum – Silicon Alloys (with A.S. Edelstein, H. Sadat-Akhavi and J. Wood), *Solid State Comm.* **41**, 139 (1982).

97. Switch, Glass (with D. Adler) McGraw-Hill Encyclopedia of Science and Technology (McGraw-Hill Book Company, 5th through 8th Editions, 1982-1994).

98. Commercial Development of Ovonic Thin Film Solar Cells, Presented at the SPIE – The International Society for Optical Engineering Symposium on Photovoltaics for Solar Energy Applications II, Arlington, VA (April 5-6, 1983); SPIE Proc. Vol. 407, p. 5.

99. Production of Tandem Amorphous Silicon Alloy Solar Cells in a Continuous Roll-to-Roll Process (with M. Izu), ibid., p. 42.

100. Innovation: Building a New Industrial Society, Presented at the American Association for the Advancement of Science (AAAS) Youth Symposium, Detroit, MI (May 26, 1983).

101. Improving the Business Environment in the Midwest for High Industry, Presented at OHMCON/83 on Hi-Technology, Hi-Growth Industries – Cultivating them in the Midwest, Detroit, MI (June 14-16, 1983).

102. Amorphous Photovoltaics – Introduction and Scientific Background, Presented at the Conference on Nonconventional Energy Sources and Summer Workshop on the Physics of Nonconventional Energy Sources, Miramare-Trieste, Italy (June 20 - July 8, 1983).

103. Amorphous Photovoltaics – Technology and Production, ibid.

104. Present Status of the Science and Technology of Amorphous Solids (with D. Adler), *Nikkei Science* (Japanese Scientific American) (August 1983) p. 60.

105. Laser-Induced Fluorescence Detection of Reactive Intermediates in Diffusion Flames and in Glow-Discharge Deposition Reactors (with H.U. Lee and J. deNeufville), Presented at the 10th International Conference on Amorphous and Liquid Semiconductors, Tokyo, Japan (August 1983); *J. Non-Cryst. Solids* **59/60**, 671 (1983).

106. The Role of Free Radicals in the Formation of Amorphous Thin Films, Proceedings of the International Ion Engineering Congress, ISIAT '83 & IPAT '83, Kyoto, Japan (September 12-16, 1983) p. 817.

107. Order Parameters in a-Si Systems (with R. Tsu, J. Gonzales-Hernandez and J. Doehler), *Solid State Comm.* **46**, 79 (1983).

108. Roll-to-Roll Plasma Deposition Machine for the Production of Tandem Amorphous Silicon Alloy Solar Cells (with M. Izu), Presented at the International Conference on Metallurgical Coatings, San Diego, CA (April 9-13, 1984); *Thin Solid Films* **119**, 55 (1984).

109. Amorphous Silicon Solar Cells, Presented at the American Vacuum Society Symposium on Coatings for Large-Scale Metallurgical, Optical, and Electronic Applications, Exxon Research and Engineering Co., Annadale, NJ (June 13, 1984); *J. Vacuum Science and Technology B* **2**, 835 (1984).

110. Roll-to-Roll Mass Production Process for a-Si Solar Cell Fabrication, Presented at the 1st International Photovoltaic Science and Engineering Conference, Kobe, Japan (November 13-16, 1984) p. 577.

111. Asymmetric Flux-Flow Behavior in Superconducting Multi-layered Composites (with A.M. Kadin, R.W. Burkhardt, J.T. Chen and J.E. Keem), Proceedings of the 17th International Conference on Low Temperature Physics, edited by U. Eckern, A. Schmid, W. Weber and W. Wühl (Elsevier Science Publishers, 1984).

112. Properties of Amorphous Semiconducting Multilayer Films (with J. Kakalios, H. Fritzsche and N. Ibaraki), *J. Non-Cryst. Solids* **66**, 339 (1984).

113. Reply to "Comment on 'Threshold Switching in Chalcogenide Glass Thin Films'," (with D. Adler, M.S. Shur and M. Silver), *J. Appl. Physics* **56**, 579 (1984).

114. Amorphous Materials – Past, Present and Future, Presented at the Symposium on Glass Science and Technology – Problems and Prospects for 2004, Vienna, Austria (July 3, 1984); *J. Non-Cryst. Solids* **73**, 395 (1985). (Kreidl Festschrift)

115. Superconducting Properties of Amorphous Multilayer Metal-Semiconductor Composites (with A.M. Kadin, R.W. Burkhardt, J.T. Chen and J.E. Keem), Presented at the Materials Research Society Meeting, Boston, MA (November 26-30, 1984); in "Layered Structures Epitaxy and Interfaces," edited by J. M. Gibon and L. R. Dawson; *Mat. Res. Soc. Symp. Proc.* **37**, 503 (1985).

116. Basic Anticrystalline Chemical Bonding Configurations and Their Structural and Physical Implications, Presented at the International Conference on the Theory of the Structures of Non-Crystalline Solids, Institute for Amorphous Studies, Bloomfield Hills, MI (June 3-6, 1985); *J. Non-Cryst. Solids* **75**, 161 (1985).

117. Chemical Bond Approach to Glass Structure (with J. Bicerano), ibid., p. 169.

118. Amorphous Photovoltaics (with D. Adler), *Chemtech* **15**, 538 (September 1985).

119. Low Pressure Microwave Glow Discharge Process for High Deposition Rate Amorphous Silicon Alloy (with S.J. Hudgens and A.G. Johncock), Presented at the 11th International Conference on Amorphous and Liquid Semiconductors, Rome, Italy (September 2-6, 1985); *J. Non-Cryst. Solids* **77/88**, 809 (1985).

120. The Chemical and Configurational Basis of High Efficiency Amorphous Photovoltaic Cells, Proceedings of the 18th IEEE Photovoltaic Specialists Conference, Las Vegas, NV (October 21-25, 1985) p. 1365.

121. Experience in Licensing, Presented at the Conference on Technology Transfer and Licensing Opportunities in the Energy Sector, Copenhagen, Denmark (November 11-13, 1985).

122. Chemical Bond Approach to the Structures of Chalcogenide Glasses with Reversible Switching Properties (with J. Bicerano), *J. Non-Cryst. Solids* **74**, 75 (1985).

123. Chemistry and Structure in Amorphous Materials: The Shape of Things to Come, in "Physics of Disordered Materials," edited by D. Adler, H. Fritzsche and S. R. Ovshinsky, Institute for Amorphous Studies Series (Plenum Press, New York, 1985) p. 37. (Mott Festschrift)

124. Critical Materials Parameters for the Development of Amorphous Silicon Alloys (with D. Adler), Presented at the 1985 Materials Research Society Spring Meeting, San Francisco, CA (April 15-18, 1985); in "Materials Issues in Applications of Amorphous Silicon Technology," D. Adler, A. Madan and M. J. Thompson, editors; *Mat. Res. Soc. Symp. Proc.* **49**, 251 (1985).

125. A Figure of Merit Evaluation of Amorphous Silicon Alloy Solar Cells (with J.A. Yang), Proceedings of the 1985 International Conference on Solar and Wind Energy Applications, China (Academic Publishers) p. 75.

126. Fundamentals of Amorphous Materials, in "Physical Properties of Amorphous Materials," edited by D. Alder, B.B. Schwartz and M.S. Steele, Institute for Amorphous Studies Series (Plenum Press, 1985) p. 105.

127. Nevill Mott Appreciation (with I.M. Ovshinsky), in "Appreciations" *Philosophical Magazine B* **52**, pp. 215-224 (1985). (Mott Festschrift)

128. A New Role for Vacuum Technology (with D. Adler), Proceedings of the 28th Annual Technical Conference of the Society of Vacuum Coaters, Washington, D.C. (1985) p. 1.

129. Superconducting Properties of Sputtered Mo-C Films and Columnar Microstructure (with J. Wood, J.E. Keem, J.T. Chen, A.M. Kadin and R.W. Burkhardt), *IEEE Transactions on Magnetics* **MAG-21**, 842 (1985).

130. Intuition and Quantum Chemistry, Proceedings of the Nobel Laureate Symposium on Applied Quantum Chemistry (in honor of G. Herzberg, R.S. Mulliken, K. Fukui, W. Lipscomb and R. Hoffman), Honolulu, HI (December 16-21, 1984); *Applied Quantum Chemistry*, edited by V. H. Smith, Jr. et al. (D. Reidel Publishing, 1986) p. 27.

131. Chemical Bonding and the Nature of Glass Structure (with J. Bicerano), ibid., p.325.

132. Amorphous Semiconductors for Microelectronics, Presented at the SPIE – The International Society for Optical Engineering on Amorphous Semiconductors for Microelectronics, Los Angeles, CA (January 21-22, 1986); SPIE Proc. Vol. 617, p. 2.

133. Macro-Engineering: The Crucial Element in Creating a Photovoltaic Industry, Presented at the American Society for Macro-Engineering conference on Macro-Engineering: The New Challenge, Washington, D.C. (March 13-14, 1986).

134. Solving the Problems of Efficiency, Stability and Production in Amorphous Photovoltaic Devices, Presented at Electronic Materials Processing, AIChE Meeting, Boston, MA (August 24-26, 1986).

135. Progress in the Science and Application of Amorphous Materials (with D. Adler), Proceedings of the International Conference on Non-Crystalline Semiconductors '86, Balatonszeplak, Hungary (September 15-20, 1986); *J. Non-Cryst. Solids* **90**, 229 (1987).

136. The Breaking of the Efficiency-Stability-Production Barrier in Amorphous Photovoltaics (with J. Yang), Presented at the SPIE – The International Society for Optical Engineering Conference on Photovoltaics for Commercial Solar Power Applications, Cambridge, MA (September 18-91,1986); SPIE Proc. Vol. 706, p. 88.

137. New Material Innovation – Birth of Synthetic Material Age, Presented at the 1ˢᵗ International New Materials Conference & Exhibition, Osaka, Japan (October 16-19, 1986).

138. Crucial Parameters in Amorphous Solar Cells (with J. Yang), Presented at the 7ᵗʰ European Photovoltaic Solar Energy Conference, University of Seville, Spain (October 27-31, 1986).

139. Effects of Transition-Metal Elements on Tellurium Alloys for Reversible Optical-Data Storage (with R. Young, D. Strand and J. Gonzales-Hernandez), *J. Appl. Physics* **60**, 4319 (1986).

140. A Simplified Summary of the ECD Model Explaining the Mechanism of High Temperature Superconductivity in "Topics in Non-Crystalline Semiconductors – In Memory of David Adler 1937 – 1987," edited by Hellmut Fritzsche and Ai-Lien Jung, Beijing University of Aeronautics and Astronautics, (1987), p. 186.

141. Amorphous Silicon Alloys – The Basis for High Efficiency, High Stability, Low Cost Photovoltaics (with J. Yang), Presented at the International Symposium-Workshop on Silicon Technology Development and its Role in the Sun-Belt Countries, Islamabad, Pakistan (June 14-18, 1987).

142. Superconductivity in Fluorinated Copper Oxide Ceramics (With R.T. Young, B.S. Chao, G. Fournier and D.A. Pawlik), Presented at the International Conference on High Temperature Superconductivity, Drexel University, Philadelphia, PA (July 29-30, 1987); *Reviews of Solid State Science* **1**, 207 (1987).

143. Fluorinated Amorphous Silicon-Germanium Alloys Deposited from Disilane-Germane Mixture (with S. Guha, J.S. Payson and S.C. Agarwal), Presented at the 12ᵗʰ International Conference on Amorphous and Liquid Semiconductors, Prague (August 24-28, 1987); *J. Non-Cryst. Solids* **97/98**, 1455 (1987).

144. Superconductivity at 155K and Room Temperature, Presented at Superconductors in Electronics Commercialization Workshop, San Francisco, CA (September 14-15, 1987).

145. 1 MW Amorphous Silicon Thin-Film PV Manufacturing Plant (with P. Nath, K. Hoffman, J. Call, C. Vogeli and M. Izu), Presented at the 3ʳᵈ International Photovoltaic Science and Engineering Conference, Tokyo, Japan (November 3-6, 1987) p. 395.

146. Continuous Web Deposition of Amorphous Photovoltaics (with P. Nath), Presented at 1ˢᵗ International Conference on Vacuum Web Coating, New Orleans, LA (November 29 - December 1, 1987).

147. Superconductivity in the Fluorinated YBaCuO (with R.T. Young, B.S. Chao, G. Fournier and D.A. Pawlik), Presented by the Materials Research Society Meeting, Boston, Massachusetts (November 30 - December 5, 1987).

148. Passivation of Dangling Bonds in Amorphous Si and Ge by Gas Absorption (with R. Tsu, D. Martin and J. Gonzalez-Hernandez), *Physical Review B* **35**, 2385 (1987).

149. The Quantum Nature of Amorphous Solids in "Disordered Semiconductors," edited by M. A. Kastner, G. A. Thomas and S. R. Ovshinsky, Institute for Amorphous Studies Series (Plenum Press, New York, 1987) p. 195. (Fritzsche Festschrift)

150. A Structural Chemical Model for High T_c Ceramic Superconductors (with S.J. Hudgens, R.L. Lintvedt and D.B. Rorabacher), *Modern Phys. Lett. B* **1**, 275 (1987).

151. Superconductivity at 155K (with R.T. Young, D.D. Allred, G. DeMaggio and G.A. Van der Leeden), *Phys. Rev. Lett.* **58**, 2579 (1987).

152. Keynote address at the Hydrogen Photo Production Workshop II, Hawaii (January 13, 1988).

153. A New, Inexpensive, Thin Film Photovoltaic Power Module (with P. Nath, K. Hoffman, C. Vogeli and K. Whelan), Presented at the 20th IEEE Photovoltaic Specialists Conference, Las Vegas, NV (September 26-30, 1988) p. 1315.

154. Yield and Performance of Amorphous Silicon Based Solar Cells Using Roll-to-Roll Deposition (with K. Hoffman, P. Nath, J. Call, G. DiDio and C. Vogeli), ibid., p. 293.

155. Conversion Process for Passivating Current Shunting Paths in Amorphous Silicon Alloy Solar Cells (with P. Nath, K. Hoffman and C. Vogeli), *Appl. Phys. Lett.* **53**, 986 (1988).

156. A Novel Design for Amorphous Silicon Alloy Solar Cells (with S. Guha, J. Yang, A. Pawlikiewicz, T. Glatfelter and R. Ross), Proceedings of the 20th IEEE PVSC (1988) p. 79.

157. A Personal Adventure in Stereochemistry, Local Order and Defects: Models for Room Temperature Superconductivity, in "Disorder and Order in the Solid State: Concepts and Devices," Institute for Amorphous Studies Series, edited by R. W. Pryor, B. B. Schwartz and S. R. Ovshinsky (Plenum Press, New York, 1988) p. 143. (Heinz Henisch Festschrift)

158. Fabrication and Performance of Amorphous Silicon Based Tandem Photovoltaic Devices and Modules (with P. Nath and K. Hoffman), Presented at the 4th International Photovoltaic Science and Engineering Conference (PVSEC-4), Sydney, Australia (February 1989).

159. Solar Energy and Superconductivity – Opposite Sides of the Same Coin, Presented at the ISES Solar World Congress, Kobe, Japan (September 4-8, 1989).

160. Band Gap Profiling for Improving the Efficiency of Amorphous Silicon Alloy Solar Cells (with S. Guha, J. Yang, A. Pawlikiewicz, T. Glatfelter and R. Ross), *Appl. Phys. Lett.* **54**, 2330 (1989).

161. This Week's Citation Classic [S.R. Ovshinsky, R.T. Young, D.D. Allred, G. DeMaggio and G.A. Van der Leeden, Superconductivity at 155K, *Phys. Rev. Lett.* **58**, 2579 (1987)], *Current Contents* **30**, 20 (February 19, 1990).

162. Production of 20 A Sec^{-1} a-Si Alloys for Use in Solar Cells (with P. Nath, K. Hoffman, J. Call and G. DiDio), Proceedings of the 21st IEEE Photovoltaic Specialists Conference, Kissimimee, FL (May 21-25, 1990).

163. Unusual Fluorination Effects of Superconducting Films (with R.T. Young), Presented at the SPIE – The International Society for Optical Engineering Symposium on Modeling of Optical Thin Films II, San Diego, CA (July 12-13, 1990); SPIE Proc. Vol. 1324, p. 32.

164. Ovonic Ni-Metal Hydride Batteries for Electric Vehicles (with S. Venkatesan, M. Fetcenko and S. Dhar), Presented at the 24th ISATA, Florence, Italy (May 21, 1991). (Awarded the Toyota Prize for Advancement)

165. Structural Changes Induced by Thermal Annealing in W/C Multilayers (with B.S. Chao, J. Gonzalez-Hernandez, D. Pawlik, J. Scholhamer, J. Wood and K. Parker), Presented at the SPIE – The International Society for Optical Engineering on Multilayer Optics for Advanced X-ray Applications, San Diego, CA (July 22-23, 91); SPIE Proc. Vol. 1547, 196 (1991).

166. An Approach to the Puzzle of High Temperature Superconductivity – A Letter to David Adler, Epilogue to "Disordered Materials: Science and Technology – Selected Papers by Stanford R. Ovshinsky," 2nd Edition, edited by David Adler, Brian B. Schwartz and Marvin Silver, Institute for Amorphous Studies Series (Plenum Press, New York, 1991).

167. The Chemical Basis of High Temperature Superconductivity: Structure and Function, *Revue Roumaine De Physique* **36**, 761 (1991). (Grigorovici Festschrift)

168. Performance Advances in Ovonic Nickel-Metal Hydride Batteries for Electric Vehicles (with S. Dhar, S. Venkatesan, M. Fetcenko, P. Gifford and D. Corrigan), Presented at the 11th International Electric Vehicle Symposium, Florence, Italy (September 1992). (Awarded best paper on batteries)

169. Amorphous Silicon Alloys – The Future Technology in Photovoltaics (with M. Izu and H.C. Ovshinsky), Presented at World Renewable Energy Congress, Reading, United Kingdom (September 1992).

170. Crystallization Studies of Ge:Sb:Te Optical Memory Materials (with J. Gonzalez-Hernandez, B. Chao, D. Strand, D. Pawlik and P. Gasiorowski), *Appl. Phys. Comm.* **11**, 557 (1992).

171. High Quality Epitaxial YBCO (F) Films Directly Deposited on Sapphire (with R. Young, K. Young and M. Muller), *Physica C* **200**, 437 (1992).

172. Optically Induced Phase Changes in Amorphous Materials, *J. Non-Cryst. Solids* **141**, 200 (1992). (Tauc Festschrift)

173. The Origin of Pairing in High-T_c Superconductors, *Chem. Phys. Lett.* **195**, 455 (1992).

174. The Relationship Between Crystal Structure and Performance as Optical Recording Media in Te-Ge-Sb Thin Films (with D. Strand, J. Gonzalez-Hernandez, B. Chao and P. Gasiorowski and D. Pawlik), *Mat. Res. Soc. Symp. Proc.* **230**, 251 (1992).

175. Toward the Elimination of Light-Induced Degradation of Amorphous Si by Fluorine Incorporation (with X. Deng, E. Mytilineou and R. Young), *Mat. Res. Soc. Symp. Proc.* **258**, 491 (1992).

176. A Mechanism for High Temperature Superconductivity, Presented at the 3rd International Conference & Exhibition, World Congress on Superconductivity, Munich, Germany (September 1992); *Applied Superconductivity* **1**, 263 (1993).

177. Advancements in Ovonic Nickel Metal Hydride Batteries for Portable and EV Applications (with P. Gifford, S. Venkatesan, M. Fetcenko, D. Corrigan and S. Dhar), Presented at the 10th International Seminar on Primary and Secondary Battery Technology and Applications, Deerfield Beach, FL (March 1993).

178. Manufacturing of Triple-Junction 4 ft^2 a-Si Alloy PV Modules (with M. Izu, X. Deng, A. Krisko, K. Whelan, R. Young, H.C. Ovshinsky and K.L. Narasimhan), Proceedings of the 23rd IEEE Photovoltaic Specialist Conference, Louisville, KY (May 10-14, 1993).

179. Continuous Roll-to-Roll Amorphous Silicon Photovoltaic Manufacturing Technology, Presented at the National Renewable Energy Laboratory Program Review Meeting, Denver, CO (October 1993).

180. A Nickel Metal Hydride Battery for Electric Vehicles (with M.A. Fetcenko and J. Ross), *Science* **260**, 176 (1993).

181. Ovonic NiMH Batteries for Electric Vehicle Application (with S.K. Dhar and M.A. Fetcenko), Presented at the Symposium of the Society of Automotive Engineers of Japan, Inc. (February 1994).

182. Ovonic NiMH Batteries for Portable and EV Applications (with S. Dhar, M. Fetcenko, S. Venkatesan, A. Holland, P. Gifford and D. Corrigan), Presented at the 11th International Seminar on Primary and Secondary Battery Technology Application (March 1, 1994).

183. Amorphous Silicon Alloy Photovoltaic Technology – From R&D to Production (with S. Guha, J. Yang, A. Banerjee, T. Glatfelter, K. Hoffman, M. Izu, H. Ovshinsky and X Deng), Presented at Materials Research Society Spring Meeting, San Francisco, CA (April 1994).

184. Historique du Changement de Phase, *Memoires Optiques & Systems*, No. 127 (September 1994) p. 65.

185. Advances in Ovonic Nickel Metal Hydride Batteries for Electric and Hybrid Vehicles (with P.R. Gifford, M.A. Fetcenko, S. Venkatesan, D.A. Corrigan, A. Holland and S.K. Dhar), Presented at the 186th Meeting of the Electrochemical Society, Miami, FL (October 1994).

186. Ovonic Nickel Metal Hydride Batteries for Consumer and Electric Vehicle Applications (with S. Venkatesan, S.K. Dhar, D.A. Corrigan, M.A. Fetcenko and P.R. Gifford), Presented at the 5th International Symposium on Advances in Electrochemical Science and Technology, Madras, India (November 24-26, 1994).

187. Roll-to-Roll Microwave PECVD Machine for High Barrier Film Coatings (with M. Izu and B. Dotter), Presented at the International Conference of Vacuum Web Coating (November 1994).

188. Ovonic Nickel-Metal Hydride Electric Vehicle Batteries: From the First 10,000 Miles to the First 10,000 Vehicles (with D.A. Corrigan, S. Venkatesan, P.R. Gifford, M.A. Fetcenko and S.K. Dhar), Presented at the 12th International Electric Vehicle Symposium, Anaheim, CA (December 1994).

189. Continuous Roll-to-Roll Serpentine Deposition for High Throughput a-Si PV Manufacturing (with M. Izu, H.C. Ovshinsky, X. Deng, A.J. Krisko, K.L. Narasimhan, R. Crucet, T. Larman and A. Myatt), Presented at the 1994 IEEE First World Conference on Photovoltaic Energy Conversion, Waikola, HI (December 5-9, 1994) p. 820.

190. Dependence of a-Si Solar Cell V$_{oc}$ on Deposition Temperatures (with X. Deng, K.L. Narasimhan, J. Evans and M. Izu), ibid., p. 678.

191. Lightweight Flexible Rooftop PV Module (with M. Izu, H.C. Ovshinsky, K. Whelan and L. Fatalski), ibid., p. 990.

192. The Material Basis of Efficiency and Stability in Amorphous Photovoltaics, *Solar Energy Materials and Solar Cells* **32**, 443 (1994). (Seraphin Festschrift)

193. Stability Test of 4 FT^2 Triple-Junction a-Si Alloy PV Production Modules (with X. Deng, M. Izu and K.L. Narasimhan), Presented at the MRS Spring Meeting on Amorphous Silicon Technology, San Francisco, CA (1994); *Mat. Res. Soc. Symp. Proc.* **336**, 699 (1994).

194. Lifting the Tyranny of the Lattice: A Revolution in Progress (with I.M. Ovshinsky), Norbert Kreidl's Festschrift, Liechtenstein (July 3-8, 1994); Proceedings of the Norbert Kreidl Symposium on Present State and Future Prospects of Glass Science and Technology Vol. 70C (1997).

195. Ovonic NiMH Battery Technology for Portable and Electric Vehicle Application (with M. Fetcenko, S. Dhar, S. Venkatesan, A. Holland, P. Gifford and D. Corrigan), Presented at the 12th International Seminar on Primary and Secondary Battery Technology Application, Deerfield Beach, FL (March 1995).

196. Using Materials Physics to Develop Novel Batteries, Presented at the March 1995 Meeting of the American Physical Society, San Jose, CA.

197. Ion and Neutral Argon Temperatures in Electron Cyclotron Resonance Plasmas by Doppler Broadened Emission Spectroscopy (with David V. Tsu, R.T. Young, C.C. Klepper* and L.A. Barry* (*Oak Ridge Natl. Lab.)), *J. Vac. Sci. Technol.* A **13**, 935 (May/June 1995).

198. Product Development Through Advances in Materials Science at ECD/OBC (with M.A. Fetcenko and S.J. Hudgens), *Daido Journal* (1995).

199. Ovonic NiMH Battery Technology for Portable and Electric Vehicle Application (with M. Fetcenko, S. Venkatesan, S. Dhar, A. Holland, R. Young, P. Gifford, D. Corrigan, A. Ng* and R. Tsang* (*GP Batteries)), Presented at the 13th International Seminar on Primary and Secondary Battery Technology and Application, Deerfield Beach, FL (March 1996).

200. PV Metal Roofing Module (with T. Ellison, L. Fatalski, R. Kopf, H. Ovshinsky, M. Izu, R. Souleyrette, K. Whelan, J. Wiehagen and L. Zarker), Presented at the 25th IEEE Photovoltaic Specialist Conference, Washington D.C. (May 13-17, 1996).

201. Ovonic NiMH Batteries Technology – Advanced Technology for Electric Vehicle and Hybrid Electric Vehicle Applications (with R.C. Stempel, S.K. Dhar, M.A. Fetcenko, P.R. Gifford, S. Venkatesan, D.A. Corrigan and R.

Young), Presented at the 29th International Symposium on Automotive Technology and Automation, Florence, Italy (June 1996).

202. Amorphous Silicon Alloys – The Optoelectronic Materials that Set the Trend for Photovoltaic Applications (with J.C. Yang), Presented at the International Materials Research Congress, Cancun, Mexico (September 1-5, 1996).

203. Ovonic Nickel-Metal Hydride EV Batteries Powering Electric Cars, Trucks, Scooters and Bicycles Worldwide (with D.A. Corrigan, S. Venkatesan, P.R. Gifford, A. Holland, M.A. Fetcenko and S.K. Dhar), Presented at 13th International Electric Vehicle Symposium (EVS-13), Osaka, Japan (October 1996).

204. The Structure of W/C (0.15< < 0.8) Multilayers Annealed in Argon or Air (with J. Gonzalez-Hernandez, B.S. Chao and D.D. Allred), *Journal of X-Ray Science and Technology* **6**, 1-31 (1996).

205. Ovonic Nickel-Metal Hydride Batteries Making Electric Vehicles Practical (with R.C. Stempel), ibid.; Proceedings of the Japanese Society of Electric Vehicles, Tokyo, Japan (February 1997).

206. Ovonic NiMH Battery Technology – Improved Energy and Performance (with M. Fetcenko, J. Im, C. Fierro, B. Reichman, K. Young, B. Chao and S. Venkatesan), Presented at the 14th International Seminar on Primary and Secondary Batteries, Ft. Lauderdale, FL (March 1997).

207. Nickel Metal Hydride Technology for Consumer and Electric Vehicle Batteries – A Review and Up-Date (with P.R. Gifford, S.K. Dhar, D.A. Corrigan, M.A. Fetcenko and S. Venkatesan), Presented at the 65th Power Sources Symposium, Brighton, England (April 1997).

208. New High Speed, Low Cost, Roll-to-Roll Antireflectivity Coating Technology (with T. Ellison, B. Dotter and M. Izu), Proceedings of the 1997 Society for Vacuum Coaters, New Orleans (April 14-17, 1997).

209. Ovonic Nickel-Metal Hydride Batteries for Electric Vehicles (with D. Corrigan, S. Venkatesan, A. Holland, P. Gifford and S. Dhar), Presented at the 30th International Symposium on Automotive Technology and Automation (ISATA), Florence, Italy (June 1997).

210. Development of a Small Scale Hydrogen Production Storage System for Hydrogen Applications (with K. Sapru, N.T. Stetson, J. Yang, G. Fritz, M. Fairlie* and A. Stuart* (*of SunFuel Energy Systems)), Presented at IECEC, Honolulu, HI (July 27-August 1, 1997).

211. Comment on "Vacuum catastrophe: An elementary exposition of the cosmological constant problem" (with H. Fritzsche), *Am. J. Phys.* **65**, 927 (September 1997).

212. Effect of hydrogen dilution on the structure of amorphous silicon alloys (with D.V. Tsu, B.S. Chao, S. Guha and J. Yang), *Appl. Phys. Lett.* **71**, 1317 (September 8, 1997).

213. Improved c-Si p-Layer and a-Si i-Layer Materials Using VHF Plasma Deposition (with X. Deng, S.J. Jones, T. Liu and M. Izu), Presented at the 26th IEEE Photovoltaic Specialists Conference, Anaheim, CA (September/October 1997).

214. Amorphous Materials – The Key to New Devices, Presented at the 20th edition of the International Semiconductor Conference (CAS '97) in Sinaia, Romania (October 1997).

215. Ovonic Phase Change Memory Making Possible New Optical and Electrical Devices, Keynote address at the 9th Symposium on Phase Change Recording, Numanzu-City, Japan (November 27-28, 1997).

216. Higher Power Ovonic Nickel-Metal Hydride Batteries for Electric and Hybrid Vehicles (with D.A. Corrigan, S. Venkatesan, A. Holland, P.R. Gifford, M.A. Fetcenko and S.K. Dhar), Presented at the 14th International Electric Vehicle Symposium (EVS-14), Orlando, FL (December 1997).

217. Advanced Ovonic High-Power Nickel-Metal Hydride Batteries for Hybrid Electric Vehicle Applications (with I. Menjak, P.H. Gow, D.A. Corrigan, S. Venkatesan, S.K. Dhar and R.C. Stempel), Presented at the 13th Annual Battery Conference on Applications and Advances, Long Beach, CA (January 1998).

218. Advanced Materials for Next Generation NiMH Portable, HEV and EV Batteries (With S.K. Dhar, M.A. Fetcenko, D.A. Corrigan, B. Reichman, K. Young, C. Fierro, S. Venkatesan, P. Gifford and J. Koch), Presented at the 15th International Seminar on Primary and Secondary Batteries, Ft. Lauderdale, FL (March 3, 1998).

219. Improved Hydride/Dehydride Process to Prepare Metal Powders for Ovonic NiMH Battery Applications (with K.H. Young, M.A. Fetcenko, S. Tang and A. Ku), Presented at PM²TEC'98 Conference on Powder Metallurgy & Particulate Materials, Las Vegas, NV (June 1998).

220. Ovonic Nickel-Metal Hydride Power for Hybrid Electric Vehicle Applications (with D. Corrigan, P. Gow, I. Menjak, S. Venkatesan, S. Dhar and R. Stempel), Presented at the 31st International Symposium on Automotive Technology and Automation, Dusseldorf, Germany (June 1998).

221. High Power Ovonic NiMH Batteries for Hybrid Electric Vehicle Applications (with D. Corrigan, P. Gow, I. Menjak, S. Venkatesan, S. Dhar and R. Stempel), Presented at the 15th International Electric Vehicle Symposium, Brussels, Belgium (October 1998).

222. Fundamentals and Implications of Amorphous and Disordered Materials, Presented at the University of Toledo (October 22, 1998).

223. Nickel Metal Hydride Batteries: The Enabling Technology for Electric and Hybrid Electric Vehicles (With R.C. Stempel, P.R. Gifford and D.A. Corrigan), *IEEE Spectrum* (November 1998).

224. Nickel Metal Hydride Batteries – The Enabling Technology for Electric and Hybrid Vehicles, Presented at the 39th Battery Symposium, Japan (November 25-27, 1998).

225. Advancing Batteries (with R.C. Stempel, S.K. Dhar and P.R. Gifford), *Electric & Hybrid Vehicle Technology* '98 (1998) p. 80.

226. *Mott's Room*, in Reminiscences and Appreciations, edited by E.A. Davis (Taylor & Francis Ltd, London, 1998) p. 282.

227. Nickel-Metal Hydride: Ready to Serve (with R.C. Stempel, P.R. Gifford and D.A. Corrigan), *IEEE Spectrum* **35**, 29 (1998).
228. Amorphous and Disordered Materials – The Basis of New Industries, Presented at Materials Research Society (MRS), Boston, MA (November 30 - December 4, 1998); *Mat. Res. Soc. Symp. Proc.* **554**, 399 (1999); *Bulk Metallic Glasses*, William L. Johnson, Akihisa Inoue and C.T. Liu (Eds.).
229. Advanced Materials for 100+ Wh/kg NiMH Batteries (with M.A. Fetcenko, K. Young, B. Reichman, C. Fierro, J. Koch, W. Mays, B. Sommers, A. Zallen, S.K. Dhar and R. Young), Presented at the Sixteenth International Seminar on Primary and Secondary Batteries, Ft. Lauderdale, FL (March 2, 1999).
230. Electric Cars and Scooters Powered by Ovonic Nickel-Metal Hydride Batteries (with N. Karditsas, D.A. Corrigan and S.K. Dhar), Presented at the 3rd International Symposium on Advanced Electromechanical Motion Systems, Patras, Greece (July 8-9, 1999).
231. The Story of Phase Change for Optical Storage, *Balzers Materials* **9**, 6 (October 1999).
232. Innovation, Corporate Strategy and Business Growth – The Challenge and Promise of the Hydrogen Economy, Keynote address at the Montreux Energy Roundtable, Cambridge, England (November 8, 1999).
233. High Temperature Charge Acceptability Improvements in Ovonic Nickel Metal Hydride Batteries (with S. Venkatesan, B. Aladjov, K. Fok, T. Hopper, B. Prasad, L. Taylor, J. Strebe, M. Amo and S. Dhar), Proceedings of the 39th Power Sources Conference, Cherry Hill, NJ (March 31, 2000) p. 278.
234. High Conductivity Negative Electrode Substrates for EV and HEV Ovonic NiMH Batteries (with S. Venkatesan, B. Prasad, B. Aladjov, D. Corrigan and S. Dhar), ibid., p. 263.
235. Metal Hydride Technologies for Fuel Cell Vehicles (with D.A. Corrigan, R.C. Young and S.K. Dhar), Presented at the Commercializing Fuel Cell Vehicles 2000 Conference, Berlin, Germany (April 12-14, 2000).
236. Performance of Ovonic NiMH Batteries with New Generation of Positive Electrode Active Materials (with S. Venkatesan, B. Aladjov, T. Hopper, K. Fok, J. Strebe, and S. Dhar), Presented at the 197th Meeting of the Electrochemical Society, Toronto, Canada (May 14-18, 2000).
237. New Developments in Optical Phase Change Memory (with W. Czubatyj), Presented at the 5th International Symposium on Optical Storage (ISOS 2000), Shanghai, China (May 22-26, 2000); *SPIE* Proc. Vol. 4085, p. 15 (2001).
238. The Road to Decarbonized Energy – Speeding towards a hydrogen economy – and the obstacles along the way, Book Review, *Nature* (August 3, 2000) p. 457.
239. Fuel Cells: Necessary But Not Sufficient, Keynote address at the Fuel Cell 2000 R&D, Philadelphia, PA (September 25-27, 2000).
240. Nickel-Metal Hydride Batteries for ZEV-Range Hybrid Electric Vehicles (with D. Corrigan, I. Menjak, B. Cleto and S. Dhar), Presented at the 17th International Electric Vehicle Symposium, Montreal, Canada (October 2000).
241. Technology's Tortoise and Hare – The sociological dynamics are now right for the electric car to eclipse its rival, book review, *Nature* (November 16, 2000)   p. 289.
242. Applications of Glasses, Amorphous, and Disordered Materials" in P. Boolchand (Ed.) *Insulating and Semiconducting Glasses*, Series on Directions in Condensed Matter Physics, Vol. 17 (World Scientific, Singapore, 2000) p. 729.
243. Effect of Alloy Composition on the Structure of Zr Based Metal Alloys (with B.S. Chao, R.C. Young, D.A. Pawlik, B. Huang, J.S. Im and *B.C. Chakoumakos), Proceedings of Materials Research Society Symposium Vol. 575, 193 (2000) [*Neutron Scattering Section, Oak Ridge National Lab., Oak Ridge, TN 37831].
244. Ovonic NiMH Batteries: The Enabling Technology for Heavy-Duty Electric & Hybrid Electric Vehicles (with R.C. Stempel, S.K. Dhar, S. Venkatesan, D. Corrigan, G. Fritz and N. Karditsas), Presented *Society of Automotive Engineers* (2000).
245. Ovonics Memories, Presented at MINATEC 2001 – The Second International Meeting on Micro and Nanotechnologies, Grenoble (April 2-6, 2001).
246. The Basic Mechanisms Unique to Amorphous and Disordered Semiconductor Devices, Keynote address at the 19th International Conference on Amorphous and Microcrystalline Semiconductors, Nice, France (August 23-31, 2001).
247. Phase Change Optical Storage, Keynote speech "given by the great father of phase-change memory, Dr. Stanford R. Ovshinsky," E*PCOS01 European Symposium on Phase Change Optical Storage, Santis, Switzerland (September 3-4, 2001).
248. The Hydrogen Economy, Keynote address at the Florida Educational Seminars, Inc. Conference on Fuel Cells for Stationary, Automotive and Portable Applications, Fort Lauderdale, FL (November 12-14, 2001).
249. Development of High Catalytic Activity Disordered Hydrogen-Storage Alloys for Electrochemical Application in Nickel-Metal Hydride Batteries (with M.A. Fetcenko), *Appl. Phys. A* **72**, 239 (2001).
250. Heterogeneity in Hydrogenated Silicon: Evidence for Intermediately Ordered Chainlike Objects (with D. Tsu, B.S. Chao, S. Jones, J. Yang, S. Guha and R. Tsu), *Phys. Rev. B* **63** (2001).
251. Solving Serious Societal Environmental Problems Through New Approaches to Catalysis, Keynote address at Symposium on Catalysis-Dependent New Commercial/Near Commercial Technologies for Improving Air Quality, 223rd American Chemical Society National Meeting, Orlando, FL (April 7-11, 2002).
252. Roadmap for the Future of Phase Change, Keynote address, E*PCOS03 European Symposium on Phase Change Optical Storage, Lake Lugano, Switzerland (March 10-11, 2003).
253. Phase Change Storage Media (with T. Ohta), *Encyclopedia of Optical Engineering* (Marcel Dekker, Inc., 2003), pp. 1939-1968. Online: www.dekker.com.

254. Phase Change Optical Storage Media (with T. Ohta), in "Photo-Induced Metastability in Amorphous Semiconductors," edited by Alexander V. Kolobov (John Wiley & Sons Canada, Ltd.) 1st edition (July 24, 2003) Ch. 18.

255. Transformative New Science and Technology Affecting Energy and Information, The Twin Pillars of our Global Society, Armstrong Lecture, Newcastle University, U.K. (October 28, 2003).

256. Phase Change Data Storage, Tutorial at the 2003 MRS Fall Symposium on Phase Change and Nonmagnetic Storage Materials for Data Storage, Boston, MA (December 1-5, 2003).

257. Optical Cognitive Information Processing – A New Field, Keynote presentation at the International Symposium on Optical Memory '03, Nara, Japan (November 4, 2003); *Japanese J. Appl. Phys.* **43**, 4695 (2004).

258. New Science and Technology - The Basis of the Hydrogen Economy, Keynote address at the 2003 Materials Research Society (MRS) Fall Symposium on Materials and Technologies for a Hydrogen Economy, Boston, MA (December 1-5, 2003); *Mat. Res. Soc. Symp. Proc.* **801**, 3 (2004).

259. Innovation Providing New Multiple Functions in Phase-Change Materials to Achieve Cognitive Computing (with B. Pashmakov), Invited talk at the 2003 MRS Fall Symposium on Phase Change and Nonmagnetic Storage Materials for Data Storage, Boston, MA (December 1-5, 2003); *Mat. Res. Soc. Symp. Proc.* **803**, 49 (2004).

260. Hydrogen-Fueled Hybrid: Pathway to a Hydrogen Economy [with R. Geiss, B. Webster, R. Stempel (ECD Ovonics), R.C. Young, Y. Li, V. Myasnikov (Ovonic Hydrogen Systems), B. Falls and A. Lutz (Quantum Technologies)], Presented at the SAE 2004 World Congress, Detroit, Michigan (March 8-11, 2004).

261. A Hydrogen ICE Vehicle Powered by Ovonic Metal Hydride Storage (with R. C. Young, B. Chao, Y. Li, V. Myasnikov, and B. Huang) , Presented at the SAE 2004 World Congress, Detroit, Michigan (March 8-11, 2004).

262. Transition Away From Fossil Fuels, panel presentation at the Bridging the Divide 2004 conference on Technology, Innovation and Learning in Developing Economies, University of California Berkley (April 1-3, 2004).

263. A new information paradigm - the Ovonic Cognitive Computer, in "Non-Crystalline Materials for Optoelectronics," Optoelectronic Materials and Devices Series, **1** (INOE Publishing House, June 2004).

264. Emerging technologies with emphasis on the workforce, skills panel at the Alternative Energy conference on "Training the Workforce of the Future," Wayne State University, Detroit (June 2, 2004).

265. Phase Change Electronic Memories: Towards Cognitive Computing, *Encyclopedia of Materials: Science and Technology* (Elsevier Science, Ltd., 2005), pp. 1-6. Online: www.sciencedirect.com.

266. Photovoltaics, the Beginning of the Hydrogen Economy, Featured speech, *Emerging Opportunities* session at "Solar 2004, A Solar Harvest: Growing Opportunities Conference," Portland, OR (July 11-13, 2004).

267. The Ovonic Cognitive Computer: A New Paradigm, Keynote address, E*PCOS[04] Third European Symposium on Phase Change and Ovonic Science (name of organization changed at E*PCOS[03] in honor of the work of S.R. Ovshinsky), Liechtenstein (September 2004).

268. Novel Storage Mechanisms Using Ovonic Phase Change Materials (with B. Pashmakov, D. Strand and T. Ohta), Presented at 2004 Asia-Pacific Data Storage Conference (APDSC'04), Taoyuan, Taiwan (September 27-30, 2004).

269. The Ovonic Regenerative Fuel Cell, A Fundamentally New Approach (with S. Venkatesan and D.A. Corrigan), Presented at the Hydrogen and Fuel Cells Conference Trade Show, Toronto, Canada (September 2004).

270. Technical Tendencies and Innovations in Fuel Cells, Invited Talk at Congress on Renewable Energy, Guanajuato, Mexico (November 8-12, 2004).

271. The Mechanism of Ovonic Phase Change Cognitive Devices, Invited talk at Glass & Optical Materials Division Fall 2004 Meeting (ISNOG XIV), Cape Canaveral, Florida (November 10, 2004).

272. The Principles of Disorder and Their Applicability to Condensed Matter Physics, Neurophysiology and Cosmology, presented at the monthly colloquium of the Michigan Center for Theoretical Physics, University of Michigan, Ann Arbor, MI (January 11, 2005).

273. Ovonic Instant Start Fuel Cells for UPS and Emergency Power Applications (with K. Fok, S. Venkatesan and D.A. Corrigan), Presented at the National Hydrogen Association Annual Conference 2005, Washington, DC (March 29-April 1, 2005).

274. Ovonic Chalcogenide Non-Binary Electrical and Optical Devices, Presented at 7th International Symposium on Optical Storage (ISOS 2005), Zhanjiang, China (April 2-6, 2005).

275. Metal Hydride Fuel Cells for UPS and Emergency Power Applications (with K. Fok, S. Venkatesan and D.A. Corrigan), Presented at Battcon 2005, Miami, FL (May 2005).

276. Metal Hydride Fuel Cells, A New Approach (with D.A. Corrigan), *Fuel Cell Magazine*, p. 25 (June/July 2005).

277. The Hydrogen Loop – The Means for Making the Hydrogen Economy Realistic, Proceedings of International Hydrogen Energy Congress and Exhibition IHEC 2005, Istanbul, Turkey (July 13-15, 2005).

278. Electro-optical investigations of Ovonic chalcogenide memory devices (with E. Mytilineou, B. Pashmakov, D. Strand and D. Jablonski), Presented at ICANS 21, Lisbon, Portugal (September 4-9, 2005).

279. The Future of Ovonic Phase Change Optical and Electrical Devices, Keynote address, E*PCOS[05] European Symposium on Phase Change and Ovonic Science, Cambridge, U.K. (September 5-6, 2005).

280. 25/30 MW Ovonic Roll-To-Roll PV Manufacturing Machines (with M. Izu), presented at 15th International Photovoltaic Science and Engineering Conference and Solar Energy Exhibition, Shanghai, China (October 10-15, 2005); presented at VacMeSS Third International Symposium on Vacuum Coatings of Metal Strips and Sheets, Dresden, Germany (September 29-30, 2005).

Neurophysiology and Neuropsychiatry

1. Combined Cortical and Cerebellar Stimulation (with F. Morin and G. Lamarche), Department of Anatomy, Wayne State University, College of Medicine, *Anat. Rec* **127**, 436 (1957).
2. A Concept of Schizophrenia, *J. Nerv. and Ment. Disease* **Vol.** 125, 578 (1957).
3. Cortical and Cerebellar Stimulation in Walking Cats, Presented before the Detroit Physiological Society (December 19, 1957).
4. Functional Aspects of Cerebellar Afferent Systems and of Cortico-Cerebellar Relationships (with F. Morin and G. Lamarche), *Laval Médical* **Vol. 26**, 633 (1958).
5. Suggested Biochemical Factors in Schizophrenia, J. *Nerv. and Ment. Disease* **127**, 180 (1958).
6. The Physical Base of Intelligence – Model Studies, Presented at the Detroit Physiological Society (December 17, 1959).
7. The Reticulo-Endothelial Systems and its Possible Significance in Schizophrenia, *J. Neuropsychiatry* **3**, 38 (1961).

Books

"Disordered Materials: Science and Technology – Selected Papers by S.R. Ovshinsky," edited by David Adler (Amorphous Institute Press, Bloomfield Hills, Michigan, 1982).
"Disordered Materials: Science and Technology – Selected Papers by Stanford R. Ovshinsky," 2nd Edition, edited by David Adler, Brian B. Schwartz and Marvin Silver, *Institute for Amorphous Studies Series* (Plenum Press, New York, 1991).

Books Edited

"Physics of Disordered Materials," edited by David Adler, Hellmut Fritzsche and Stanford R. Ovshinsky, *Institute for Amorphous Studies Series* (Plenum Press, New York, 1985).
"Disordered Semiconductors," edited by Marc A. Kastner, Gordon A. Thomas and Stanford R. Ovshinsky, *Institute for Amorphous Studies Series* (Plenum Press, New York, 1987).
"Disorder and Order in the Solid State – Concept and Devices," edited by Roger W. Pryor, Brian B. Schwartz and Stanford R. Ovshinsky, *Institute for Amorphous Studies Series* (Plenum Press, New York, 1988).

About the Author

George S. Howard is a Professor of Psychology at the University of Notre Dame. He has served as Chairman, Department of Psychology and Director, Laboratory for Social Research at Notre Dame, as well as the Joseph Morahan Director of College Seminar. He served as President, Division of Theoretical and Philosophical Psychology and President, Division of Humanistic Psychology of the American Psychological Association. He also was the 1998 winner of Notre Dame's *Faculty Award*. Author of 11 other books and over 170 scientific articles and chapters, his specialties include philosophical psychology, research methodology, narrative psychology and environmental psychology. *Stan Ovshinsky and the Hydrogen Economy* is his first biography. His wife, Nancy Gulanick, is also a psychologist and his sons, John Gulanick and Greg Howard, are currently enjoying college.